Fibs, Facts and Farces
Tales from the Arab World

Fibs, Facts and Farces: Tales from the Arab World

Published by
Barzipan Publishing
www.barzipan.com

© John Carter 2012

ISBN 978-0-9567081-4-5

Printed and bound by Short Run Press Ltd, Exeter

CIP Data: A catalogue record for this book is available from the British Library.

Fibs, Facts and Farces
Tales from the Arab World

John Carter

Barzipan Publishing
not what you'd expect

Dedication

This book is dedicated with love to Galen, who has shared it all.

Contents

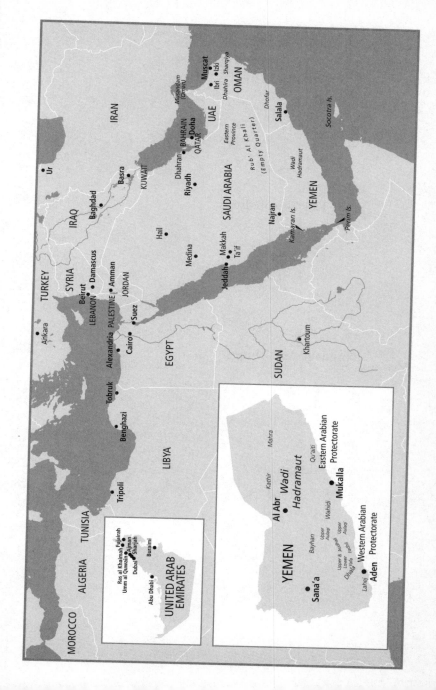

FOREWORD

Anyone who tells the truth is bound to be found out sooner or later.

Oscar Wilde

Follow the liar to the gate of his house.

Egyptian Proverb

It is something of a truism that a good story should never be spoilt by over-assiduous attachment to the truth. These stories have been collected together with this in mind, and with the purpose of demonstrating that the people of the Middle East who, though they have their own foibles and idiosyncrasies aplenty, have by and large put up with British and Western interference with notable patience, politeness, and good humour. The West in general, and the British in particular, have given ample cause for merriment; one has only to remember Noel Coward's delightful ditty, *Mad Dogs and Englishmen,* which hits the nail on the head with devastating accuracy. Western behaviour has also given rise to many charming stories – perhaps not so innocent but nevertheless beguiling.

It is amusing to consider how the British on the one hand pride themselves on their sense of humour, yet on the other seem to remain completely oblivious to the fact that other people have one too. Arabs actually have a terrific sense of humour – and they need it to put up with the Brits! Sadly, it is little known outside the Middle East. The American sense of humour is another thing altogether. Most of the stories recorded here concern the British in one way or another, but our allies in two World Wars also have a large part to play, both with us and against us. There is no doubt they do find us very irritating at times.

It is also important to highlight the differences in humour within the region itself. It has been said that the British and the Sudanese got on so well together simply because they shared a sense of humour. On the other hand, the French get on very well with the Egyptians because they share a sense of wit – a nice distinction. However, it is not recorded whether the Sudanese found it amusing when the Mahdi's head was forwarded to the Royal College of Surgeons, and his fingernails to White's Club in London, following the Battle of Omdurman.

An important adjunct to many of these stories is a British characteristic that was frequently found in their official institutions and diplomatic representatives. As Michela Wrong put it, albeit with reference to Africa:

> *There is a type of resolutely silly humour at which clever English people of a certain class and education excel. Based on a keen appreciation of the absurd, it is associated with achingly bad puns, dirty limericks, quotations from the poems of Hilaire Belloc, vainglorious Latin mottos, and a propensity for reciting long sections from* Alice in Wonderland.

This collection has also been compiled in a spirit of fairness, so that if the Arabs, the British and the Americans feel they have been insulted, at least the others have been equally so. Many of these tales contain an element of fiction; some are quite obviously fiction from beginning to end but are included for merriment's sake. Quite a few are, however, completely true! But mostly they stem from an earlier age when somehow things *seem* to have been gentler but which has nevertheless led inexorably to the events of today. They show how much we have all changed. It is unforgivably patronising to talk endlessly about Arabian Progress while failing to mention that the West had been going through similar, if not always such convulsive and rapid changes. After all, Baghdad had street lighting and mains drainage seven hundred years before London did.

Some stories have circulated in more than one version and it is often worth recording the differences. Naturally, that famous raconteur, Baron Munchausen, has put his oar in from time to time; so too has the imaginative Walter Mitty.

Lynette Crouch, when helping her husband (an Adviser in the Eastern Aden Protectorate) with his memoirs, would often remark, 'But it wasn't like that at all! Don't you remember?' Yes, memory plays strange tricks.

The British became involved in the area long before the discovery of oil. The Americans arrived later, and one forbears to comment, but quite early on the Arabs made their own efforts in the direction of the United States. The then Ruler of Oman sent a dhow to New York in the 19th century, which probably elicited the question in Manhattan, 'Where the hell's that come from?'

The British were busy taking care of business and maintaining communication with the Crown Jewel of the Raj – India – suzerainty over which they acquired entirely by mistake in the first place simply because the East India Company went bust. Having acquired it, they had to establish a number of what amounted to little more than a series of bus stops, so that they could get safely from London and Liverpool to Bombay and back, and protect trade routes within what was then the Persian Gulf. In this way, Suez, the Red Sea ports, Aden, South Arabia and the many sheikhdoms of the Gulf, Syria, Iraq and Iran came into the orbit of the British Interest.

Readers unfamiliar with the local history and geography may wonder how the top end of the Gulf could possibly be thought of as being on the way from Liverpool to Bombay. Well, the Suez Canal didn't exist, so the overland route via Syria and Iraq was the only way – other than rowing round Africa (which, incidentally, had already been done by the Portuguese). This is why some time later the British got terribly excited when people like the German Kaiser wanted to build railways between Constantinople, Damascus and Baghdad, which would have outflanked the Suez Canal. They also realised that once they'd got hold of the bus stops, it would be necessary to prevent unfriendly people using them. To continue the analogy, there were other, non-British bus companies involved. These were either trade competitors like France and Holland, or political interlopers like Russia, and eventually Germany; and of course local foreigners, who simply didn't play cricket and whose trustworthiness was deeply suspect, giving rise to the pejorative epithet 'Wily Oriental Gentleman': an epithet whose acronym has become particularly insulting but whose components would not seem at all uncomplimentary, but pretty accurate! The main local player in the region was the Ottoman Empire, referred to romantically, or maybe sarcastically, as the Sublime Porte. All this generated a feeling of unearned and undeserved superiority on the part of the British – a feeling still apparent today in some quarters.

In looking after their bus stops and keeping competitors out, the British devised a rather jolly policy of offering 'Protection' to various people and states, who were reckoned to own the bus stops. This was long before Al Capone, of course. The deal was simple: the Rulers – the bus stop owners, real or imagined – could carry on as they wished on their own turf, but the British would take care of their foreign policy. From the British point of view this would deal with French and Dutch competition splendidly, and doubtless expensive involvement with internal affairs would be avoided. The locals could build their own roads, schools and hospitals, couldn't they? From the Arabian point of view, it meant that the Rulers would be protected from sundry local powers who had claims on their territory, valid or otherwise. Thus, in southern Arabia they would be protected from the nasty designs of the Yemeni Imams, against whom several of them had already successfully rebelled. In the Gulf, the locals would be freed from what they saw as the threat from the House of Saud, or the Persians, or indeed most of their other neighbours. The rest of the Middle East was ruled by the

Turks, who had to be looked after to keep the Russians out. In general this suited everyone very well.

Naturally, the British wanted their involvement to be cloaked in respectability and altruism. So they blew up the pirates and stamped out slavery while they were at it, thus severely damaging, if not actually destroying, several economies in the area – a policy they and their allies enthusiastically continued into the late 20th century! We should add that they probably blew up either the wrong pirates or people who weren't pirates at all. However the epithet 'Pirate Coast', sometimes applied to the Lower Gulf, as late as 1959 led to the Political Agent on one occasion being addressed as HM Piratical Agent.

As for slavery, the clever locals merely readjusted the slave routes. The eccentric Englishman, John Keane, who travelled to Makkah and Medina in the late 19th century, mounted a robust defence of slavery. Of slaves in Arabia he wrote (and remember that political correctness had not yet been invented): 'There the Negro finds himself in his proper place, an easily managed useful worker. Slavery made men of them, even superior men'. This 'making of men' was absolutely in line with the British public school ethos and so was clearly A Good Thing. It is essential to make men out of even the most unpromising material, which is why public schools are so popular! Incidentally, the descendants of some of those unjustly accused of maritime robbery eventually came to supply the red asphalt that covers the road outside Buckingham Palace – so no grudges there then.

Just to add to the confusion faced by the modern reader, the Brits cunningly called quite a few of their bus stops 'factories', which they clearly were not as they never actually made anything at all, except perhaps money. The British Empire expanded magnificently and the bus stops became almost forgotten in the pomp that ensued. By the end of the 19th century almost all European countries had an Empire too. But Great Britain's was the biggest, and towards the end of the century they were prepared to be just slightly magnanimous. It was even mooted in some circles that maybe a bit of sharing would be in order – perhaps the Middle East could be fairly and justly divided between those who mattered? France could have Morocco, Italy Tripoli, England Egypt, Germany Syria and Asia Minor, Russia Persia; and Austria could have Constantinople to avenge the siege of Vienna by the Turks.

The British, unsurprisingly, also laboured under a number of misconceptions. One of the more obvious was the muddle over Arabian titles and honorifics. Titles are much admired by the British – even devoted Socialists often wholeheartedly embrace a peerage when given the chance. So, when confronted by a 'Sultan', they immediately pictured a grand, romantic, rich and powerful being, dripping with gems, a character from *One Thousand and One Nights*, like the Sultan of Turkey himself maybe. Someone who could do lots of things, particularly in bed, that they were either too shy to do or lacked the imagination to try. They were therefore rather nonplussed, especially in South Arabia, to come across Sultans aplenty living in conditions of real poverty, devoid of dancing girls, jewels, huge harems and multitudes of slaves. A couple, however, did at least look the part, notably the Abdali Rulers of Lahej and the Al-Qu'aiti Sultans of Mukalla who, having had close contact with the India of the Raj, had great presence and tailoring to match.

The word 'sultan' merely means authority and a Sultan is therefore a chap with authority. However, in the search for potentates to have Treaties with, British ignorance over what titles meant led to bungles and misunderstandings. For instance, they signed a Treaty with the then Sharif of Bayhan although he didn't actually have anything to do with ruling that area, which wasn't really a state either! A member of the Sharifian family living in Bayhan apparently visited Aden on the off chance of getting a handout. He not only got the handout but, to his delight, got recognised as an independent Ruler as well. So the British inadvertently created a new state and a new Ruler. This diddling of the

British Government is today a great source of amusement and pride to the Sharif's descendants. The British copy of this Treaty is said to have been eaten by white ants in the Government Archive, leaving the Sharif Hussein, grandson of the original signatory, in possession of the only copy. This he kept in the pocket of his sports jacket to be whisked out if there was any argument, secure in the knowledge that no one on the British side could contradict him!

The British also got it wrong when they met a small family in Lower Yafa', who had the appearance of being almost destitute goatherds, the Afif. This family suddenly found themselves dignified as the Sultans of Lower Yafa' because the British failed to understand the difference between appointed Suzerains like the Rulers of Dhala, Lahej and Mukalla, and an elected tribal chief with the same title. In the case of Lower Yafa' the real Sultanic family, the Afif, though indigent, was of impeccable and very noble lineage indeed stretching back to the ancient Kingdoms of pre-Islamic Arabia. In the case of the Amir of Dhala, failure to recognise the exact reach of his claimed hegemony led to endless friction with the Bani Qutayb tribe, likely descendants of another ancient Kingdom, Qataban – a failure that defrauded them of recognition which should arguably have been theirs.

An omission which led to decades of discontent and finally erupted in the Radfan Campaign of the mid-1960s. After an earlier rebellion in the 1930s which was quelled with light but inaccurate bombing by the Royal Air Force, the Bani Qutayb sent a stiff letter to the Government in Aden complaining that it was difficult for them to consider a Protectorate Treaty, even if one was offered, with an inept government which was clearly unable to bomb people properly.

As the years have gone by, the opportunity for muddle has been increased by the Arabs themselves. Inflation has struck! Sheikhs have become Emirs and Sultans are now Kings. He who once was a Highness is now a Majesty. Mind you, this has been going on for a while. The Sheikh of Diriyah became the Emir of Riyadh and a couple of decades later transmogrified into the Sultan of Nejd. The holder of this title eventually became the King of Saudi Arabia and with all due modesty called the geographical entity that this title applied to after his own family. It is as though the British lived in Windsorland. To be fair, the daughter of a long line of German Princes and Kinglets became the Queen of England, Scotland, Ireland and Wales. Then, at the insistence of her Prime Minister Benjamin Disraeli, she became Empress of India – they thought at the time that the English themselves would not accept their Head of State being an Empress because of their Cromwellian Protestant heritage of self-effacement and diffidence, but as she was only a woman it would be all right for the Indians.

Further confusion is caused because Sultan is not only a title but also an ordinary forename. It is thus possible to have a Sultan Sultan, or to meet someone called Sultan Muhammad who isn't a Sultan but just Sultan, son of Muhammad. Get it? These confusions continue happily right up to today. A book published as recently as 2005 awarded King Faisal of Saudi Arabia an extra son, when the person is actually the King's grandson. His title was also confused with his name. Thus Amir bin Faisal should have been the Amir Amr bin Muhammad bin Faisal.

One of the many attractions of Arabia rarely, if ever, mentioned is that Arabians are even worse snobs than the British, which is saying something. At a Reception in Saudi Arabia, a visiting English banker related with great pride how his forebears had arrived in England with William the Conqueror. His Saudi client enquired politely who this William might be. On having it all explained and being given the magic date of 1066, the Saudi Arabian looked unimpressed and told the banker that he himself was descended from Adam. Arabs from the Arabian Peninsula rather look down on Arabs from the north, west and east of themselves – a sentiment heartily returned by these objects of contempt who, if pressed, characterise their Peninsular brethren as uncivilised, unwashed, uneducated stay-at-home barbarians. Indeed, the British have a similar attitude to the Australians, Canadians and (especially) the Americans, which is likewise heartily reciprocated. The British passion for pedigrees – a passion they extend to their dogs, cats, horses, cattle and even budgerigars and pet mice – is quite different to the Arabs'. The Arabs use pedigree to define social structure, and structures can be changed, re-invented or, perish the thought, forged!

Though it seems odd to us now, a cardinal principle of the British Raj was that it just wasn't the done thing to mix with the natives. Naturally, some communication other than down the barrel of a gun was necessary from time to time, and rather sweetly the Raj solved the problem by frequently using such junior people to do the communicating that senior and important people were not involved in too embarrassingly an intimate way. Harold Ingrams, whose efforts at bringing peace to the Wadi Hadhramaut earned him deserved and lasting fame, was the most eminent official to hold a contrary view. Scandalously, he made friends with the Arabians! This attracted the disapproval of the Governor of Aden, Sir Charles Johnston, who explained the position perfectly when he said of Ingrams, 'I could never follow him in his view that the Englishman in Arabia must try to think as an Arab.'

Perhaps the prime example of this is to be found in the person of Lawrence of Arabia. This daring and dashing archaeologist was the first media-made celebrity and ended up a Colonel before eschewing all the trappings of fame. However, while leading the Arab Revolt he was a mere Captain and his careless attitude to military uniform appalled three-quarters of the British officer corps. Nevertheless, he liked the Arabs enormously and it is doubtless his knowledge that they were to be betrayed that led him to enlist as an aircraftsman in the RAF.

This official attitude to the natives was again expressed by no less a personage than the august Lord Grey. As Foreign Secretary, Grey – who had never been further abroad than Paris but was nevertheless a paladin among holders of that office – simply could not grasp the importance of reports on Abdulaziz Al Saud received from Captain Shakespear, Al Saud's military adviser. Shakespear had endeared himself to the man who was to become King of Saudi Arabia and, indeed, was killed fighting for him. He reported that Abdulaziz was certainly the man for Britain to back. For his pains, Lord Grey merely sent him a reprimand for wearing British military uniform while wandering around the Nejd – a lack of comprehension bordering on incompetence that was a factor in the loss of Saudi oil to the Americans. Admittedly, by ignoring Abdulaziz the British were able to reach agreements with the Ottomans and obtain access to the Iraqi and Iranian oil fields and establish the Anglo-Persian Oil Company; so not quite all was lost!

This incident underlines the fact that Empires old and new have no friends, they only have interests. A British problem in the world of Arabia, if nowhere else, was that their Men on the Spot did have friends. Which party was right in the long run historians will decide, but one feels that the moral right lies with the Men on the Spot. Amorality is the preserve of Empire: remember Mahatma Gandhi's reply to an American journalist who asked him what he thought of Western Civilization. The Mahatma replied that he thought it would be a good thing!

As the Raj faded and finally disappeared altogether, the process of insulation from the natives went into reverse. The needs of competitive commerce grew as imperial preference faded, and throughout the Western world frantic, often spurious, courses were run on the topic of 'understanding the natives'. Businessmen from California to Basingstoke were taught that they should never expose the soles of their feet to an Arab, and so on. It is odd that there never seem to have been any courses in Arabia on understanding the Westerner. Maybe they knew us too well to need it! It is ironic that the imperial drive to export the benefits of what the Victorians believed to be civilisation often gave way to a selfless dedication on the part of the British working on the ground to enable people to rule themselves and become independent of the British Government and the Colonial Office. Sir Hugh Foot (then Governor of Cyprus) aptly remarked in the 1950s that the Colonial Service should really be called the Anti-Colonial Service.

All this meant that eccentrics and adventurers got mixed up with the serious matter of government on the one hand, and local powers (already odd enough by European standards) on the other. In addition, the Men on the Spot frequently exhibited a strangely proprietorial attitude towards the Arabs. It was common to hear them talking about 'my sultan', for instance. These British, selflessly devoted as they frequently were, nevertheless developed another irritating characteristic which started as soon as they arrived in the area and became almost a tradition: anyone who arrived after you, not only fellow Britons but *all* foreigners, were resented and despised. The epithet 'Old Hand' to describe the first arrivals is a signpost to warn the unwary. You'll have heard of the 'Old Sudan Hand' or the 'Old China Hand'. Note the troubles faced by the Bents while journeying in the Hadramaut at the end of the 19th century from English officials in the Aden Protectorates – a tradition that continued into the next century when Freya Stark suffered a few similar problems. There were, nevertheless, sometimes sound reasons for this attitude, in that wandering visitors could get into difficulties from which overburdened local officials would have to rescue them. Perhaps the reason for establishing what were in effect dozens of mini empires may well be that the Brits are all little larval emperors.

In Oman, the arrival of the oil company in the 1950s had a surprising effect on the Men on the Spot in Muscat. These worthies clearly resented the intrusion but put on a brave face, realising in their hearts how important the oil company's activities were to the future of their beloved Sultanate. One wife put it succinctly when she remarked, 'Oil really must not be allowed to upset the happy little Omani donkey cart'. What is funny is that at that time the oil company was the only properly modern commercial company in the place. It was even known in Arabic as 'The Company'. Of course, when oil was eventually produced successfully many other Western companies flocked into the Sultanate to help the locals spend their newfound wealth. The Oil Company took the same view of these johnnies-come-lately as the old British Establishment had taken of them only a couple of decades previously, and the Oil Company looked down their noses on the newcomers just as they had once been looked down upon.

The Arabs themselves held a perfectly understandable point of view with regard to Western travellers, whom they considered to be spies. In many cases, they were absolutely right, and even when they were wrong the information collected by quite innocent travellers was put to use by the British Government. Geographical, botanical and zoological data collected for purely scientific purposes became classified information to Naval Intelligence. Otherwise, such tourists were viewed as treasure hunters or worse.

So many episodes in Middle Eastern history have an air of déjà vu and frequently made one think, 'Here we go again'. This makes it difficult to extract much amusement from them. The tragedy in the way the Government at Westminster has been constrained not only to betray its obligations to Arabs but also to let down its own people on the ground as well makes the laughs sound hollow, and leave a bittersweet taste.

The people of England have been led in Mesopotamia into a trap from which it will be hard to escape with dignity and honour. They have been tricked into it by a steady withholding of information. The Baghdad communiqués are belated, insincere, incomplete. Things have been far worse than we have been told, our administration more bloody and inefficient than the public knows. It is a disgrace to our imperial record, and may soon be too inflamed for any ordinary cure. We are today not far from a disaster.

T. E. Lawrence's words in the *Sunday Times* of August 1920 have lost none of their relevance and resonance, and have been repeatedly quoted by reporters in the context of the 21st-century wars in Iraq.

Naturally, the stories recorded here are recorded from an English perspective and those about the English themselves reflect our predilection for telling stories against ourselves. This trait has been elevated to a virtue, and we have come to think we are the only self-effacing people, that it's the foreigners who boast endlessly about their skills, prowess and glittering achievements. The fact that this self-deprecation is embarrassingly and accurately seen as preposterous hypocrisy by most of the rest of the world is something the English sublimely ignore.

To rub this lesson in, Arabian jokes have been added where it has been thought appropriate. Many of them bear a strong resemblance to the kind of political humour behind the Iron Curtain, which is a consequence of having so many more authoritarian regimes in the region. However, it also follows in a very old tradition dating from the days of the earliest Caliphates. This predilection for admiring and perpetuating the style of classical literature and music is an important facet of Arabian life. For instance, they adored the Egyptian singer Umm Kulthum, who serenaded the whole of the Middle East with ancient poetry set to music which brought the whole area to a standstill every Thursday night. And this despite her somewhat murderous reputation with regard to potential rivals. It was rather as though Elvis Presley sang verses from *The Canterbury Tales*. This propensity extends to other facets of history and forms an important similarity with the Irish.

The Arabs never forget anything, either. When the British first arrived in Bayhan in South Arabia one of the older inhabitants told them that they were not in fact the first 'Franks' to get there. When, rather sniffily, the British asked who had arrived before them, reference was made to Aelius Gallus, a Roman general who turned up in 24 BC and clearly made quite an impression. Similar historical 'memories' sometimes get skewed in order to impress. In the latter half of the 20th century, many small boys in the Hejaz, born at least three decades after T. E. Lawrence's death, were wont to approach European visitors swearing blind that they knew Lawrence of Arabia personally and asked after his health and to be remembered to him!

There has also been a long tradition of storytelling and poetry recital in Arabia. Although largely replaced by cinema and television, it still survives in Morocco and odd corners of the Middle East where you can hear gripping stories of the adventures of the Arabian hero Antar and extracts from *The Arabian Nights*. The storyteller always stops at the most exciting moment so that his audience will return the following day for the next instalment. An ancient tradition of using poetry as political comment is also alive and well. This has recently been splendidly recorded from Jordan where the tradition has been maintained by Bedouin poets writing in the vernacular. The rise of the House of Saud in comparison to the glories of Jordanian desert society is described caustically by the couplet:

> *These miserable sparrows – now who would have thought it?*
> *Over peregrine falcons have started to lord it.*

Ghassan Surur Al Sbaylat

To date, events have also been captured not only orally or written in the traditional way, but also in imitation of 'rap' and Texan American! In 2004 a poem entitled *Oh Condoleeza Rais!* was published in the Arabian newspaper *Al Ittijah*. President Bush is speaking in this small extract:

> *Bring some gin with y'all, and some whisky and some beer,*
> *With good ole Condoleezza: bring 'em all over here!*
> *Cos Ah'm gonna have a drink and Ah'm gonna raise a holler,*
> *Tell the A-rabs, up and dance, when Ah sing they will foller!*

Muhammad Fanatil Al Hajaya Al Dayjami

The writer recommends the reader to consult the work of Khalid Kishtainy, but reminds him that the stories may not always be true.

It is the Egyptians who have a well-deserved reputation for wit and political satire, and a rich tradition of taking the mickey out of authority. So pointed and devastatingly accurate have been the barbs aimed at successive Rulers of Egypt, from the Pharaoh Rameses onwards, that it is amazing any of them have been able to stay in power and survive the laughter of their subjects. The last of their kings, Farouk (who gave his name to a particularly garish variation of French furnishing, Louis Farouk), was eventually moved to remark that shortly there would only be five kings left – the King of England and the four in a pack of cards.

There is another who trips lightly across the Middle Eastern stage, a character little known in the West but who lives laughingly in every Arab child's heart. His name is Joha in the Arabian world; in Turkey he appears as Hoja or Khoja and in Egypt he is Goha. In the Indian sub-continent he is called Mullah Nasruddin. Joha is a famous character in Arabic popular literature. He is known for being a funny character who sometimes behaves in very strange, hilarious, or even ridiculous ways. He is famous in different cultures, and the character has been adapted to different settings and different ages. He has many comments to make on this and that, and some of them are included here to carry the fun along.

It is a terrible irony that more often than not, when the peoples of the Middle East join enthusiastically in what they perceive to be a thoroughly worthwhile and progressive revolution, they end up jumping straight out of the frying pan into the fire – which leads before long to yet another upheaval. This all makes the old tyrants, whether indigenous or British, look rather endearing when viewed through the rose-tinted spectacles of hindsight.

The collision of all these factors has resulted in a series of incidents, clashes, and misunderstandings over the years, tales of which have been repeated often. In the repetition the accounts have been embroidered and embellished to such an extent that it is now impossible to be sure about the truth of the matter. What began as part of a grand imperial enterprise ended with revolution, betrayal, and political disintegration – but, most marvellously, a continuing friendship despite all and the growth of mutual affection and respect. But all have together contributed to the general air of raging dottiness that has come to be such an important characteristic of British and Western relations with the Middle East.

The stories have been accumulated over the years. Some of them feature in written sources, but most have been handed down by way of the happy reminiscences of Englishmen sitting on sand dunes, in London clubs, in oil company bars, at university seminars and at reunions, and even casually on trains. In Arabia the gossip is passed from mouth to ear in every market, every sitting room, every university, and the foyers of splendid new hotels, where languid young men with doctorates in Business Administration from Harvard, who quite recently ran about barefoot outside their fathers' tents, complain about the vichyssoise. Maddeningly (and unlike most Brits), they can spell it perfectly. All personal sources must remain anonymous of course.

There is, however, one important difference between the British stories and the Arabian ones. The British stories will all have been repeated from man to man. The Arabian stories are often repeated from man to woman to woman to man. This is because Arabs tell their wives what they have heard during the day, and the wives get on the phone and tell their sisters who then tell their husbands. The author has no wish to repeat the betrayals and stupidities of British politicians, nor private confidences, and should perhaps best be described as Collector rather than Author.

Enough to think that Truth can be;
Come sit we where the roses glow,

Indeed he knows not how to know
Who knows not also how to unknow.
>   Sir Richard Burton, *The Kasidah of Haji Abdu el Yezidi*

The Arabs are surviving the tsunami of change with amazing calm when one considers their own history of the last fifty years – a period that equates to the five hundred years the West took to reach what it thinks is the same place. The stories collected together here are just a small snapshot of quite a short period and part of that history.

1917–1956: Britain's Moment in the Middle East.
>   Elizabeth Monroe

Readers will notice that most stories originate in the last half-century or so. This is because storytellers from earlier decades are dead and not saying anything very much. And earlier authors were not concerned with jokes.

Glencairn Balfour-Paul captures these threads in describing a stone mason:

Enough for this man that his skill had truth by the forelock. In his tough credo, whatever was indisputably valid was also good for a laugh.

'No Good Story is All True'

To cheer up the Jeddah taxi drivers who are much reviled for their rapacity, here is a quotation from Marcus Tullius Cicero (106–43 BC):

You must look out in Britain that you are not cheated by the charioteers.

And just to be fair, here's the Syrian poet Abu 'l'Ala, who died in

AD 1057, sadly just missing the invasion of England by William the Conqueror:

I lift my voice to utter lies absurd
For when I speak the truth, my hushed tones scarce are heard.

I have heard it claimed that the Arabs (Palestinians) invented the quip, 'Why did the English have an Empire upon which the sun never set?' Answer, 'Because even God would not trust them in the dark'. The original quote, in fact, comes from Duncan Spaeth, who phrased it slightly differently: 'I know why the sun never sets on the British Empire: God wouldn't trust an Englishman in the dark'.

Finally, I would like to add that anything written about the Middle East is almost always greeted with fits of fury from all sides. Fellow Arabists sneer: one Festival of Islam in the 1970s was enlivened by geriatric but savage Arabists who, half a century earlier, had disagreed about some arcane point of grammar, and on meeting again went at it with renewed rage, hoisting their Zimmer frames like lances as they joined battle. Arabs are also affronted when mentioned personally, though they delight in reading about other Arabs! So, in propitiation, I take refuge in a quotation from the eccentric Wilfrid Blunt, poet, arabophile and diplomat, who wrote in a Preface to his long-suffering wife's book *The Bedouin Tribes of the Euphrates*:

In conclusion, and while protesting complete submission to the learned on all matters connected with Oriental lore, I take my stand against the merely untravelled critic in the words of the excellent Arabic proverb, which says, 'The off forefoot of my donkey stands upon the centre of the earth. If you don't believe me, go and measure for yourself.

PART ONE

ARABIAN ATTRIBUTES AND TRADITIONS

Their sense of humour: a unifying force

Arab Unity is a much misunderstood subject. The Arabs will probably never attain a unity that accords with the West's notion of it. You might think there is a similar lack of unity in the West, but they already have an Arabian kind of unity, which is something they would do well to understand. Perhaps the following explanations will make it clear what I mean.

The twenty-three Arab States have a sort of circular system in which the Lebanese laugh at the Syrians, who laugh at the Iraqis, who laugh at the Saudis and the Egyptians, who laugh, with superb fairness, at all the Gulf States who, chortling among themselves, laugh at the Kuwaitis, who fall about laughing at the Tunisians, the Libyans, the Algerians and the Moroccans, who all kill themselves with merriment over the Lebanese, and round again we go. However, just to show how united they all are, everyone laughs at the Yemenis. The historian Al Wasi'i rubs this in more than somewhat. Writing in the 1920s he reports on the ignorance of tribes in the north of Yemen, describing them as being up to their necks in barbarism, violent, heartless and dissolute. They tried to eat soap, and thought that sugar cones were artillery shells. Another writer says that the Yemenis threw rice away thinking it was maggots and, never having seen themselves in a mirror, shot at their own reflections.

****

A young Egyptian accountant in Jeddah expressed the idea of fraternal unity and affection rather well at a time when Egypt was in hot water with the Arab League for coming to an accommodation with Israel which culminated in an exchange of ambassadors. The Arab world was fizzing with anti-Egyptian rhetoric. The accountant said, 'What do these Bloody Arabs know about it?' We should point out that the epithet 'Arab' can itself be a bit confusing. In the Middle East, it usually means 'bedouin', and the noble descendants of Byzantium in Syria and the Levant, and the descendants of the Pharaohs in Egypt, though both having been conquered by the 'Arabs' in the past, do like to make a distinction!

Cairo writes, Beirut publishes, Baghdad reads.

Arab saying

By implication the rest are unable to do any of these things.

◎ ◎ ◎

The following tale might make the idea of Unity plainer still. After the move of the Arab League headquarters to Tunisia, a young man was seen sitting on the wall outside their splendid new offices with a trumpet in his lap. When asked what he was doing he explained that this was his new job. He was paid fifty dollars a month, and when Arab Unity took place through the good offices of the Arab League, he was to blow the trumpet to let the whole world know the good news. When his questioner commented that the salary appeared to be on the low side the young man replied, 'Yes, but it is a job for life'.

****

In Nasser's day, Unity was a really hot topic and most years there was a Unity Conference held in Cairo. These usually produced some hilarity, like stories that President Gaddafi of Libya had pulled a gun on King Hussein of Jordan. On one occasion President Arif of Iraq attended after a somewhat traumatic experience back home. The story goes that he had paid a visit to the Presidential privy and had just left it when there was a shattering explosion that could not possibly have been produced by Baghdad plumbing alone. It transpired that a disaffected Hunter pilot in the Iraqi Air Force, British-trained naturally, had fired a rocket at the Presidential Palace. Fortuitously, the missile went straight through the lavatory window. So, when he arrived in Cairo the Iraqi President's nerves were not in good shape. This was why all the delegates were astonished to see him suddenly flying horizontally across the room to land, quivering, behind a sofa. Apparently, King Hussein of Jordan had taken out a cigarette and lit it with his Zippo lighter. The noise of the flame being ignited had frightened the wits out of the nervous President, who promptly took off for safety in uncharacteristically athletic fashion.

This story comments not only on the West but also on the Arab world, and it is perhaps no surprise that the Deity is involved. Allah once asked the Angel Gabriel to show him what had happened to the World he had made. The Angel first of all showed Him America, Disneyland, Hollywood, skyscrapers and so on. God was amazed. Then Gabriel showed God England, the disused railway lines and the empty factories and silent shipyards. Again God was amazed. Gabriel guided God to all the other countries in the World and God was full of wonder at each one. Then finally Gabriel showed God the Yemen. 'Oh yes,' said God, 'I recognise this place, it's just as I made it'. The poor Yemenis always seem to get it in the neck.

◈ ◈ ◈

The acting skills fostered during the centuries of the Caliphates are justly famous, as is the great tradition of the modern Egyptian theatre. However Arabians frequently have a marvellous talent for mimicry. Sir William Luce and his wife were much entertained during a visit to the Eastern Aden Protectorate by their host's driver. This man had a reputation for his acting skills and beautifully mimicked Harold Ingrams, probably the most famous of the British Agents in that part of the world, talking to the Al Kaf Sayyid. This was followed by a brilliantly funny take-off of a lady typist in Aden. The poor woman was continually being distracted by telephone calls, and the driver only used a very small vocabulary of English words, such as 'Hullo', 'How are You?', 'Yes', 'No', and 'Oh!' However the best part of the act was the mimicking of the typewriter itself, with splendid carriage returns and the ringing of the bell.

In Oman a Harsusi called Muhammad, who worked spasmodically as a driver for the oil company, would reduce whole floors of the headquarters offices to convulsions of mirth by imitating the walk of secretaries in high-heeled shoes; he was also of the opinion that he could do the managing director's job with no trouble. Obviously he could easily live in the large house and be driven to work each morning, and shout at people until it was time to be driven home again!

Another company driver in the interior of Oman was deaf and dumb. His name was Abid and he performed a brilliant, if ribald, act. He would mimic getting into a Land Rover, and would start it up and travel up the road. He would stop to give a girl a lift. He would fondle her and eventually bring the car to a halt, and help her out of the cab. They would make love beside the road and finally get back into the Land Rover, and continue the journey. This was all done in complete silence. The act entertained everyone enormously.

This talent is not confined to Arabian drivers. No less a person than the great King Abdulaziz of Saudi Arabia was wont to reduce attendees at his majlis to paroxysms of mirth by imitating the bossy voice and manner of the great Gertrude Bell, who played such a large part in Iraq after the First World War.

Manners, hospitality and generosity

Toujours la politesse

King Idris of Libya was in the habit of stopping his car if he saw a foreigner beside the road, and asking if they liked being in his Kingdom. It frequently happened that the cloud of dust thrown up by the motorcade meant the escorting cars failed to see that the King's car had stopped, and so sped on across the desert without him. On one occasion, the King saw a young airman from the RAF Station at El Adem near Tobruk and, having stopped and alighted from his limousine, he asked the young man if he was happy in Libya. The airman, having no idea who his questioner was, replied that he thought the place was a complete dump, it was hot, nasty, unpleasant and devoid of pubs, but full of flies and sand – and, furthermore, he had had to leave his newly-wedded wife behind in England as there were no married quarters available. Admittedly, the airman's vocabulary was not exactly as recorded here, being rather more colloquial, and the King was absolutely horrified.

His escort had by now realised that they had lost their King, and returned hotfoot – if one can do such a thing in a Mercedes. The

King got back in his car and ordered an immediate return to the palace, from where he urgently and furiously contacted the British Ambassador. The King expressed his huge displeasure and demanded that something be done at once to alleviate the boy's unhappiness. The British Ambassador got in touch with the Foreign Secretary who, sensing a serious rupture in Anglo-Libyan relations, contacted the Ministry of Defence and the Prime Minister. Counsel was taken and the airman posted elsewhere as fast as possible. Certainly faster than waiting for a married quarter to become available.

Arabs can be very touchy over remarks that Westerners find quite ordinary and normal. They frequently take offence over things we feel to be quite trivial. However, in the field of deliberately giving offence by firing off a thunderingly insulting piece of rudery they are masters of the art of insult. For instance, an Arabian would shrink from anything so crude as to call someone a bastard. Instead he makes a delicate enquiry as to whether or not the person concerned was aware which of the many pairs of shoes outside his mother's door belonged to his father.

***

Stephen Day tells a tale which nicely illustrates how the story itself can get a bit distorted and of the Arabian traditions of hospitality taking no account of cost. Having served as British Ambassador in Qatar, he became head of the Foreign Office's Middle East Department and was temporarily attached to the Royal Household to help in the planning of the first visit to Arabia by Prince Charles. On a subsequent visit he was in a taxi which passed a small single-storied house on the beach nestling among the forest of new skyscrapers. The taxi driver pointed this out, saying somewhat inaccurately, 'That's Bayt Diana, where the Princess spent her holiday with the man from Harrod's'. Stephen Day corrected this remark saying, 'Oh no, that's where the Princess and her husband, our future King, spent his birthday. I know because I arranged it.' The taxi driver was impressed.

The visit had been a wonderful opportunity for the ex-Ambassador to experience the magnificence of Arabian hospitality at its very best, and he had put on the cover of the brief for the Royal couple a picture of the Field of the Cloth of Gold, that splendid medieval pageant when Henry VIII out-dazzled the King of France. This suitably illustrated how our Arabian hosts would view the tour. It happened that Prince Charles' birthday fell on a Friday in the middle of the tour, and Stephen Day knew that HH Sheikh Khalifa, the Ruler of Qatar, would like his guests to have an opportunity to rest and celebrate the birthday quietly on the beach, before returning to the public stage for the grand banquet in the evening. The little villa on the beach was built in three months, a feat seemingly only achievable in Qatar, and fulfilled its function perfectly. It still stands as a testament to the hospitality of the Qatari people.

🏛 🏛 🏛

The history books record that in the time of the first Queen Elizabeth an eminent nobleman, the Earl of Oxford, committed the social solecism of breaking wind while attending the Court. The poor man was mortified and left the capital for his country estates to escape the consequent ribaldry of London society. Seven years later, when he supposed that all had been forgotten, he ventured back to Town. On meeting the Queen once more she apparently welcomed him, and said that it was nice to see him again and she had quite forgotten the fart.

An Arabian equivalent to this anecdote comes from the Fadhli Sultanate of the old Western Aden Protectorate and is important because it is the only instance of a Southern Arabian mention in the tales of *One Thousand and One Nights*. In Arabian society, the public breaking of wind is even more frowned upon than it is in Europe. It is told that a young Fadhli called Abu Hasan, from a good family, so far lost control of his bowels as to let loose an enormous and loud fart at his own wedding party. Covered in shame, Abu Hasan fled the country.

Eventually he fetched up in India where he took up a military post with an Indian prince, and after many years achieved high rank, position and wealth. However the guilt of his offence remained with him and, wanting to retire to his homeland, he resolved to return disguised as a religious pilgrim to see if he had been forgotten; if so it would of course be safe for him to return permanently. However, while sitting outside a hut he heard a young woman inside ask her mother when she had been born because she needed to know the date so that her horoscope could be read. The mother replied that she had been born on the same night that Abu Hasan had farted. Abu Hasan, much cast down, returned to India.

Tales like these betray an almost universal preoccupation with alimentary explosions. There is a very similar one, collected as the result of a quite casual conversation, that comes from Hail in northern Saudi Arabia. It appears that a young Shammari tribesman called Salman farted in the majlis of the Rashidi Amir. In order to escape the consequences of disgrace he fled to Damascus, where he became a prosperous merchant and lived for the next forty years. After this length of time he thought all would have been forgotten, so he journeyed back to his homeland. He stopped at a well between Al Ula and Hail, two days' ride from the capital, to water his camel. There he met a Bedu woman who asked him about his travels. In answer to her queries he told her that he had been away from Hail and the marches of the Nafud Al Kabir for over thirty years. 'Good Heavens', responded the woman, 'You haven't been home since Salman farted in the Emir's majlis'.

Of course, it isn't only mankind that suffers this sort of thing. Apparently the historian Al Nahrawali relates the story that once Yemeni forces retreated because their commander's donkey farted, this action being reckoned to bring ill fortune. In which case there must be a lot of bad luck about in the lands of Arabia as donkeys seem to be particularly good at it.

The Arabs are famous for their courtesy. It has been said that they always say 'Excuse me' before they shoot you. The march of progress has had a marked effect on this aspect of life. In the good old days it often took ages to get through a door because there were so many 'After yous' and 'No, please do me the honour of going firsts' and gentle friendly argument like that. Once in Oman after the discovery of oil and the establishment of a progressive government in 1971 enabled the country to advance rapidly, an old man met a young one at the entrance to a fort in the interior. The old man politely deferred to the younger man, fully expecting to go through the usual ritual. To his astonished disgust the young man swept past him through the door without a word. The old man shouted 'Peasant!' at the miscreant's back.

And this in a country which has its own national style of coffee-pot, an object much used in following the courteous traditions of the Sultanate. The Omani pot is one of great elegance and distinction and has two little dangling silver 'earrings' and little stones enclosed in its lid. This is so that when coffee has been made and the pot is shaken the tinkling can be heard out in the street. This alerts passersby that coffee is ready and they are invited in for a cup.

In the days of King Saud Bin Abdulaziz, the Shah of Iran paid a State Visit to Riyadh. The Saudi monarch strictly adhered to the tenets of Wahabi Islam, and smoking and drinking were absolutely forbidden in the Nasiriya palace. Heralded by brilliantly uniformed staff and guards, as well as a band playing the two national anthems (which music later changed to an enthusiastic rendition of *Don't Fence Me In*), the Shah arrived in the Palace Reception Hall to be greeted by the King. Orange juice was served, followed by coffee. The two monarchs spoke fitfully for a little while and then the Shah took out a gold cigarette case and extracted a smoke. A shocked silence fell over the room. However, immaculately covering up his feelings the King hastily gave a whispered command to have an ashtray brought for his guest. The only one in the place belonged to the American steward and was tastefully engraved with an edelweiss design and inscribed 'Souvenir of Switzerland'. This was swiftly brought in together with a can of air freshener aerosol. The King's aide presented the Shah with the ashtray, and then stationed himself behind the Persian monarch. The Shah smiled when he saw the inscription on the ashtray, but the smile vanished when he took his first puff and immediately the aide squirted him with air freshener. The Shah did not however give in and resolutely continued to smoke, each puff attracting another cloud of air freshener. The King waited patiently until the Shah had finished, and then escorted him into the Banqueting Hall.

King Saud's staff had to face at least one test of their skills in the field of politesse. This was occasioned by the State visit of the Egyptian President Nasser, which also coincided with a visit by President Al Quwatli of Syria. A State Banquet was planned to be held in the Al Hamra Palace and a suitably exotic menu was approved. It listed such delicacies as *paté de fois gras, canard à la presse sous cloche, carottes*

Vichy, pommes Parisiennes, salade Napoléon, riz pilaf sauce suprême, and *vol-au-vent à la Reine.* The menu was rushed to the printer on the day of the feast and he promised a proof by midday. It duly arrived for approval. It had superb Arabian calligraphy, with the Egyptian and Saudi flags embossed in gold. The Steward sent the proof, with an Arabic translation of the basic dishes, to the Palace Superintendent, who approved it and sent it back to the printer. By early afternoon the finished menus were delivered.

The Palace Superintendent then looked at them again and pointing at *pommes Parisiennes* asked if the menus were in English. The Steward said No, it was French.

'Why French?', asked the Superintendent. 'Our Guest is Egyptian, and the French are supporting Israel against us. We can't have that kind of writing – throw these menus away and do them again in Arabic. We must have only Arabic names for the dishes.' In vain did the Steward protest that there were no Arabic names for the dishes. The Superintendent ordered that they be given Arabic names nevertheless, remarking that God would help. Thus *pommes Parisiennes* became Cairo Potatoes; *salade Napoléon* became Rameses Salad, and on it went with, Pressed Duck under Pyramid Covers, Chopped Alexandria Goose Livers, Theban Carrots and, perhaps rather unfortunately, Nile Tarts. The new text was rushed to the printer and the results returned in record speed by four o'clock. Disaster! The new menus had not had time to dry and were irreparably smeared. A new batch was printed and delivered just ten minutes before the banquet was due to start. As the Egyptian President arrived, a Secretary rushed in to say that no provision had been made for the Syrian party. Apart from a terrible effect on the seating plan, the menus had to be destroyed yet again as they had no Syrian flag on them.

****

During the Civil War in the Yemen it was felt in some quarters that the Royalist cause would be given no end of a boost if they could lob some explosives at the Republican Presidential Palace in Sana'a. Accordingly a box of twenty-four mortar shells, and a small mortar to go with them, were loaded onto a donkey. Travelling only by night to avoid the attentions of the Egyptian Air Force, the precious cargo took a little over a month to reach a suitable site within range of the Palace. To add to the PR side of things it was arranged that a Royal prince should be present and perhaps let off the first round. The tribesmen were so impressed by this honour that when the prince arrived they fired off a Royal Salute of twenty-one mortar bombs into the mountainside. This fusillade alerted the Egyptian Air Force, which immediately took to the air, and there was only just time for the remaining three bombs to be hastily sent in the direction of the target before everyone had to race for cover. It was reported that several windows were in fact broken, so, with a bit of exaggeration, the object of the exercise could be said to have been successfully achieved.

❁ ❁ ❁

By April 1966 the flow of Yemeni refugees into Saudi Arabia increased following the withdrawal of the Imam Badr to Taif, the resort south of Makkah, and the extension of the Egyptian occupation of Yemen. There the Imam spent several months in hospital recovering from the rigours of living in caves and fighting the war. He left his cousin Saif Al Islam Muhammad Bin Hassan in charge within Yemen itself. The Quraish Palace Hotel in Jeddah was the place where most of the refugees stayed in that city, at first being put up by the Saudi Government. This hotel was a splendid relic of the Ottoman period but had taken on a somewhat seedy appearance by the late 1960s. Vestiges of former glory could still be made out: a wonderful staircase criss-crossing the building, first of all leading to the reception desk on the first floor; two courtyards, floor to ceiling mirrors, chandeliers and Syrian furniture in the Louis Farouk style; and all now mismanaged by a corpulent Alexandrine Greek called Nikko, with help from his slightly less corpulent spouse, who prided herself with total self-delusion that she was mistress of both good husbandry and hygiene. Here eventually both the supporters of the Imam Badr and the assassins of his grandfather were accommodated amicably side by side, much to the amazement of Western observers.

****

Later, just as the British were leaving Aden, the National Liberation Front shelled Government House and the military headquarters. They used three-inch mortars for the first target and two-inch mortars for the second. As the last High Commissioner, Sir Humphrey Trevelyan, remarked, 'At least protocol was observed'.

Sheikh Zayd had not long become President of the United Arab Emirates when he made a visit to the UK. The Presidential plane stood on the tarmac of Abu Dhabi Airport and an impressive guard of honour smartly lined the red carpet leading to the steps. The President alighted from his limousine and, gracefully acknowledging the salute, began a stately walk up the carpet. Suddenly a scruffy Bedouin leading a camel burst through the left-hand line of soldiers.

'Hello Zayd,' he said.

'Hello Muhammad', answered the President. 'How are you? How is the family? What's the news?'

'Praise be to God, there is nothing but what's good,' replied Muhammad. 'How are you, Zayd?' he continued. So it went on for several minutes. Eventually Sheikh Zayd said,'You must come with me as we have so much to talk about,' and, taking the halter of the camel, he passed it to a most surprised airport manager with an instruction to look after the animal until he got back. With that the Presidential party, accompanied by a quite unmoved Muhammad, proceeded into the plane. It wasn't until they were flying over Cairo that the thought passed around as to what would happen at Heathrow when they all got there. Muhammad had no passport, no spare clothes, and nowhere to stay. Fortunately the wonders of radio resolved the difficulties, but Muhammad was accompanied tactfully to the Dorchester where the workings of the plumbing were gently explained.

♜ ♜ ♜

During the final years of British control in South Arabia some members of the National Liberation Front occasionally were caught by the authorities. Following the inevitable questions, the British interrogator would tell the prisoner that he didn't mind him being a Communist as long as the miscreant was happy with what had happened to so many of Lenin's friends by 1920. One other thing the prisoner might like to reflect on was the incontrovertible fact that only one man ever won a revolution. If the prisoner was that man then all would be well, but if he was not, he would have to look out. The prisoner was then taken back to his cell.

Many years later this same interrogator was walking through the Market in Riyadh, when a plump tailor busily making the long white cotton clothes for Saudi men saw him. The man jumped over his sewing machine into the lane in front of the Englishman and embraced him warmly. The Englishman responded to this display rather diffidently as he naturally had no idea who the plump man was – whereupon the tailor said that the Englishman must remember him, because he had put him in prison. Feeling somewhat nervous at this, the Englishman began a conversation to find out more. The plump tailor thanked him profusely for saving his life because when the British left Aden there had been a huge celebration, particularly amongst released prisoners. After the first day their friend Salim was missing. On the second day Ali disappeared, and then the following day no one could say what had happened to Muhammad. The remaining partygoers looked at one another and remembered the words of that Imperialist English interrogator: none of them was the new President! The imperialist colonialist running dog had been right. So they all decamped as fast as they could to Saudi Arabia. The plump tailor explained that this was how they had survived.

He invited the Englishman to his house that evening. When he arrived he was a little perturbed because there were nearly a dozen former enemies of Britain there in the sitting room. However he quickly recovered when his host indicated that as a thank-you he should help himself to a whisky from the two cases that were put on the carpet. Bearing in mind that the price of one bottle was at that time about £150, it was an enormous expense for his host to have gone to.

****

The romance of the desert and the attraction of its people has exerted an enormous pull on the minds of many Westerners, in particular the English. Some have been completely distracted but most retain some sense of proportion about their feelings; but the march of progress has displaced much of both the romance and the landscapes that evoked it. However a couple of vignettes serve to record something of the wonder that was created in the quite recent past – a wonder that perhaps will not re-appear. The rules of hospitality laid down by centuries of desert life are fast disappearing, along with that life itself.

Wilfred Thesiger records that on one of his tremendous journeys his party was stopped in the Empty Quarter by a small boy of about eleven years of age. He was not much over four feet tall and wore a white shirt and headcloth with a dagger at his waist. He had run to catch up with Thesiger's camels and, after exchanging the customary greetings, the little fellow stood in front of them with his arms out and told them that they could not proceed. Thesiger thought, 'Damn! Are we to be stopped by this child'? Thesiger's companions said nothing and the boy repeated, 'You may not go on'. Pointing to some dunes about five or six miles away he said, 'You must come to my tents. I will kill a camel for your lunch. I will give you fat and meat.' Thesiger and his party protested that they had a long way to go before sunset, but the boy insisted. Finally he gave way saying, 'This is all wrong, but what more can I do?'

An oil company man travelling in the same area many years later found two young men of the Rawashid tribe camping in the dunes. They had a small bivouac tent and insisted on making coffee for their guest. After conversation, the exchange of news and the drinking of the coffee, in which last his two hosts did not join, the oil company man prepared to continue on his way. He asked the lads if he could give them some food but they both refused. However, when he got into his Land Rover, and the temperature was about a hundred and thirty in the shade, it became apparent why the lads hadn't joined their guest in having a cup of coffee. Clearly disapproved of by his colleague, one of the lads put his hand on the oil man's arm and asked if he had any water. He explained that they hadn't drunk for three days. They had given up the very last drops they had to entertain their guest. If he could give them nothing, if one of them hadn't asked, they would both have been dead in a day.

❀ ❀ ❀

When the Six-Day War was more or less over, one of the English schoolteachers in Jeddah, contrary to Embassy advice, was forced to go to the souk due to sheer hunger. Needing some cups and saucers, he went first to a shop selling crockery where the radio was blaring out Egyptian propaganda to the effect that the Egyptians had triumphantly shot down four hundred Israeli planes, or some such. The proprietor of the shop naturally offered his customer tea and asked the tea-boy to turn off the radio. When the teacher asked why, he said that it was well known that the English and the Americans were friends of the Israelis, and he felt that the programme would be displeasing to his guest.

Another incident at another time underscores the innate courtesy of Arabians. The artist Henry Hemming relates how, when on his way from Amman to Baghdad shortly after the 2003 invasion of Iraq, he and his companion travelled by bus, and their British passports attracted a considerable amount of active antagonism at the border crossing. However their Arabian travelling companions on the bus took the view that they were guests, and took care of them as best they could, sharing food with them.

****

If there is one quality for which Arabians are most justly famous it is their generosity. In the good old days they used to steal camels – an activity frowned on by Westerners, who would naturally never think of doing such a thing! Little did they realise that the stealing of a camel enabled the Arabian to be generous because he then had something to give away.

During the 1970s in London an attractive young English businesswoman decided to have a girls' night out with a friend. They agreed to meet up in the foyer of the Garden House Hotel in Kensington. As the first to arrive was sitting in the foyer, as arranged, she was approached by an exceptionally good-looking young Arabian. He smilingly accosted her offering a handsome £100 but she was naturally put out and told him that she wasn't that sort of girl. The young man looked disappointed and walked away. The girl's friend still did not arrive and so, after about a quarter of an hour, the Arabian lad saw her still alone and approached her once more, offering a £1,000. The English girl became quite annoyed and told the young man that she would complain to hotel security if he persisted. A further half hour passed and the girl's friend had still failed to appear. Just then, the receptionist crossed over to her to tell her that her friend had telephoned to say that she would be unable to make their appointment after all.

Collecting her coat, she was once again approached by the handsome young Arabian who offered her £100,000. He was very good looking and the English girl thought, well why not. The young man took her to the restaurant where he bought her a wonderful dinner, and then they went up to his suite. In the morning the girl awoke to find herself all alone. The young man had gone. She thought, 'So that's that!' Never mind, he had been a kind and terrific lover. Then she noticed an envelope pinned to his pillow with her name on it. Inside was a cheque for £200,000 on a private city bank. The girl went to the bank and to her surprise the cashier calmly put the money into a bag for her. Blushing, she asked him who had signed the cheque. She wanted to contact him because their agreement had been for only half the sum written on the cheque. The cashier told her that he was not allowed to do that. The girl kept the extra hundred thousand for over a year but she was never able to find out who her beautiful lover was.

Status, loyalty and rivalry

Who do you think I am? The Sheikh of Ajman?
Sultan Said Bin Taimur, enraged at being belittled and acidly
making comparison with the most insignificant and smallest of his
northern neighbours

What do I need PR for? Everybody knows me already.
attributed to Sultan Said Bin Taimur, a Ruler of Dubai, a Ruler of
Kuwait and at least three important merchants in Jeddah

Beware the Evil of the one to whom you have done good.
Arabian proverb

Ruler in Disguise

Sultan Ghalib Bin Awadh Al Qu'aiti of the Hadramaut was educated
at Millfield, where he developed an interest in sports. On his return to
Mukalla he continued to try to keep fit and astonished the Bedouin
visiting the town by jogging in singlet and shorts on the beach. He was
followed at a respectable distance by some bodyguards. This activity
was something of a family tradition: his bulky grandfather, Sultan Salih
Bin Ghalib, was wont to take brisk early morning walks in pursuit of the
same objective. Sultan Ghalib's grandfather's uncle and predecessor,
Sultan Umar Bin Awadh, used to make incognito visits to the less
salubrious and more dangerous parts of the town, accompanied at a
respectful distance by some guards.

Followed discreetly by his Equerry and Chief Bodyguard Salih
Ali al Khulaqi, he would at times join gangs of coolies engaged by
local merchants to carry smuggled merchandise and stack it in their
godowns. Sultan Umar would then take up the matter with the

merchant concerned. Only a few such conversations were needed to discourage the merchants from these activities.

Also rather like Harun Al Rashid and his Wazir, Ja'far Al Barmaki, in Abbasid Baghdad, Sultan Ghalib, following his forebear's example, used to disguise himself to find out how his people lived and what they thought about things. His chief cook would smear ash from the kitchens over his Ruler's face before he and a very worried bodyguard, who had vainly tried to dissuade the Sultan, set out. On one occasion Sultan Ghalib found it difficult to keep a straight face. It was afternoon and he and his guard were visiting a coffee shop in a suburb of Mukalla, and one of the other customers began to bully a lad waiting at a nearby table. The boy responded by saying, 'Stop or I will report you to Ghalib'. However, Ghalib's disguise was seen through on this occasion by an official who worked at the British Residency, Abdul Qadir Ali Hakim, who by chance was sitting at a neighbouring table. Ghalib's bodyguard found it difficult to prevent Abdul Qadir from giving the game away by greeting the Sultan with customary respect.

Sultan Ghalib was also in the habit of openly joining labour gangs working on the roads. This was done in order to give his people the message that, contrary to socialist propaganda which emphasised how the upper classes lived off the blood and sweat of the workers, their Sultan, in keeping with Islamic teaching, saw no difference between one class and another. He actually enjoyed missing his siesta and the comforts of his palace during the hottest part of the day so that he could share the tribulations of the workers.

🏛 🏛 🏛

It is told that an American Admiral paid a visit to the Ruler of Bahrain. On arrival, the Admiral was not only met by the Ruler himself but also the Ruler's teenage son, who politely held out his hand to shake. The Admiral, thinking the lad was a servant, immediately put his hat into the boy's hand, as did the two American officials following him. On subsequent visits the Americans were surprised by the way their hats were grabbed the moment they entered the Ruler's Reception Room.

The Millionaire

The lazy person has no legs.

Egyptian Proverb

In Aden a beggar was so successful at his trade that he became a millionaire. He used his wealth to build a beautiful large house in Crater under Jebel Shamsan, and to send his boys to England to be educated at an expensive private school. In his old age he missed his companions of begging days and used to escape from the house to sit with them once more on the pavement. While catching up on the gossip he would put out his begging bowl to earn a few coins as he had been used to doing. After all why waste the opportunity? This behaviour embarrassed his family dreadfully, and it was quite a sight to see a Rolls-Royce arrive and young men in Savile Row suits jump out to grab the old man and bundle him, protesting volubly, into the car to be taken home and respectably hidden.

****

The Yafa'i Sultan Mahmud Ibn Aidrus Al Afifi was regarded by the British as being the closest thing South Arabia had to Lenin himself. But, as an instance of different attitudes to things, this story perhaps demonstrates just how wrong the British were. It can scarcely be called a story about Communism red in tooth and claw!

Sultan Mahmud was visiting London in 1958, during a period when he was still talking to Her Majesty's Government, and one evening in his hotel he was horrified to see a white girl leaving the foyer in the company of a black man. The Sultan rushed up to Reception and demanded to know if the girl's family knew that their daughter was going out with one of the servants!

A propos of this, I recall presenting a Prince of the House of Saud with a copy of *Burke's Royal Families of the World, Volume II, Africa and the Middle East*. I jokingly told the Prince that by being in this book clearly the Al Saud had at last become respectable! His Royal Highness looked at the volume for a couple of minutes and then remarked that of course he was honoured to see his family details there, but he did have reservations about being in the same volume as the servants!

There is a not dissimilar tale from far away in South Arabia. It is just as politically incorrect. When, in November 1963, the British mounted an expedition to tame the unrepentantly belligerent tribes of the Mahri Sultanate, their arrival outside the town of Al Ghaydah on the coast was met with sullen, silent non-cooperation. A stalemate ensued that was really a classic in the annals of sending people to Coventry. The Mahri tribesmen steadfastly refused to have anything to do with the British party. Into this standoff arrived a small party of Mahris who had been working overseas in Africa. Doubtless the mind-broadening effects of foreign travel enabled them to ignore for the moment their compatriots' policy of total non-communication with the British, and they strolled over to the Army encampment to see what was what. At that time Africa was going through its own period of anti-colonial strife and revolution and the cry of Uhuru ('Freedom') was loud in that continent. The returning Mahris brought news of all this and in effect reported that Africa was going down the drain. 'You know what's happening?' they asked. 'The Christians have been beaten and the slaves are taking over.'

****

After oil had been found and Sheikh Zayd had replaced his brother as Ruler of Abu Dhabi, becoming also President of the UAE, eager developers obtained a contract to build a wonderful corniche along the beach by Abu Dhabi town where for years an Englishwoman had, perhaps rather oddly, been running a fish and chip shop from a caravan at one end of the beach. Zayd, by then one of the richest men in the world and a formidable global financial force, patronised the lady and her fish and chips. He refused to give permission for the work to begin because that would mean that she would lose her livelihood. The Abu Dhabi Corniche was only begun when she retired, and was finished in 1980. Sheikh Zayd's reticence in this matter is all the more remarkable when one considers that, having seen the Corniche at Alexandria over a decade before, he had at once set his heart on having one at home in Abu Dhabi.

♔ ♔ ♔

Formal meetings with King Idris of Libya were bedevilled by the attention that had to be paid to his slippers. This was because King Idris was convinced that his brother had been poisoned by the Italians, who had put a lethal drug in his brother's slippers. The sofa on which the King perched during formal occasions was so high that the King's feet swung free of the floor. Consequently, his slippers frequently fell off. It was crucial that they were retrieved with all speed lest an Italian be lurking behind the sofa with a fatal dose at the ready. These occasions, otherwise full of gravitas, were thus enlivened by the sight of eminent officials grovelling on the floor putting carefully inspected slippers back on the royal feet.

****

Whose Side Are You On?

Joha was sitting on the river bank when someone on the distant side shouted across at him, 'How do I get to the other side?' Standing up, Joha shouted back, 'You are already on the other side,' and then muttered to himself, 'It's amazing how stupid some people are'.

The idea of who is on whose side is often a very personal matter in Arabia and leads to misunderstanding in Western societies. In the mid sixties the authorities in Aden were astonished to have a fellow in the full uniform of a Colonel in the Yemeni Republican Army turn up at the Rock Hotel for breakfast .The reader should know that the effect on the British was similar to what it would have been in London in 1940 if an SS Colonel had similarly appeared in the Ritz. Taking the advice that too precipitate a course of action might be unwise, an officer was dispatched to join the good Colonel, and perhaps find out what he was doing.

The UK was not actually at war with the Republic, of course. It transpired that the man was going home to spend his leave with his family in Bayhan State. Despite protestations in some quarters that the man was clearly a traitor and should be locked up at once, the Colonel was taken to see his Ruler, the Amir of Bayhan, who would make a decision. As the Colonel walked through the door of the Amir's office the Amir rose from his chair and greeted him warmly, asking how he was, for news of his brothers and how long he could stay. He then authorised the issue of a free ticket to fly the Colonel up to Bayhan and home.

Taking up a career as a mercenary has long been perfectly acceptable in Arabia and, if handled tactfully, does not often create unpleasant frictions. Indeed in the field of the dissemination of news can frequently be very useful, as the Amir realised only too well.

Rory Stewart records, from another place and another time, how, just before he left Iraq in 2004, he was descending the Ziggurat of Ur one evening with some Iraqi friends. One of them, who had attacked the British compound and Rory himself only five weeks previously, told him how much he would be missed when he left. He was much admired by everyone for his hard work and they didn't want him to go. He was their hero. Rory Stewart asked the Iraqi what he was talking about, as so recently he had tried to kill him. The Iraqi replied with a grin that that was nothing personal.

I gave up shooting when Yemenis went out of season.
A British Adviser, Western Aden Protectorate

The Middle Eastern states aren't nations, they're quarrels with borders.
P.J. O'Rourke

There are three superpowers – America, Russia and Kuwait.
King Faisal of Saudi Arabia, teasing the Kuwaitis for their perceived self importance

Me against my brother. My brother and I against the family. The family against the world.
Old Arabian saying

Development in the Trucial States

In the early days of oil wealth the Trucial States were the target of sharks of all shapes and sizes, all intent on getting their teeth into some of the action. It is true that quite a lot of the feeding frenzy was unwittingly encouraged by local government itself. Traditional rivalries found expression in competition for building contracts. It was in the field of roundabout construction that some of the more bizarre manifestations occurred.

There had been decades of rivalry between Abu Dhabi and Dubai, and in the late 1940s they had actually been at war; and in both their territories enthusiastic consultants had produced grandiose road schemes, even if there weren't very many places to go to. However, as is the wont of roads they interconnect from time to time and the need arose for roundabouts. Sheikh Zayd would be persuaded that a life-sized replica of, say, Big Ben, would be an ideal and impressive thing to erect on the latest roundabout. Naturally on completion there would have to be a reception and an opening ceremony; and top of the guest list would be Sheikh Rashid of Dubai, who would thus have his nose put out of joint, seriously losing out on points.

Returning home, Sheikh Rashid would immediately plot revenge. Consultants gladly drew up plans for another road that would, though itself going nowhere, provide a site for a roundabout. On one occasion a brilliant riposte was planned. The roundabout would have a huge arch under which would burn 'The Eternal Flame', fuelled by gas from the oil field. All was prepared and Sheikh Zayd arrived for the opening ceremony looking a bit discomfited. Sheikh Rashid stood up and delivered a magnificent speech. He grandiloquently described the enormous contribution Arab culture had made, and was continuing to make, to global civilisation. Dubai was playing a noble part in this effort and was leading the States of the Trucial Coast, if not the whole Arab World, in this respect. Lesser states were following this glowing example and doing their best to emulate the triumphs of Dubai.

Sheikh Zayd looked distinctly put out by all this. At last Sheikh Rashid finished speaking, and a golden Dunhill lighter was proffered on a golden salver. The tap under the flame head was turned on. Sheikh Rashid flicked a flame from the lighter and held it to the burner. Nothing happened. The connection to the gas supply was blocked and Sheikh Zayd began to smile slightly. An aide, seeing what had happened, jumped forward and told Sheikh Rashid to deliver the speech again as the people at the back of his audience hadn't heard it properly. An engineer was sent off hotfoot to obtain a little gas cylinder, the sort that campers use, and instructed to return and install it in the pipe in ten minutes flat. Just as the Sheikh finished speaking for the second time all was accomplished, and again the lighter was proffered. It worked, and the eternal flame lasted just long enough for the ceremony to be completed successfully. Sheikh Zayd, scowling a bit, went off to see what his people could now do. And so it all went on and on!

A Great War

The managing director of the company responsible for appointing Sheikh Muhammad's Adviser was persuaded to visit the Trucial Coast to see how things were going. The plane journey was just about satisfactory but, after a bumpy, dusty and tiresome journey to his room in the Fujairah fort, the MD was worn out. After being entertained by Sheikh Muhammad he retired to the guest suite where he was followed by the Sheikh and his guards for a goodnight coffee in an outer room. To the consternation of the MD, a huge flying cockroach came in through the window and fell on its back in front of him. Righting itself, the insect then began to march towards the Sheikh, whereupon one of the guards trod on it.

During the night the MD had a nightmare and yelled out what sounded like the Arabic word for cockroach in those parts, 'Yaal!' This shout of alarm woke up one of the sentries who at once thought that an attack was being mounted from the neighbouring State of Sharjah. Sure that fire from Fujairah would persuade the men of Sharjah to discontinue their attack, a furious fusillade was let off in the direction of the neighbours, with whom there had been much recent tension. They of course had been sleeping the sleep of the righteous and were much put out to be so rudely awakened. Leaping to their weapons they returned fire. It was only the approach of dawn and some small investigation by the Adviser that enabled matters to be put to rights, and an uncertain peace to break out again, in time for breakfast. This had not been as easy as it might seem because, taking advantage of the uproar, the gallant men of Sharjah had succeeded in abducting several ladies of Fujairah. At the same time, redoubtable Fujairan warriors had succeeded in running off with a few flocks of Sharjan sheep. This gave the Adviser something of a bargaining chip, but it is not recorded how many sheep a Fujairan lady was worth, or indeed vice versa.

****

Sheikh Muhammad of Fujairah was also an ambitious builder whenever he got the chance, and was proud to own the longest Majlis, or reception room, in the Middle East. He had a Lebanese First Minister to help with the administration of his territory, and this gentleman, to alleviate the loneliness of his position, tilled a small rose garden which was positioned outside the end of the Majlis. Sadly, whenever Sheikh Muhammad heard on his transistor radio that King Faisal of Saudi Arabia, for instance, had just completed a new palace with a Majlis a few yards longer than his, the Sheikh would immediately instruct that the end wall of the Majlis be pulled down, and the building extended to make it longer than the Saudi King's. This reduced his First Minister to tears as his beloved rose-garden was uprooted yet again.

🏛 🏛 🏛

During the 1960s it became increasingly important that the Federal Government of South Arabia address the problems of a Constitution both urgently and seriously. This story has been passed on by David Ledger.

Facing an impending visit from the United Nations to look into things, a meeting of the Supreme Council was held. This was attended by the then High Commissioner, Sir Richard Turnbull, and chaired by Sheikh Ali Atif, Minister of Health, who opened proceedings by saying that as this was an Arabian matter it should be dealt with in an Arabian way. All present agreed. Ali Atif continued, 'It is well known that the most successful Arabian monarch of recent times was King Abdulaziz of Saudi Arabia'. Again everyone nodded their agreement. 'He united Saudi Arabia, and the way he did it was to marry a girl from each of the tribes. If the President of South Arabia is to unite this country then he must marry a girl from each of the seventeen states'. So far so good, and all would have probably gone on all right had it not been that a Member from Little Aden overheard a remark made by Foreign Minister Muhammad Farid Al Aulaqi at this point, 'Well that lets out our Adeni friends', he said. 'They can't manage one woman, let alone seventeen'.

The Member from Little Aden was outraged and banged furiously on the table with a large glass ashtray. 'I have had fourteen children from one wife. Can anyone beat that?' Someone interjected that it was performance that was wanted, not production. Taking advantage of the ensuing laughter Sheikh Ali continued by offering his services. He said he didn't want to push himself forward, but he was perfectly capable of fulfilling the task; furthermore, everything should be above board and the girls should be inspected regularly. He then suggested that the Permanent Secretary should be given this job. 'Certainly not,' yelled his colleagues. 'We must have a neutral doctor, one from the Royal Air Force!'

A barking dog is more useful than a sleeping lion.
Arabian Proverb

****

The merging of the Aden Protectorate States in the 1960s was much criticised in many quarters, including the House of Commons. However, some of the most vocal attacks on the policy came from the Decolonisation Committee of the UN in New York. The Federal Government thought that their cause should not be unsupported, so they deputed Sheikh Muhammad Farid Al Aulaqi, newly-appointed Foreign Minister, to fly to America to present the Federal case. This he did most ably with both moderation and common sense. In the delegates' lounge after the meeting he was seen having coffee with Sheikh Hani Al Habshi, a leader of one of the more extreme nationalist parties, the South Arabian League. This man's politics had forced him to leave Aden some years previously, and he was now living in the Egypt of President Nasser! He and Muhammad Farid were actually old friends, but their amicable meeting deeply upset members of the Decolonisation Committee, who had no idea how things work in Arabia. One, amusingly enough from an Eastern European country, even went so far as to approach the couple to tell them that they should not be on speaking terms.

◈ ◈ ◈

The only witticism so far recorded as coming from King Fahd dates to the time before he ascended the throne, when he was the Crown Prince. He was chairing a conference of sociologists in Riyadh when a young American asked him why the Saudi Government didn't give Iraqi refugees citizenship, and allow them to settle permanently in the Kingdom. Prince Fahd replied that the reason was that the Saudis didn't want to end up like the Red Indians.

Religion

The Saudi Government has had to cope with many unforeseen difficulties. For instance the Holy Territory comprising the area which is forbidden to non-Muslims was easy enough to delineate on the ground, until the invention of the aeroplane. The question then arose as to how high up the boundary went into the air. This matter came to a head when a German company was inadvertently awarded the contract to build new roads to cope with the increase in pilgrim traffic. They employed Muslim Pakistani labour, as naturally it was impossible for Christians to work there. Then how could they be supervised? The answer was that someone could give them orders by megaphone from a helicopter. The religious authorities decided that the vertical boundary of the Holy Territory exactly corresponded to the height from which a megaphone could audibly reach the ground.

Incidentally the preferred spelling of the name of the Holy City in the Kingdom is 'Makkah' rather than 'Mecca'. This is because the Saudi authorities discovered that the British company of that name is involved in dancing and gambling, that is to say the sinful activity of bingo!

****

The brave Arabians have been assailed by British politicians, travellers, sociologists and businessmen doing their best to live up to the Viking view of commerce. However, reaching the very summit of Mount Eccentricity must be the Reverend Joseph Wolff. This wonderful man was a Jew by birth but had taken Holy Orders in the Church of England. Clutching Arabic translations of *The Pilgrim's Progress*, the New Testament and *Robinson Crusoe*, he arrived in Sana'a in Yemen in 1836. He had persuaded himself that the Arhab Tribe of the Bakil Confederation were in fact the Rechabites, a teetotal nomadic tribe of the Hebrews; and he was intent on bringing the Arhab back into the fold of the Church of England. It is reported that, while his reception was cool, he suffered no harm but he had no takers. Later, after an abortive trip to Bokhara to rescue two Englishmen who had been thrown into jail by the irascible and suspicious Emir Nasrullah Khan, he returned to his parish in Somerset, never to leave the shores of Britain again. Incidentally, the two Englishmen had been executed before the Reverend Wolff arrived at the Emir's court, but he escaped their fate because the Emir was hugely amused to see the parson dressed in full academic uniform of gown and mortar board.

> *'He is crazed with the spell of far Arabia,*
> *They have stolen his wits away.'*
>
> From *Arabia* by Walter de la Mare

Victoria for Caliph?

However remote and bizarre a possibility it might seem that the British Sovereign would be considered as a Muslim ruler, it was nevertheless something that occurred to the Ottoman Sultan in 1904.

While lunching with Wilfrid, the self-serving husband of Lady Anne Blunt, the Mufti of Egypt, Muhammad Abdu, told a story which shows how ideas can get about. During his exile in Damascus in 1883, the Mufti related that a parson, the Rev Isaac Taylor who lived in London, had conceived the idea of a union between Islam and the English Reformed Church, based on their shared monotheism. The parson was encouraged in this idea by an old Persian gentleman, Mirza Bakr, who on his return to Syria after a visit to the British capital circulated the concept in a supportive way. This activity attracted some sympathy from the exiled Mufti who, in company with a couple of the Syrian religious establishment, wrote a letter to Reverend Taylor. He was naturally thrilled, and immediately published it, without mentioning the names of the signatories, as representing the view of the Muslim clerics of Damascus, putting forward the opinion that the union between Islam and Christianity was about to become fact.

The article somehow came to the notice of the Ottoman Sultan (who, after all, was the Caliph at that time), who at once contacted his Ambassador in London to find out who had signed the letter from Damascus. The Ambassador got in touch with the Rev Taylor who, not for a second realising the possible consequences, naïvely told the Ambassador the names of the signatories of the letter; consequently, they were immediately thrown out of Syria. Before leaving, the Mufti did have a chance to talk to the authorities. It emerged that the Sultan had become alarmed because he thought that, should England become converted to Islam, the British Sovereign, Queen Victoria, would then become the most powerful ruler in the Muslim World, and so claim the Caliphate, to the detriment of the House of Osman in Turkey.

****

A bedouin encampment in Libya was being visited by an Englishman who was much gratified to see the whole local population crammed into the Sheikh's tent, to meet him so he thought. The Sheikh himself was away but the honours were performed by his brother, and his daughter poured out the tea. As her veil slipped slightly her exceptionally beautiful face was momentarily revealed, and murmurs of 'Allah Allah' went appreciatively round the tent. In this context, the name of God would be appropriately translated as 'Cor!' in colloquial English! To the Englishman's chagrin he realised that it wasn't him they had all crowded in to see. Meanwhile, the call to prayer was heard and all bar the Englishman left the tent, amid a noticeable air of suppressed and amused expectation.

A small itinerant beggar interjected himself to lead the prayers and began to loudly criticise the Almighty. The little man yelled that God was unfair if not downright unjust. Here he was, a poor beggarman with a family to support, and what did God do? Nothing. The beggar had faithfully followed God's commandments all his life. He had obeyed every word of the God-given Quran, and followed the precepts of God's Holy Prophet (Upon Whom Be Peace) loyally and without complaint. What was his reward? Nothing! Nevertheless, God never held back from looking after the King, Idris al Sanusi. God had provided the King with palaces and wealth. The King didn't have to walk everywhere, having all those cars, but the little beggar couldn't even afford a camel. Even Sheikhs lived in expensive tents, and never went short while the little beggar had to creep into a tiny hovel with scarcely enough space for him and his wife to lie down to sleep. Then there were the King's ministers who lacked for nothing, as their waistlines testified.

These comments on the harshness and rigours of his life extracted a rising tide of mirth from the congregation of onlookers. Giggles turned to guffaws and then the little man, judging that he had elicited sufficient sympathy and amusement to make it worthwhile, made the rounds and collected a spoonful of tea here, a spoonful of sugar there. Eventually he had collected quite a haul of gifts, and he stopped in front of the Englishman, who could only offer a ten piastre note, which was avidly accepted.

A couple of weeks later the Guardroom at RAF El Adem telephoned the Englishman to tell him that a scruffy little chap had appeared at the gate asking for him. When he went down to the gate there was the little beggar, who greeted him warmly calling him 'The Lord of Ten Piastres'. When the Englishman asked why he had come, the little chap insouciantly replied that he wondered if the Lord of Ten Piastres would like to become the Lord of Twenty Piastres, or maybe even Fifty?

This story echoes the experiences of the Pakistani poet Muhammad Iqbal. Writing in Urdu, his poem *Shikwa* (Complaint) also moans about God's treatment of mortals. Iqbal had a fatwa issued against him for his pains, and two years later wrote another poem called *Jawab al Shikwa* (Reply to the Complaint), but it isn't recorded if he received any piastres.

****

There are a couple of tales about Joha which fit here.

A doctor, a rich merchant and a lawyer were praying in the front row in the Grand Mosque. They prostrated themselves, confessing the deepest devotion and repentance. Each one repeatedly cried out that he was unworthy. Then Joha, dressed in rags, came in and, seeing the mighty abasing themselves, joined them and cried out that he too was unworthy. The doctor, looking at the merchant and the lawyer said contemptuously, 'Look who thinks himself unworthy'.

Joha was poor. One day he was standing in the market, his wretched clothes patched and his shoes full of holes. He saw a man entering the market astride a fine horse. He was dressed in clothes of the most expensive silk that fitted his well-fed frame to perfection. 'Who is that?' asked Joha. 'He is the Sultan's servant,' one of the bystanders told him. Joha turned his eyes skywards and said, 'God, look at the Sultan's servant and then look at yours'.

Superstitions

Sheikh Muhammad Al Sharqi of Fujairah

Ruler of a Trucial State that was divided inconveniently into three tiny pieces, Sheikh Muhammad, known by the affectionate nickname Fudge, actually lived most of the time in a house he rented in Dubai. There he was in a continual state of concern because, should the site be sold and developed by his landlord, it was likely that bulldozers would unearth the remains of people who had crossed his path, and who had been removed from this world and buried in the courtyard. Such a discovery could only lead to the need for embarrassing explanations.

Back in his own State, there were other worries as he was prone to bouts of being the Gulf's answer to various world heroes. A feeling that he was a reincarnation of Alexander the Great or Napoleon would lead to several weeks of planning a huge military campaign, and the sourcing of the appropriate weaponry. However, it was in one of his periods of doing good and clothing himself in the mantle of Louis Pasteur that he attracted a flock of consultants to his side. Sheikh Muhammad became very excited at the prospect of providing his people with a beautiful hospital, and the consultants looked forward to a very lucrative contract, despite the fact that the Sheikh actually had no money.

Everything proceeded well and the time for signing the contract approached. It was at this point that it occurred to the Sheikh that he should ask the consultants where exactly the hospital was to be built. Eagerly plans were unfurled and the exact position of the hospital proudly pointed out.

'No,' said Sheikh Muhammad. 'You can't put it there because there is a water well there, and my people must have water,' he explained, a trifle lamely. Crestfallen, the consultants quickly assured the Sheikh that an alternative well could easily be dug and no one would go short of water. However Sheikh Muhammad was adamant, and the whole scheme came to a halt. If only the consultants had done their homework a bit more assiduously!

A few years before all this, Sheikh Muhammad noticed that when visiting one of the three bits of his Sheikhdom he always got an attack of rheumatism. This never happened when he visited the other two parts. He determined to find out the reason and caused enquiries to be made. It transpired that he had antagonised a man called Al Baluchi, who had travelled south into Oman to the city of Nizwa to enlist the aid of a famous witch, so that he could get his own back on the Sheikh. Having accepted payment in advance, the Witch of Nizwa set to work and, exerting all his powers, put a curse on Sheikh Muhammad. However, the curse could only reach that part of Fujairah nearest Nizwa and not all three parts of the Sheikhdom. Having the explanation to hand, Sheikh Muhammad considered how to take countermeasures, and decided to invite the witch to a meeting.

A messenger was sent to Nizwa to tell the witch that Sheikh Muhammad had heard of his skill and fame, had an important job for him, and would pay very handsomely indeed. The cupidity of the witch was aroused and, feeling sure that Sheikh Muhammad was unaware of his work for Al Baluchi, he set off for Fujairah on his donkey. On arrival he entered the fort where Sheikh Muhammad was sitting in his reception hall and announced himself obsequiously.

'Are you really the famous Witch of Nizwa?' enquired Sheikh Muhammd.

'Yes my Lord, I am,' answered the witch with confidence. Whereupon Sheikh Muhammad yelled at his men to seize the witch, cut his throat and toss the body down the well. After this, Sheikh Muhammad recovered completely from his rheumatics, but remained fearful that the body would be discovered. It was of course the very well that would be dug up if the hospital was built. There appears to be no extant record of how the devoted and loyal subjects of Sheikh Muhammad enjoyed the flavour of decomposing witch in their coffee.

There is a charming little story which is quite untrue, but everyone in Oman seems to know it. Like many Arabian stories it is rather inconsequential. During the Jebel War of the 1950s British soldiers in Fahud, where the first oil was found, caught a devil. They put it in a box and sent it to London Zoo. Omanis visiting London in the seventies and eighties frequently asked either to go to the Zoo to see the devil, or enquired after its welfare.

◇ ◇ ◇

People's beliefs, often regarded as superstitious by the supposedly superior, can be both amusing and also invade the hallowed sanctuaries of 20th-century personnel management. Most westerners will have heard of the Jinn, especially the sort that live in a bottle and carry the westernised epithet of Genie. These beings were very real. The writer has described the acting talents of Muhammad Al Harsusi but this man, while on his way to a market town, caught a Dhab lizard. The meat of the tail of this animal is delicious and tastes like chicken. However when caught it must be eaten before sunset because after that time it becomes a companion, so cannot be eaten. As Muhammad got near the town he decided to leave his lizard tied to a tree; he could then go on to the market unencumbered. On his return he found his lizard standing upright balanced on the tip of its tail. This clearly indicated that it was no ordinary lizard, so Muhammad released it as it was almost certainly a Jinn in disguise.

Jinn also had a potentially dramatic effect on the oil company.

They decided to drill a new well in the Duru' area at a place called Ghabar, aptly 'the place of dust'. When the Duru' labourers heard of this plan they immediately refused to move to Ghabar, as they had heard that the area was inhabited by Jinn, rather nasty Jinn at that. Nevertheless, they agreed that if a Christian went and camped in the area and survived, then they would reluctantly consent to work there – it being clear that if the Jinn refused to eat an infidel, then surely it wouldn't eat one of the Faithful.

Accordingly, armed with a bottle of Christian milk, a personnel man from the company set up camp at Ghabar. After the sun went down anxious Duru' labourers got lifts from their colleagues and kept watch all night from the rocky rim around Ghabar to see what happened. In the event all was well and drilling went ahead.

Misunderstandings

An Important Visitor

In the Yemen of the Imams, the northern Zaidi tribes were divided into two parts, known as the Wings of the Imamate. The first Wing was the Hashid, whose Sheikhs were on the Republican side in the Civil War because they had a blood feud with the family of the Imam (although some of its tribes were on the Royalist side). The second

Wing was The Bakil, who were largely on the Royalist side. In the sixties an Arabist in Aden flew up to Bayhan to meet the Sheikh of these last, Naji Ali Al Ghadir, to pick up news of the Royalist cause. The Sheikh was a most striking man to meet due to an extraordinary dual appearance. With his hat on he looked like a dear old Arabian Father Christmas. Without it, he looked like the Devil incarnate. Sheikh Naji was well aware of this, and whisked his hat on and off to suit the points he was making in conversation. The interview went off very well and the Arabist flew back down to Aden.

Back at his flat a couple of weeks later, the Arabist, after seeing his very small daughter off to bed, was having a shower before having dinner. The front door bell rang and his wife answered it. She had to rush back to the bathroom and call her husband as there was a crowd of fully-armed Arabians on the landing. Hastily wrapping a towel round himself, the Arabist went to the door where he found Sheikh Naji who, accompanied by his wounded son, was asked to come in and taken to the sitting room. Sheikh Naji ordered his companions to sit down where they were on the landing. Quickly getting dressed, the Arabist arranged for his guests to be plied with tea, hard-boiled eggs and biscuits, which was all he had to offer.

On asking his visitor why he had called, the reply was that as the Arabist had visited the Sheikh in Bayhan, the Sheikh was returning the call. We should mention that, because there was a serious terrorist situation in Aden Colony at this time, the carrying of arms in the Colony was strictly forbidden. In addition, the flat had no telephone and the nearest one was in a Yemeni grocery, six storeys down and on the opposite side of the road – and the lift wasn't working. As the last plate of biscuits was almost finished an ethereal voice floated up out of the night. It asked in educated tones whether all was well in number twenty-four. The Arabist went out onto the little balcony and, peering down, saw to his dismay that the flats were surrounded by armoured cars with an officer standing beside one of them with a loud hailer.

Realising that a neighbour must have reported the armed men on the landing, and that the garrison troops were probably intent on arresting them, something had to be done quickly to prevent things getting out of hand. The Arabist went back to the sitting room and told his wife and Sheikh Naji that he just had to pop across the road to get some more biscuits. He flew down the stairs, across the road and into the grocery. Borrowing the phone in the shop, he called the garrison to explain the situation, picked up half a dozen packets of biscuits and rushed back across the road and up six flights of stairs. On the landing he gave four packets to the lads sitting there polishing their Kalashnikovs and let himself into the flat. In about five minutes the sound of departing armoured cars wafted up from below, and then Sheikh Naji took his leave, calmly flagging down enough taxis to take him and his party off to see the Sharif Hussein of Bayhan with whom he was apparently staying.

It was quite a problem receiving visitors in a flat at this time, although perhaps not often as dramatic as the incident described here. Various visitors adhering to different factions gave cause for a certain amount of concern. Luckily the Arabist's houseboy neatly solved the most obvious difficulties. He put Royalists on the comfortable chairs in the sitting room. Republicans were parked on the hard chairs in the dining room, and the don't knows were parked on the roof until an accurate opinion could be gained as to whether or not they warranted comfy or hard chairs.

Women

The question of Arabian treatment of women has been a sore point in the West in general and the UK in particular. While Western opinion is largely seen in the Kingdom of Saudi Arabia as rather impertinent nosiness, it is good to be able to relate a few stories that indicate something a little closer to reality.

The usual Western view has frequently been so inflexible that it has perhaps stood against our own national interest. The Foreign Office for years advised against sending HM the Queen to Saudi Arabia because it was thought that she would not be treated with proper respect, despite the experience of an informal visit by Princess Alice, Countess of Athlone as early as 1938 – a visit that led to King Abdulaziz sitting down to eat with a woman for the first time. The Princess was treated with consummate courtesy and generosity throughout her visit. In the event, when a State Visit for Queen Elizabeth II was eventually arranged in 1979 it emerged that the Saudis were perfectly aware, down to the smallest detail, of who was who, and indeed what. For instance, in their bedroom in the Riyadh Palace the Queen's bed was raised a bit higher on a dais than that of the Duke of Edinburgh.

However, during the preparations for the visit some potential for problems arose. These were handled on the British side by Sir John Wilton, the Ambassador, who guided the British officials and explained to the Saudis that Her Majesty needed to have an exact and precise timetable some six months in advance. This need for precise to-the-minute timing was initially greeted by the Saudi officials with some surprise and they clearly thought it was dangerously close to challenging the will of God. However, in the event punctuality was precisely observed and everything happened exactly as planned, making the visit a most memorable success.

◈ ◈ ◈

When Queen Elizabeth was due to visit Aden in 1954, the British were anxious about how the Rulers in the Protectorates would react to receiving a woman, despite the pleasant experience of Princess Alice described above The British were aware that within Islam just touching a woman at her trying time of the month would nullify a man's purification between prayers, a matter which the authorities were in no position to ascertain, and which put them therefore in something of a quandary. After some discussion they decided that after the Queen's arrival she should be driven around to fill in the time until after afternoon prayers. She could then safely shake hands with the Arabian Rulers whatever the state of her health. Unfortunately, Aden was not a large place and Her Majesty soon recognised buildings she had passed earlier, leading her to ask why they had to go round one particular roundabout twice.

****

There is a nice story about a very wealthy merchant in Riyadh who had refused for a year or more to give in to his son's repeated pleas that the family business should buy a private jet. At last, to the young man's joy, his father gave in. But when asked over lunch why he had waited so long the old man replied that his son had got the costings wrong. The plane itself was priced at a million pounds but it would actually cost the family two million pounds. He explained that his son had forgotten about his sister. If he gave his son the price of the plane he would have to give his daughter the same. With that he pulled a cheque for a million pounds out of his pocket and passed it across the table to his daughter suggesting that she pop over to Paris and buy some jewellery. Why Paris? The old man represented the French aircraft industry in the Kingdom.

❖ ❖ ❖

The Saudi Royal Family is deliberately, if slowly, turning the tide of reaction and liberalising life in the Kingdom. Today the movement to allow women to drive by themselves is gaining momentum with not infrequent flouting of the rules by independent-minded girls.

The subject of the veil does have an unexpected aspect too. A Saudi Princess was talking to the author and out of the blue asked him to make sure that Germaine Greer be kept out of the Kingdom. He answered that it wasn't in his power to do so, and enquired what was Her Royal Highness's reason for making this demand. 'Oh,' she replied, 'All this fuss about her sisters suffering behind the veil. Doesn't she realise that with our veils we can have as many lovers as we like? Without them we have problems.'

Cultural differences can be a lifesaver

In the territory of the old Wahidi Sultanate of the Eastern Aden Protectorate there are some magnificent Himyaritic remains. Before the Second World War these were visited by the intrepid Freya Stark. The local Bedouin took the gravest exception to her presence and decided to shoot her. Freya Stark told them, without batting an eyelid, that they couldn't do this because she was a woman. The Bedouin were most surprised to hear this because, as she was wearing trousers, they had naturally assumed she was a man.

🏛 🏛 🏛

Perhaps the subject of underwear is not exactly foremost in anyone's mind when writing about Saudi Arabia. Recently, however, it was something of an eye-catcher to read the headline, '*Saudi Arabia*

Orders Men Out of Women's Clothing. This turned out to be not about transvestites but an article recounting the difficulties faced by a lady in Jeddah called Fatma Qaroub. Whenever Fatma went shopping for clothes she was faced by male shop assistants who asked her all kinds of personal questions about her size, marital status and so on. Fatma started a Facebook campaign entitled 'Enough Embarrassment' and, having gathered no fewer than 11,000 supporters, was joined by other women intent on boycotting women's clothing shops that had no female staff. Fatma's efforts swiftly bore fruit, and within a few weeks His Majesty King Abdullah issued decrees to improve the prospects for female employment in the Kingdom, including one ordering the feminisation of women's clothing shops.

****

Is thy mother-in-law quarrelsome? Divorce her daughter.

Egyptian Proverb

Weddings between Arabians and the English have been uncommon. It is a matter that usually leads to unhappiness on both sides. Some years before the withdrawal of the British from South Arabia, the government decided that the few English ladies married to Arabians in the Federation should be discreetly visited and their passports sorted out in case the British left. The few wives there were had arrived due to what had become quite a regular migration of South Arabians to the UK. If you inherit the hundredth part of a palm tree you can't earn a living from that. Accordingly the Arabian concerned would work his passage to Cardiff, Liverpool or Sunderland, and go into business, usually as a greengrocer. When established, they would fall for the charms of a young blonde local girl and eventually take her home to South Arabia – blonde hair driving most Arabians to paroxysms of desire.

One such girl lived in a small mud house in Dhala State. She was most upset that anyone should think she might want to leave her husband, with whom she had had ten children. As time had passed he had shrunk to become a wisp of an elf, and she had become enormous. Her delicate arms, almost solidly covered in gold bangles, were the size of a rugby player's thigh! She explained that her girlfriends back in Sunderland didn't get their Chanel No. 5 in a bloody bucket. On being asked how she got on with her husband's family, in particular his mother, she simply recalled that on her first arrival she had seen that there was going to be trouble with her mother-in-law. So, she took the old lady round the back of the house and thumped her. She then settled down to life with her adored and adoring husband without any further trouble, and eventually ruled the entire village!

In the 1930s a British Political Officer in Bayhan, Peter Davey, married a relative of the Sharifian family but this met with official horror, and he was told that as she could not come down to the Colony he had better divorce her. Sadly this was what happened.

Another Yemeni gentleman married a girl while he was working in Hull. They had two daughters and when his wife died the bereaved father took the girls home to Yemen. There one of them caught the eye of the Imam Ahmad, who married her. She became a devoted and favourite wife who helped him to overcome his addiction to the morphine prescribed by his Italian doctor.

The most publicised difficulties thrown up by marriages between Western women and Arabian men concern the ownership of the children in the event of a breakdown, and the fact that in entering into a marriage with a hawk-eyed son of the desert the Western bride is all too often totally ignorant of the fact that she is actually marrying his whole family! However, there are other, perhaps more mundane, matters which can give rise to both irritation and amusement.

One Western wife who married into a very important merchant family in Jeddah did not at first come up against any difficulties due to the cosmopolitan nature of her husband's family and their friends. After living in Saudi Arabia for some months she had not had to veil her face once. Then her husband had to fly to Riyadh. The two of them were sitting comfortably in the VIP lounge at the airport when, without warning, several princes appeared. Hastily her husband asked her to cover her face. Somewhat flustered, she did this with the chiffon scarf she had around her head. Then the need to smoke a comforting cigarette arose. Desperately the lady asked her husband how she was supposed to smoke with the headscarf covering her face. The reply was that she should lift up the side of the scarf and insert the cigarette sideways into her mouth. The consequent contortions that this evoked reduced an old family nurse travelling with them to hysterics.

This sudden immersion into Arabian society was repeated at the Riyadh hotel where they were all staying. She found that she had to sit facing the wall in a corner of the dining room to eat her meal. The headscarf still having to remain in place, she also had to eat sideways! Later, during summer, they drove through the desert on a magnificent trip to Taif following a summons to meet the King. Because she was a Christian, they had had to go around Makkah to comply with the rule that Christians cannot enter the Holy City. On arrival in Taif they put up at a fabulous hotel and, after changing, went out to dinner at the villa of one of the Court officials.

The following morning her husband went off to see the King after breakfast and his wife was left to her own devices in the hotel suite. She was told that should she want anything all she had to do was ask a faithful family retainer who was sitting in the corridor outside the suite. After a while the telephone rang and to the wife's surprise the caller turned out to be the British Ambassador. His Excellency asked who she was and then welcomed her to the Kingdom and expressed his hope that she and her husband would come to dinner with him soon. When her husband returned from his meeting with the King his wife told him about the telephone call saying that she had been amazed to get a call from the Ambassador himself and had thought that a secretary might have done it. Her husband replied in lofty tones that she would soon discover that secretaries didn't telephone him. This was how she learned just how eminent a man she had married.

Probably the greatest difficulties faced by intermarriage between partners from the Arabian world and the West have been faced by Sheikh Abdullah Bin Isa Al Khalifa in Bahrain. He had fallen in love with a beautiful Swedish blonde called Dana. Her father had worked in Tsarist Russia and had married a Russian girl. After the revolution the family went back to Scandinavia and in the 1950s their daughter Dana went to the University of California. There she met an Arabian student, Isa Bin Abdullah Al Khalifa, and after a year they became engaged. Soon they were married and their first child, a daughter, arrived. At this point Isa decided to go back to Bahrain to square the family. This proved impossible, and his treatment at their hands was little short of draconian because the then Ruler, Sheikh Salman, decided to make an example of him. His passport was confiscated, as was all his property, and they even refused him permission to use the family name, Al Khalifa.

Dana was living in Beirut with no money at all. Isa cooked up a plot to enable him to get funds from his family: he pretended to divorce Dana. However the family would not relent and Isa hawked himself round the Middle East desperately looking for a job. No one would help until at last an Englishman in Beirut offered him a teaching post. It turned out that the family had banked on him failing to get employment and that this would force him to come home with his tail between his legs. When he got the teaching job their stratagem had clearly failed, so they sent him a telegram forgiving him. However, Dana wasn't included in the arrangement so the couple took up residence in the Eastern Province of Saudi Arabia, from where Isa commuted to work in Bahrain. Altogether this put a strain on the family and Dana moved to Cairo, where she indulged her passion for Arabian horses. There in the days of Colonel Nasser there were still difficulties but some were hilarious.

One day Dana was approached by a young lad wanting a tip because he had put a tap on her phone! Her daughter's American passport caused problems, and the girl was dragged out of their house; it seems that only a miracle enabled Dana to retrieve her from the police station.

In the end, Isa was able to strike a bargain with his family. If he took a second wife, from the Al Khalifa family, Dana would be allowed to come to Bahrain. But that was not the end of the story. Isa was sent off to London on a year's course accompanied by his Al Khalifa second wife. After a year alone on the island Dana passed the test of separation set by the family, and then Sheikh Salman died. His successor, Sheikh Isa, took a much more lenient view and allowed Dana to look after his horses which were in a poor state. However Isa, Dana's husband, continued living with his Al Khalifa wife, visiting Dana every day.

Marriage and the Problem with Polygamy

Sweet night of joyous merriment
Beside the swerving stream I spent,
Beside the maid about whose wrist
So sweet it swerved her bracelet's twist:

She loosed her robe, that I might see
Her body, lissom as a tree:
The calyx opened in that hour
And Oh, the beauty of my flower!

Al Mu'tamid, King of Seville 1068-1091

In past years the Arabians defended the practice of having many wives – at least only four at a time – by telling you that one wife is always nagging you, two gang up on you, and with three there is never any peace in the house as two of them side up together and fight with the third. So four is the ideal number! It is a practice becoming increasingly uncommon. But in any case there are grounds for saying that Islam has in fact always frowned on the practice. It can be held that polygamy was only allowable if all four wives were treated equally, a course which the Holy Book says is impossible. However, a multiplicity of spouses can lead to unforeseen complications, as Harold Ingrams tells of the respected Sayid Tayib Al Attas of Huraydha in the Hadramaut. It was said of the old man that when you saw him smartly dressed in silken robes and he had dyed his beard bright red, you knew he was about to get married again. At the claimed age of ninety-two he had had no fewer than fifty-eight wives, and must have suffered a failing memory at times. All of his wives were recorded in a special book because, as the old man said, he would otherwise forget them!

****

Another consequence of excessive polygyny is underlined by the following account. After the withdrawal of the British from Aden and the consequent impossibility of doing good business under the government of the Communist National Liberation Front in the new workers' paradise, an Adeni contractor removed to Jeddah and started a new company there. He prospered greatly and got married as often as he could. Consequently his family rapidly increased enormously in number. Many sons grew up, got married and needed houses of their own, and their father just put another house on the end of his own for the first lad, and then one on the end of that as the second boy got married, and so on. Eventually a whole, long street was erected. The old man used to wander about complaining that he was surrounded by people he didn't know, all of whom claimed to be his relatives and descendants.

There is a charming story about a family of Saudi bankers whose founding father moved to Jeddah, where he lived in a tiny house that had a single bedroom reached by a ladder up to a very small landing. His business did well from the start and he married four wives in quick succession. Bearing in mind the Islamic instruction that he should treat all his wives equally he had a double bed in the bedroom, and three camp beds on the landing. The bedroom also contained one wardrobe with four doors and a chest of four drawers. Wife number one would accompany the man of the house in the double bed while the other three slept on the landing.

The next night the first wife retired to the landing and the second wife moved into the bedroom. And so on, every wife scrupulously taking her turn, with one space in the wardrobe and one drawer in the chest of drawers. Eventually the man prospered hugely. His sons opened banks throughout the Kingdom and in his old age he moved to the capital Riyadh. Each wife now had her own palace. They were all in a row and looked rather like copies of Buckingham Palace. Each one had the same coloured geraniums growing in identical pots outside, and the old man was solemnly driven in a white Rolls-Royce in exact rotation to a different Palace each evening.

This scrupulous attention to the idea that one should treat all ones wives equally is very common, so common in fact that visiting businessmen from the West often came a cropper because they were unaware of it. A famous Bond Street jeweller had for sale a huge diamond. He took this beautiful and fabulous stone to an exhibition in Riyadh in the belief that only there would he find customers with sufficient wealth to buy it. The writer had a bet with the jeweller that he wouldn't sell the stone. He won. The jeweller sadly recounted that several old men had expressed an interest but sauntered away when the jeweller told them he only had the one stone. Others did tell him they would buy it if he cut it into four.

All this helps to explain why the Arabians don't go in for birthdays. The Olympians in the marriage stakes are of course the members of the Saudi Royal Family itself, and their exact numbers are unknown. However it has been estimated that there could be as many as four thousand descendants of King Abdulaziz Al Saud, boys as well as girls. If they all sent a card to each other, that would make sixteen million cards a year, which would be good business for the greetings card industry!

****

It was possibly much more satisfactory in the Omani Desert, and here the reader needs to understand that employing a Bedouin really means that you acquire a son. An Englishman working for the oil company there hired a young tribesman as a driver. The man's grandfather's dhow had been destroyed by British naval gunfire off the island of Zanzibar for involvement in the slave trade and it was felt that we owed him something. He was also one of the tallest people in Oman and, while an Arabian sneer is pretty lethal from a normal height, it was positively atomic from a height of six foot six, and would be useful in negotiations with his smaller compatriots. After only a couple of weeks the man announced that he was to be married. It soon emerged that his boss was expected to cough up the price of a celebratory sheep and other necessary rations, provide the transport and generally be responsible for the wedding reception. With as much good grace as possible this was accomplished, and the lad was given part of his annual leave entitlement to get his marriage underway.

After a month the lad informed his boss that the marriage had been unsuccessful, and he had divorced the girl and put in a bid for another. The whole performance was gone through again. When there was a request for providing for a third wedding the Englishman remonstrated with his driver and told him that things could be organised better – the lad should try to make friends with his wife, as wives were really quite a permanent sort of thing and not, as it were, just for Christmas, and he felt that in future he could only run to helping out with one wedding a year. The driver replied that he couldn't understand the Christian way of doing things. His way meant that all the young men got to try out all the girls and all the girls got to try out all the young men. In the end everyone could make a sensible, informed and final choice.

From the Western Aden Protectorate, Adviser Nigel Groom records the wedding in Bayhan state of Captain Thabit Qassim, an officer in the Government Guards. The ease with which the necessary arrangements were made impressed Groom's clerk, Nabih, who though he had a family back in Aden, felt the loss of conjugal comforts while on duty up country. Accordingly arrangements were set in train. The reader needs to be aware that the prospective bridegroom has to rely on the reports of friends for an idea as to what the bride actually looks like. He will not see her face until the celebrations are all over and he is at last alone with his bride.

One day Nigel Groom got a note from Nabih, who had been left behind to look after the office. The note informed his boss that a wedding had been arranged and the girl had been recommended by Sharif Awadh, the Ruler's brother. It was known that Sharif Awadh had a racy and rascally sense of humour and although this engendered a feeling of unease it wasn't possible to warn Nabih. When he returned, Nigel Groom found a downcast clerk who informed him that all Bayhanis were crooks. Sharif Awadh had sworn to him that the girl was a young and lovely virgin. 'Everyone said I was marrying the most beautiful girl in Bayhan,' he sorrowfully recounted. 'After the feast I was very excited as it is a terrible life we lead here without women. I approached her and she took off her veil. She was at least seventy years old and she laughed at me, showing that she had no teeth. She was hideous. I divorced her at once but had to stay in the room until the morning because the bedroom door had been locked.' Nabih never lived it all down.

There is a curious sideline to the previous stories which marks the inexorable march of progress. In 2011 the Sunday Times contained a piece by Theo Padnos about Western men converting to Islam and marrying Yemeni brides. Apparently, while researching the article, he discovered that the market shopkeepers in Sana'a displayed bridal undergarments. These were often fantastic creations. There were bras with flashing red lights over the nipples, strings of fake diamonds and revolving sunflowers, and Sex Kitten suits made from strips of red leather and adangle with glass jewels. Panties had remote-control buzzers and massage equipment built into the crotches, and some were even edible!

It seems a bit unfair to pass on the following, as it looks as though the Yemenis are being made a regular target. It was reported by a visiting photographer that in the 1930s ladies on the Tihama coast not only danced with their husbands, but also did it in public, and unveiled. The recorder of this disgraceful behaviour goes on to say that he asked if it also took place on the island of Kamaran, which was at the time safely under British control. Mercifully for the British reputation for single-minded support of virtue and probity, the answer was that the Qadi on the island would not permit such a thing.

Desert Comforts

The social conventions in Arabia involving the fair sex, who are meticulously protected from unwelcome masculine attentions, to the extent that they are never mentioned directly even in greetings, and are veiled in public, leads the observer to think that there can be no naughty ladies in the Arab lands. This is not so, as the following anecdotes relate.

In the Dhahira of the Omani interior there was a lady whose husband had died and left her all alone at Natih, a desert area close to the oil fields. In order to support herself, and not wanting to remarry, she sold her last remaining possession: herself. She was easy to see, as she wore a white *abaya* (cloak) rather than the black favoured by her sisters, and in addition she was always surrounded by the largest herd of goats for miles around. This last was because she charged one goat for her services not specifying the sex of the goat; and as she engagingly explained, goats did what men did and so her herd increased of itself, and the widow became exceedingly wealthy. This wealth enabled her to have an extraordinary independence and eventually she was able to choose her second husband from a position of strength, and to retire happily from her commercial activities.

Further to the south, in the Sharqiya by the Wadi Halfayn, there lived a lady of the Harasis called Safi, which means 'purity'. She was so fierce and formidable that all the men were afraid to marry her. The oil company representative stored a barrel of petrol at Safi's encampment sure that it would be safe with her. So indeed it was. One day a geological party passed by and, seeing the petrol barrel under a bush, thought that the bedu had stolen it, and stopped to fill up their Land Rovers as a way of retrieving the 'stolen' petrol. No sooner had they got out of their vehicles than there was a screech from the thorn bushes and out sprang Safi armed with a tent pole, which was stolen, and our redoubtable heroine began to belabour the geologists until they fled.

Safi was amused to be called Dhahab Safi, meaning 'pure gold'. She appreciated the double entendre as a tribute to the financial aspects of the trade she followed, otherwise than by guarding oil company petrol barrels. Later she moved to Abu Dhabi, where her strength of character attracted the attention of the Ruler, Sheikh Zayd. He gave her a licence and she became the only lady taxi-driver in the Trucial States. It needs to be said that life in the desert was much freer than in the towns, and Safi's sisters, though encumbered with rigid masks to their faces that make them resemble strange crow-like birds in profile, were never stopped from hilarious flirting. When sipping coffee they had to raise the mask a little, and this gave them the chance to throw out a quick sideways wink. The mask somehow enhanced the effect.

Some years earlier it was reported from the Western Aden Protectorate that a lady called Bint Issa had come into Aden Colony from the hinterland to found a thriving business as a procuress. This was so successful that she was able to invest the profits and become a substantial and wealthy merchant. Eventually Bint Issa became well known to the authorities because of her shrill and penetrating voice. This, combined with a domineering and brassy temperament, came to official notice when she daily assailed the relevant government offices, stridently pursuing payment of a debt incurred by an up-country sheikh who had welshed on his financial responsibilities after taking advantage of Bint Issa's stock-in-trade.

The Colony also supported the commercial activities of another lady, who came from Somalia. She was known only as Maalla Mary, so called after the area of her operations. She drove a Mercedes taxi and as she weighed at least twenty stone it was always possible to identify her vehicle with ease. It was the one cruising along with the passenger side up in the air.

****

A Naib in the Audhali Sultanate of the Western Aden Protectorate, created a certain amount of ribald amusement. He had taken a shine to his driver's wife. He arranged to assuage his amorous yearnings by sending the driver on long journeys so that there was plenty of time to indulge his passion. However, on one occasion the driver left his sunglasses behind and returned unexpectedly. The Naib had only one avenue to escape discovery. This was the bedroom window, out of which he hurriedly leapt into the top of a conveniently placed pawpaw tree. Sadly the weight of the Naib was too much for the little tree, which promptly snapped, and deposited the Naib unceremoniously on the ground in an undignified heap. Here, following the noise of the snapping tree, he attracted quite a lot of unwelcome attention.

Shortly after the 1971 coup, when an air of euphoria pervaded the Sultanate of Oman, whose new Government was busy bringing to the country freedoms unheard of under old Sultan Said, a German lady sociologist is reported to have obtained a visa to visit and write about a colony of transvestites in Sib. These gentlemen dressed in black *abayas* and their faces were masked. It was thus very difficult for an outsider to recognise what gender they were as they sauntered through the palm trees. The decision to let in the sociologist was swiftly regretted when the authorities realised the possible implications of the ensuing revelations to the world at large. It would certainly be very embarrassing, particularly amongst their neighbours. In the event she was allowed to proceed as long as no mention was made in her report of the geographical location.

Local stories are often innocently hilarious, if a bit 'improper' to the English mind. Arabs are much more frank about these things than the British. The Omanis have the tale of the young man who was taking a bath in the men's place at the *falaj*, or water channel. This particular *falaj* ran underground and it so chanced that the girls' washing place was downstream. The young man peered down through the gloom to see some twenty girls also taking a bath. He became so excited that he ejaculated into the water, and thus impregnated all twenty girls at once!

During the 1970s the *Daily Mirror* carried a front page picture of Queen Elizabeth the Queen Mother arriving at the Royal Opera House in London. The picture was taken from the top of the steps as Her Majesty alighted from her car, and showed a splendid view of the royal bosom magnificently if scantily obscured by a large diamond necklace. Copies of the paper were distributed worldwide as usual, but despite the appreciative comments from everywhere else round the globe, there was one place where the picture was not greeted with praise and delight. This was Dubai. Here the local censors were horrified. Reaching for their black ink they painted over the middle of the Queen Mother's picture in every copy, so that the sight of her generous attributes wouldn't upset the delicate sensitivities of the local inhabitants (though the delicacy of the sensitivities of the inhabitants of Dubai is open to question).

When informed, Her Majesty was much amused that she should be considered less than respectable, at least somewhere in the world, as indeed were all the other members of her family.

This was perhaps a strange reaction when one considers the devotion shown by the whole of Arabia to the Maria Theresa Dollar. Perpetually dated 1780 following the death of the Empress, this substantial silver coin was the main silver currency in the region for two centuries, finally being replaced by national currencies as various countries obtained their independence. It depicts the Holy Roman Empress with a truly imperial bust and, when, following her husband's death, she was shown wearing a widow's costume which obscured this noble characteristic there were howls of protest from throughout the Middle East! It is rather fun to think that the mother of the ill-fated Marie Antoinette survived as the pin-up girl of most of Arabia for over twenty decades.

There is also amusement to be derived from the story of another coin. During the Yemeni Civil War the Saudis generously supplied the Royalists not only with huge quantities of Maria Theresa dollars but also with Gold Sovereigns. These were all dated 1915 and carried the portrait of the King Emperor, George V. However they were all minted in Beirut and were forgeries. Not only that, but their gold content was better than the British original.

Alcohol

The moth a merry caper
Around my flagon turned,
Supposing it a taper
That in the shadow burned.

With beating wings he hung him
About the flame it shed,
Until the flagon flung him
Upon the carpet, dead.
Abu Yahya of Cordoba, 13th century

The subject of alcohol also calls up quite a lot of hypocritical excuses and while allusion has been made to this topic in other stories it is a subject that deserves a bit of space of its own. The following anecdotes have clearly been embroidered and by their nature are prone to some occasional exaggeration. All the world knows that it is strictly forbidden for a Muslim to drink alcohol. It is also widely known that huge numbers of them do drink, often very enthusiastically. It is consequently cause for much derision from non-Muslims, who draw attention to the hypocrisy involved. Nevertheless here are some happy stories which are told with no wish to cause offence.

It is reported that as long ago as the start of the Arab Revolt, a Major Vickery, being part of a British party being entertained by the Emir Faisal, and trying to overcome a British revulsion to Arabian food, took a swig from his whisky flask and then passed it round. T.E. Lawrence, who was present, took a dim view of this as he thought it was disrespectful. The Emir however thought it amusing! The government of Qatar with great understanding permitted the Gulf Hotel in Doha to serve drink, but only secretly and tactfully.

Westerners visiting Doha and in the know had only to ask at Reception for a key to Room 501. The Bar!

The Bahrainis are very realistic people and, when asked, published a statistic stating that there were 8,000 alcoholics on the island. The same question asked in Saudi Arabia elicited the response that there were none because there was no alcohol in the Kingdom, a statement somewhat contradicted by another that stated that more whisky was consumed in Saudi Arabia than in any other country on God's earth. It is interesting that alcohol as a word is actually derived from Arabic! But it is the word they use for their 'eye-shadow', *kohl*, and so not quite as bad as it seems.

A visitor in Saudi Arabia was offered whisky in a bucket, his Saudi host reasonably explaining that this would obviate his having to get up and refill his guest's glass all the time!

On another occasion, during an evening conversation with a prominent merchant, the phone rang. When the merchant finished his call and replaced the receiver he looked rather sad and his visitor enquired if everything was all right. The merchant replied with a straight face that the call was from the Customs in the port. It appeared that his container of Italian furniture was leaking! There seems to have been something about containers of furniture. The British Embassy when in Jeddah once had the same problem with a container of their furniture, but in this version it was in fact a crate containing a piano for the Embassy.

The Arabs can be charmingly solicitous of the needs of visitors. An Englishman arrived in Kuwait in the 1970s. Knowing the rules well, his luggage was quite devoid of any bottles. A smart young Kuwaiti Customs officer nevertheless scrupulously searched through every nook and cranny. Finding nothing, he ceremoniously chalked the visitor's luggage and welcomed him to Kuwait with a friendly smile. As the Englishman was getting into a taxi in the airport car park he was tapped on the shoulder. It was the young customs man. 'I know you haven't got any drink,' he said. 'Would you like some?' A bottle was later delivered to the Englishman's hotel, without charge.

****

'Bring wine!' I said;
But she that sped
Bore wine and roses beautiful.
Now from her lip
Sweet wine I sip,
And from her cheeks red roses cull.
From Al Adab wa'l Fann

The happy tale is told that in the latter part of the 20th century one of the main routes into the Kingdom of Saudi Arabia for drink was through the northern border. The Frontier Police came under the authority of the Minister of the Interior at that time and the way things worked is reported to have been as follows. The buyer of the alcohol would arrange for his purchases in the Lebanon, and the goods would be loaded onto a lorry bought for the purpose; a young Lebanese driver, willing to take a risk, would be engaged and he would set off southwards. On reaching the Saudi border the police stopped one in ten of the lorries and – surprise, surprise – discovered the contraband, which was of course confiscated. The hapless driver would be arrested and sent to prison for a year. On release the driver was deported back home penniless. If however, he was one of the nine lucky ones, he passed into the Kingdom unscathed and, after delivering his consignment to the original purchaser, he would be given the lorry in lieu of a cash payment. Thus the wayward citizens maintained their supply of scotch and the Minister was ensured of his own supply for nothing. Incidentally it is felt by some that as whisky was not invented until well after the Prophet's time, his strictures on the subject of drink don't really apply to this particular beverage.

An Arabic-speaking English visitor to the Kingdom happened to be looking at the books in a Riyadh bookshop when he was approached by one of the holier inhabitants. These people can easily be recognised because they wear white hats and the hem of their garments is some six inches or so above their ankles. The religious gentleman was clearly surprised to see a foreigner looking at Arabic books and engaged him in conversation. Assuming that the visitor was a Christian believer, he at once brought up the subject of the Trinity which, as it divides the Deity into three, is regarded as the most heinous blasphemy by Muslims. Not wishing to have a possibly heated discussion in public, the visitor readily accepted the holy man's invitation to come to his house.

After they were seated the host thoughtfully set out a European tea service, and asked his guest how he liked his tea. On being told that he liked it with milk and sugar this was how the holy man poured it out. His visitor was surprised that while the tea looked normal the milk was distinctly colourless and the sugar translucent. On sipping from his cup he discovered that he had been given a whisky and water with ice. Mentioning politely that there seemed to be a bit of hypocrisy about, the Englishman was amused to be told with a guffaw of laughter, 'I fooled you, didn't I?'

****

After the establishment of the Republic in Yemen a famous military author was shown a collection of South African brandy bottles which, he was told, only went to show how decadent the Imam's regime had been. As a fortuitous piece of tit for tat, after the Revolution someone blew up the Egyptian Intelligence officer's whisky in a town to the south of the capital. The strong smell of a well-used bar floated over the town, and advantage was taken to spread leaflets around drawing the attention of the town's inhabitants to the ungodly nature of both Egyptians and the Republic.

Out in the Omani desert the writer was camped out for the night with his driver at the edge of the Empty Quarter, when they saw a small convoy of about half a dozen strange vehicles draw up about half a mile distant. As at that time only the Sultan's Army and the oil company were allowed to have motor vehicles, the strangers were obviously of interest. After perhaps half an hour a Land Rover detached itself from the group and drove over to the writer's little camp. The visitor was a handsome young man in spotless white clothes and was greeted with the best and most polite Arabic. He replied in perfect English that 'He had just popped over, old boy, to see if you have, by any chance, a couple of spare bottles of soda. Our servants forgot to pack any and we only have plain water to put in the scotch'. It emerged that he was part of a hunting party down from the Trucial Coast.

I myself found I had acquired unwarranted attention simply because chatting to Bedouin all day can be rather tiring, and a small scotch – disguised in an opaque Arabian coffee cup to avoid giving offence – worked wonders. My drivers kept the secret for over two years, telling any enquirer that it was the boss's medicine – which was at least partly true. When the whole truth did finally emerge, I felt constrained to say that the contents of the coffee cup were Christian Milk. This was generally accepted with great amusement.

However, many years later I was travelling north on a plane from Dubai to Qatar. My travelling companion in the next seat was a young Qatari going home on leave from his job driving truckloads of building materials into Oman from Dubai. When the flight attendant came by with his trolley, without thinking I asked my travelling companion if he would like some Christian Milk. The young man responded, calling me by name and telling me that I was very famous. Naturally I enquired why this was, and the young man told me that all the Bedouin in Oman called whisky Christian Milk, and when asked why they said it was because that's what I had called it.

During King Idris' time in Libya, the Arab League placed a boycott on all things French in support of the Algerians, who were having their own anti-colonial revolution at that time. This meant that no French wines could be imported into the Kingdom. This was not good, since quite the nastiest wine ever made by man was the locally produced 'Libyan Claret', which tasted as though it would dissolve the glass bottle that contained it. The King, following the example of St Augustine who prayed that God should make him virtuous, but not yet, informed all Embassies, the American Wheelus Air Base, the British Army at Derna and the RAF at El Adem that he would support the boycott with all his strength; but not for a month! Enough wine was stockpiled to last until the overthrow of French rule and the establishment of the independent Algerian Republic.

In the Omani mountains lives a tribe of great antiquity and impeccable lineage, the Bani Riyam. They figured largely in the Jebel War of the late 1950s, fighting Sultan Said Bin Taimur, and were only defeated with difficulty. Their aristocratic ancestry confers on them an aura of respectable gravitas that is hard to beat. However, after the appalling horror of Libyan claret the reader is now asked to contemplate the dreadfulness of Bani Riyam brandy. Yes, not only do they make wine but they distil it too! As many of them live at an altitude of several thousand feet on top of the Green Mountain, Jebel Akhdar, it may be that they need this sustenance to keep them from the winter cold.

In the same general part of the Sultanate, in the Wadi Sumayl, live many other very distinguished people. This great valley is in fact the main route south through the mountains of Oman connecting the interior with the Batinah coast, and it was chosen as the best route through which the oil produced in the interior of the country could be brought to the coast by pipeline. The right of way for this pipeline had to be negotiated through each tribal territory. During one meeting the sheikh of the tribe concerned was assisted by an ancient Qadi, whose long beard almost hid the even more ancient dagger at his waist. He looked like some predatory vulture with bright beady eyes. The old man turned out to be the most pedantic, irascible, difficult, casuistical, awkward, troublesome and argumentative character imaginable. He prolonged the discussions from nine in the morning to sunset with lengthy quotations from the Quran, the Traditions of the Prophet and the most obscure legal texts; and as the sun went down the oil company negotiator was finding it very difficult to keep calm, polite and friendly. The sheikh was no help at all: he was rather stupid and had to have everything explained at least three times, and over each of the three times the Qadi would think of some new obstacle.

Finally all was settled and the oil company negotiator wearily climbed into his Land Rover buoyed up by the thought that before too long his flagging energies would be revived in the company club down on the coast. However, no sooner had he put the key into the ignition than the Qadi appeared at his door, with beard afloat on the evening breeze.

'Can you give me a lift home?' he asked. The company man, feeling that he would rather strangle the old goat, felt he had to agree even though it transpired that the Qadi lived about thirty miles away in the opposite direction. Off they went down bumpy, dusty tracks through the palm trees. On arrival at the Qadi's modest mud-brick residence the old man invited the company man in.

'We have both had a long day,' he said. 'I know I need a drink and I am sure you could do with one too. I think you did very well – there aren't that many Christians who know much about our Holy Book and Laws.' It was a comforting glass or two of whisky that was generously produced, and the oil company man rather took to the old ancient, always trying to visit him when duty took him in that direction again.

Sheikh Muhammad Al Sharqi of Fujairah, in the merry days before his little state was subsumed into the United Arab Emirates, was able to use his territory to import whisky. This enterprise allowed him to augment what really were rather slender resources. So successful was he that he was soon able to afford a holiday. This he took amongst the fleshpots of Alexandria. However, while he was twiddling the sheikhly toes in the Mediterranean war broke out and the Israelis assaulted Egypt. Demonstrating a tribesman's canniness, Sheikh Muhammad felt he could not place much trust in the ability of the Egyptian Army to defend the Suez Canal, let alone Alexandria, and impulsively fled back to Fujairah. However, the only available route was via Riyadh, where he had to change planes. On landing he was given a message from no less a person than King Faisal. This told Sheikh Muhammad that the King did not look kindly on his commercial activities and would be much gratified if they ceased at once.

Now seriously rattled, Sheikh Muhammad continued his journey and became frantically alarmed when, on arrival home, the first thing he saw outside his fort was a Bedford 3-ton truck loaded with cartons bearing the magic word 'Haig'. In a panicky effort to hide the evidence from the all-seeing King of Saudi Arabia, he told the driver to leave at once and take the truck to Dubai, the neighbouring state where the import of booze was illegal. Grim consequences. Sheikh Muhammad lost the whole consignment and was forced to make rather unconvincing explanations to the Ruler of Dubai, Sheikh Rashid, who had himself not long before seen fit to impose a ban on the import of alcohol himself. Following the fall of the Shah of Iran and his replacement by the Ayatollah Khomeini, the new Iranian government had sent a representative to Dubai who had told Sheikh Rashid how happy the Ayatollah would be to hear that alcohol had been banned in Dubai. Because of the large number of his citizens who were of Persian descent, Sheikh Rashid had agreed and accordingly had forbidden the import of drink to his state. There was an outcry and one hotelier even called on Sheikh Rashid and threw his hotel keys on the floor in front of him telling the startled Sheikh that he might as well have the hotel as it was no longer of any use to him. As a consequence, the law was amended and licensed foreigners could have facilities for the purchase of a tipple.

Christian Solace and Hospitality

The British have always been quite adept at getting agreement for sundry comforts for their officials. During the days of the Ottoman Empire the Sublime Porte agreed that British citizens committing misdemeanours in their territory could only be tried by British Law, thus initiating the idea of the Capitulations. Much later the Sultan of Oman, when making arrangements for the oil company to prospect for oil in his country, is said to have kindly agreed that the European employees could have either 'women' or 'booze', but not both. In the event the company chose the drink!

Embassies and outposts were all permitted to import alcohol but, in a strange but apocryphally-told twist, things were a little odd in Aden, with regard not to the British but to the Americans. This story seems to be a compilation of several different memories and anecdotes. The American Navy is dry and, as valued allies in War but bitter rivals in the field of oil exploration, the British were only too pleased to offer them a drop or two of hospitality when they called. However, it has untruthfully been related that, while Aden was ideal for hosting visits from the American Indian Ocean Fleet, the Americans could not go there. They could not go to Aden as it was a Colony and the USA strongly disapproved of Colonies. Perhaps it made them feel guilty or shamefaced to see what they had missed. Accordingly the British entertained their allies informally at Mukalla, three hundred and fifty miles east up the coast. The Americans could safely call there as it was a port in the Eastern Aden Protectorate: this nomenclature didn't raise any hackles in Washington, and the visits were in any case unofficial. It did, of course, entail the expensive transport of the necessities in small aircraft all the way up to Mukalla.

On one such occasion, so it has been told, the Mukalla Resident, expecting an informal visit, had arranged for the drink, and a football match to be played between the American sailors and the Hadrami Bedouin Legion, as was usual. Having enjoyed a glass or two at lunch on the day in question he retired for his siesta before the coming evening's events. As he relaxed under his mosquito net the Hadrami Bedouin Legion started a mortar practice on the beach. Sleepily the Resident began to count the explosions. One, two, then up to ten. On went the bangs, fifteen, nineteen, twenty and finally twenty one; and then they stopped. A Royal Salute! Hastily waking up from his boozy snooze the Resident surmised that the explosions must have been fired by the American Fleet, who for some extraordinary reason had turned the occasion into a formal visit. The Resident flew out of bed wildly, getting his cocked hat out of its tin, shaking out his white coat and buckskins, and dusting his sword. Buttoning and buckling everything together as fast as he could, he raced into the street, rousing the boatmen who would now have to row him out to give formal welcome to the Americans.

Such inhabitants of Mukalla who were awake at that time in the afternoon were doubtless astonished at the sight. The Resident, resplendent if breathless, was soon bobbing out to the great grey ships which had arrived in Mukalla Roads. They saw the bright figure approaching, and swearing somewhat because the goddamn Limeys had clearly decided to make this a formal visit, they decided to respond with a Royal Salute. Their great guns began to fire. Hearing the noise, the Hadrami Bedouin Legion on the beach looked up from packing up after their mortar practice and saw out at sea the great grey ships. They immediately decided that they were being attacked, and attacked moreover by a force that they would have no chance of resisting successfully. They therefore felt there would be no loss of honour, and promptly fled into the hills, and so it naturally followed that the football match had to be cancelled.

Eventually mutual explanations were made and the Americans and the British settled down to a convivial evening. It so happened, however, that the Americans fired a further single round on departure the following morning. This was to disguise the magic number of twenty one from the accountants in Washington; so that the whole episode could be passed off as gunnery practice.

As has been said, this story is almost certainly apocryphal, but it may have its origins in a real occasion written about by John Harding in his *Roads to Nowhere*. The sequence of events was however rather different.

Following a valedictory visit to Mukalla by the Governor of Aden, Sir William Luce, the town was shaken by a salvo of heavy gunfire.

The Resident furiously said that it must be the Yankee warship USS *Duxbury Bay* calling again, but this time with an admiral aboard. The Americans it was, and they invited six of the British staff to lunch. Accordingly, an ancient Mercedes car was brought into service to provide suitable conveyance of the British party down to the harbour. The choice of which staff should accompany the Resident proved a bit of a problem. Someone with a military background was clearly needed, then someone with an American wife was included. One man was excluded because of his known antipathy to the United States. Down at the harbour two gleaming launches awaited the British guests. The combined weight of the Residency contingent sank the smaller of the two boats, so everyone had to transfer to the other, and off to lunch they went.

On board they found to their chagrin that the American Navy is dry, which fact on their return to the Residency elicited the rather ungrateful comment from the Resident that the Yanks couldn't even be trusted with a can of lager! Things now took an awkward turn because in order to meet the locals the Americans asked to play a football match. Protocol demanded that an Assistant Adviser who would normally have refereed the game would now have to look after the American Admiral on the touchline, while his cook did the refereeing. It was overlooked that this Assistant Adviser was the very one who had been excluded from the lunch party due to his disenchantment with all things American.

A huge crowd from Mukalla town turned out to support their team, but these heroes seemed to be but tiny imps in comparison to the huge American footballers. The game started well enough but eventually another Assistant Adviser who had been co-opted in support of the home side, forgetting that the rules had been changed since he last played, floored the USS *Duxbury Bay*'s goalie with a shoulder barge when that unfortunate was in possession of the ball. The Assistant Adviser was immediately surrounded by enormous

American seamen who threatened to fill him in, and the cook/referee told him that another infringement would lead to his being sent off. It is a matter of no little interest that this may be the only occasion in the entire history of the British Empire that a cook has been in the position to order his superior about in this way! But it transpired that the small stature of the Mukalla players proved to be an advantage, and in the end they triumphed due to their speed and nimbleness, the Americans losing 2-0.

The truth of the matter, however, still seems to be a bit obscure, as the following also amply demonstrates, and only goes to show how embellishment, failing memory and the passage of time conspire to improve stories in improbable ways. Assistant Adviser Michael Crouch records a sequence of events which individually are amusing enough in their own right. First of all a Royal Naval frigate arrived off Mukalla and fired a thirteen-gun salute, which was officially meant to be answered by a Sultanic salute. To achieve this, an ancient gun, probably dreadfully out of date in the time of Lord Nelson and normally used to warn the faithful during Ramadan that it was time for them to break their fast, was brought into play. This return salute consisted of nine guns and was to be fired as the visiting frigate moved gracefully to her moorings. On this occasion proceedings began with a single but huge bang. Dogs barked, children burst into tears, the whole town rattled and amidst a cloud of dust a flock of panic-stricken pigeons fluttered frantically over all. The gun had now to be reloaded. This was a lengthy process and consequently it took an age to get through the official nine-gun salute. Indeed it took so long that the frigate was forced to sail on at least once and circle back.

A further anecdote includes some elements of the previous tales and the reader will see how different versions came to be created so easily.

The Residency staff were relaxing with a few comforting pink gins in hand when there was a dramatic explosion just as the USS 'Ducksbury' came into view. (The reader might like to note that the change in the spelling of this ship's name in the various stories may be explained by one of the uses to which she was put. But read on.) Misunderstanding the bang, the Resident rushed upstairs and struggled into his uniform to await the Admiral's arrival at the Residency. The Assistant Adviser hastily donned a suit and went down to the jetty to greet the American party. There he found the Americans arrayed in Hawaiian shirts and a few tactful questions elicited the information that the visit was indeed an unofficial one. Actually the US ship was a seaplane tender and quite bereft of guns but it was nevertheless the Admiral's Flagship. It had been chosen for this august position because of its shallow draft which enabled the Admiral to creep into shallow inlets and indulge his passion for duck shooting. The gun that had been fired, causing the initial misapprehension, was not however the one used to warn the inhabitants of Mukalla during Ramadan of the setting of the sun so that they could break their daytime fast. It was in fact the State's Mukalla Regular Army indulging in practice with a three-inch mortar on the beach. (The Mukalla Regular Army was a quite distinct Force and had nothing to do with the Hadrami Bedouin Legion.)

Royal Naval visits were magnificently and generously endowed with drink by both the ships and the Residency. But rules are rules, and American visits were more constrained, with the American response to the Residency booze consisting of a deluge of fruit juice and Coca-Cola.

Sir Donald Hawley reported that the USS *Duxbury Bay* visited Dubai in mid-January 1959 carrying Admiral Flaherty, Commander of the American Middle East Force. In Dubai, Sheikh Rashid gave everyone lunch. Wearing what he called his Napoleon uniform, Sir Donald had attended a return meal on the USS *Duxbury Bay* where in his capacity as Political Officer he had inspected a Guard of Honour, and he commented that in their aluminium helmets the American sailors had looked like spacemen. All this Imperial pomp was suitably taken down a peg when the Political Officer's launch got stuck on a sandbank on its return journey.

Business, money and corruption

You are too nice for the Arab World. You will be taken for a ride.
N.S. Doniach, editor of the Oxford English-Arabic Dictionary, to Leslie McLoughlin

The failed businessman knows a conman.
Arabian Saying

My son, if you meet a man interested in coins of silver and gold, then sell him my son, for he was born to be sold.
Advice given by an Arabian merchant to his son

Who wants a thing is blind.
Egyptian Proverb

A Jew found meat at a low price. 'It stinks,' he said.
Egyptian Proverb

In God and the Americans we trust. The rest, cash.
Anonymous

The Englishman had sauntered up Abu Dhabi High Street with an old man, Lutfallah by name, as he went from bank to bank casually borrowing a million pounds or so from each. When some ten million had easily and comfortably been collected, together they went back to the old man's shop for a coffee. The old man made a couple of phone calls to arrange for a consignment of gold bars to be paid for and delivered to his dhow for onward (and illegal) transit to India. If only one shipload in three got through he would make a handsome profit.

This trade depended on the bizarre fact that while the Indian rupee was at that time the currency of the area as well as of India, the rupee coin was worth twice as much in the Gulf as it was in India – though the one rupee note was worth the same in both places. Accordingly, the merchants of the Trucial Coast loaded up their boats with gold, sent them off to India, and exchanged the gold for rupee notes which they then changed into coin in Bombay banks. On return to the Gulf these coins were then exchanged again for twice as many rupee notes. Half of these notes were then converted into sterling for the purchase of more gold, making a profit of 100% which would be divided among all the shareholders in the business. Incidentally, the shareholders comprised the entire population, from the Ruler downwards.

Looking out of the window, Luftullah suddenly asked where all the English had gone. Surprised, his visitor replied that they were still present, and all one had to do to see them was to look at the people outside wearing shorts with pink knees.

'No', said Luftullah. 'Those aren't the English I know.' 'In the old days when a young airman from the British base in Sharjah went home to get married he was usually broke because he had spent all his money celebrating in the NAAFI with his friends. I always let him choose anything he wanted for his new wife from my gold stock, because I knew he would always pay me back as soon as he could. I wouldn't even take a cheque from that lot out there.' *Sic transit gloria!*

It is a sad fact that many Arabians, thinking that all Britons were as honest as the devoted Colonial Officers and military men they had known, were fleeced by unscrupulous vultures from the UK.

****

Long before Colonel Nasser swept the Brits out of the Canal Zone, the Egyptians had successfully developed a means of getting their own back by combining a bit of business enterprise with low cunning. The hawkers sold canaries to the posh people on their way back from India. It wasn't until the Sahibs and Memsahibs got to Southampton that the little yellow birds moulted and reverted to being sparrows. This ruse was adopted in subsequent years by Adeni merchants who sold fake Rolex watches to tourists on their way to Ceylon and the Far East. The liners were well away when the tourist found out that his beautiful cheap Rolex had no insides and the gold plating rubbed off when lightly wiped with a hankie. However, selling the wrong thing can sometimes turn out to be the right thing. In the 1950s an English salesman of refrigerators arrived in Jeddah. He sold out with great speed to Bedouin customers from the desert. Knowing that they had no electricity at that time he then left as quickly as he could, before they found out that their wonderful new fridges couldn't work. His success led his company to send him out once more, and he was somewhat fearful on his return to Jeddah. To his surprise, he was besieged with dozens more customers demanding refrigerators. So he bravely asked one of them why, when they couldn't use the things. The reply came that they only wanted the doors. They took these off and threw away the rest. It turned out that the doors were the best possible trays for their rice and boiled goat.

It has been often been part of the briefing given to British businessmen before embarking on a trip to the Kingdom that they should beware of the taxi drivers. They were told, not entirely in jest, that should their taxi get involved in an accident they should get out at once, putting as much distance between themselves and the taxi as possible, as quickly as possible. The reason for this was that they would be blamed for the accident. Quite reasonably, the taxi driver would say that if the businessman hadn't hired the taxi the accident would not have occurred. So it was the businessman's fault and he should pay for any damage.

The Market in Second-Hand Goods

The markets of Arabia are an Aladdin's cave of surprising treasures. In Damascus was to be found wondrous Imperial Russian porcelain, Kuwaiti merchants stock Persian carpets and miniatures of supreme quality, and in Muscat a Danish archaeologist found red clay pots that had been made on the island of Socotra; while in Salala they still make gold jewellery exactly like that made by the ancient Sabaeans and Himyarites.

Just as surprising are these discoveries.

A British author living in Sana'a, Tim Mackintosh-Smith, was surprised and delighted to find a small Yemeni wearing the very blazer he had had at school back in England. Identification was confirmed by recognition of a unique biro stain on the breast pocket.

A Political Officer serving in the Western Aden Protectorate during the 1960s discovered quite large quantities of old British military uniforms, as well as an Egyptian one dating to the period of the Khedivate, in local markets. It must have been quite a jolt to come across infantry scarlet tunics of the First World War belonging to the Gloucesters, Inniskillins, Welsh Borderers and Somersets. But possibly best of all was the Full Dress Uniform of the Coldstream Guards, which was to delight the Colonel of their 1st Battalion, when worn by the Political Officer's retainers on the occasion of the Colonel's visit. How these uniforms reached South Arabia is a mystery, but it is possible that some of them might have been looted from the British Ordnance Depot at Tel Al Kabir, in the Canal Zone, when the British left Egypt in 1955. It seems unbelievable that they would have been left behind, but in fact the store was abandoned intact. It was not however only uniforms of historical and military interest that were forgotten. During the insurgency preceding British withdrawal, mine-laying in the Protectorate was quite a problem. After detonation it was found that the base plates all bore British numbering, which enabled them to be assigned accurately to the precise shelf in the Tel Al Kebir Depot whence they had come. The British kept the records but not the explosives, which some might say was careless. In another incident a British officer carelessly lost his tank during the landings at Port Said in 1956. However he found it again in 1973 in Sinai, but repainted with Egyptian markings.

****

The British have never ruled in Saudi Arabia and we often feel that their Royal Family's involvement in commerce is somehow rather disgraceful. Royalty should not soil its hands by involving itself in something so unsavoury as trade! It is something that leads to disapproving harrumphs from the average Englishman – an attitude that betrays a somewhat woeful ignorance of practicalities, and indeed history.

The position was expressed rather nicely by Adnan Khashoggi during the Lockheed scandal, when this American company was accused of using bribery to gain a very substantial contract to supply military aircraft to the Saudi Government. AK, as he is known, was being interviewed by Robin Day on British television when Day accused AK of being corrupt, and taking bribes to ensure the success of Lockheed's bid for an immense defence contract. Naturally AK strongly denied any misdoing and stated categorically that the charge was a nasty and entirely unjustified calumny. He then paused and smilingly told Robin Day that in this life one nevertheless always had to pay for services rendered. This episode involving an American company should be read while keeping in mind more recent and very similar matters involving British Aerospace and the storm of complaints from the USA!

There can be little doubt that a lot of highly dubious commercial activity has gone on over the years and there are plenty of reasons why this takes place. In the West we do get mesmerised by large numbers and become hypocritically hysterical. Perhaps Prince Bandar put the whole question into perspective when he told an American programme that between 1971 and 2001 the Saudi Government had spent $350 billion in building the country, out of an income of $400 billion. If the fifty billion change went on corruption, so what? After all, when someone accepts a bribe, someone else has to pay it.

Of course the British are absolutely in the clear and always take the utmost care to be completely free of even the tiniest whiff of corruption. Sir Donald Hawley gave us the rules for the acceptance of gifts when in government service as a Political Agent. Any gift accepted had to be declared, handed in to the Residency and a value placed upon it. If the recipient wished to keep the gift, he had to pay for it at that valuation. The money would be put into a fund called the Toshkhana. If he didn't want it, the gift itself was put into the Toshkhana, and eventually a suitable return gift was given to the original donor, paid for out of the funds in the Toshkhana. It is noteworthy that this slightly complicated procedure did not cover the gift of swords or daggers. These items were considered to be exceptionally personal!

A young teacher who was devoid of any kind of talent was devastated when his uncle, the Minister of Education in Cairo, introduced an examination that the young man could never pass. Very troubled, the nephew went to see his uncle and explained the situation. His uncle said that the only way out of the difficulty was to make the young man Chairman of the Examinations Board.

The representative of a foreign company was approached by a Moroccan engineer and asked to lob in a thousand dollars to ensure the award of a contract. The representative was horrified and reported the matter to the minister. The minister was furious and said that the engineer had no right to award any contract. However, if the representative would give him two thousand dollars, the minister would sack the engineer and give him the contract. The representative then told a Member of the Moroccan Parliament this story. The MP was livid and said this was no way to run national affairs. He told the representative that if he was given four thousand dollars he would bring down the government and give him the contract. The representative now went to the Prime Minister and told him the whole sorry story. The PM said the situation was untenable and preposterous. If the representative would give him eight thousand dollars he would dissolve parliament and after holding new elections award him the contract.

The introduction of the telephone followed by the tidal wave of foreign businessmen that beset the Kingdom created appalling difficulties. It was impossible to make a telephone call as the lines were all blocked all the time. However, one Jeddah businessman solved the difficulty by simply keeping his line open to his New York broker twenty-four hours a day; thus setting up a world record for the most expensive call in the world. Apparently the line stayed open for several years!

At this time visitors needing to contact their head offices in the UK had to resort to a certain amount of cunning. The key to this involved the amazing sight presented by the cars parked outside the Riyadh telephone exchange. The vehicles were a collection of the most expensive Cadillacs and an observer could be forgiven for thinking that the King himself must be visiting the exchange. Not a bit of it! Delicate enquiry led to the information that these magnificent vehicles actually belonged to the telephone operators, each one of whom picked up a paltry salary from the telephone company but huge sums on the side from Saudi merchants. The trick was to find out which operator was working for which merchant, and when they were on duty. In this way it was possible to build up a timetable that enabled you to make calls instantly at any time of the day or night. All you needed to do was ring the exchange, consult your list and ask for Salih or whoever and tell him that Sheikh Muhammad had told you to call at that time. You would be put through in seconds to the remotest parts of the globe.

A similar system was put into operation by at least one bank in Cairo, a city afflicted by the same sort of telephonic constipation. Leslie McLoughlin reports that they went straight to the heart of the matter and came to an arrangement with the President's personal telephone operator. Every month a shoebox full of dollars was discreetly left at a convenient place for collection.

Throw him into the river and he will rise with a fish in his mouth.
Egyptian Proverb

Education and the world of work

Sultan Said Bin Taimur didn't object to education per se. It was just that almost all troublemakers and revolutionaries had observably been to school, so he was on the whole against it. He did let Omanis send their children abroad for schooling but he wouldn't let them back in afterwards.

The oil company did manage to get permission to send one young Omani student to Cairo. At this point it needs to be explained that the word for 'blanket' in Oman is very similar to the word for 'bomb' in the rest of the Arab World. It is much colder in Cairo than it is in Muscat. So, the boy sent a postcard home asking his parents to send him blankets. The Egyptian authorities naturally read all outgoing mail and assumed the worst. They reckoned they had caught a small but lethal terrorist red-handed. It took quite a while to explain all this to the Egyptian police and to get them to understand that the lad really posed no threat at all to Egyptian security.

Another Omani student was eventually sent to Beirut by the oil company, and carefully instructed as to how he should ask for blankets if he needed them. However, he was only rather casually taught how to ask to leave the room in school if he needed to relieve himself. He was told, 'Just raise your arm to attract the teacher's attention and ask to leave the class'. The lad interpreted this to be a universal thing and not at all confined to classroom use. Not long after his arrival in the Lebanon a pathetic communication was received in Oman. Caught short in the street, the boy had raised his arm as instructed and no one took the slightest notice.

This is not the only occasion when Arabians have been caught out with misunderstandings involving their own language. Author Madawi Al Rasheed has recorded a story about no less a potentate than King Saud of Saudi Arabia. It appears that the King was disturbed in his majlis by hearing a racket produced by lorries working outside the palace. He asked what the noise was all about and was told that it was lorry traffic. The Arabic word for lorries is very similar to the word used for insurrection and revolution. His Majesty erroneously understood that there were insurgents outside. Accordingly he decamped as fast as dignity would permit to his private quarters, where he calmed down after having things gently explained to him.

◇ ◇ ◇

Following the leap into the modern world and the embracing of liberty that the Iraqi revolution so triumphantly announced, the Iraqi government offered free education to students from other Arabian countries. This was so that the young people, having completed their courses, could return home and spread the revolutionary word. However, the Iraqis were apparently not too sure of the quality of the education they were giving to the young hopefuls, because each diploma was firmly stamped 'Not For Use in Iraq'.

This lack of self confidence in their educational attainments shown by the Iraqi government of the time is probably justified, as the following report indicates. Rory Stewart records that in a hall of the Republican Palace in Baghdad there are Arab proverbs carved in marble by way of decoration. One, citing Saddam Hussein as the author, reads as follows, 'Ask not what your Country can do for you but what you can do for your Country'! As an instance of the old adage that imitation is the sincerest form of flattery this takes the biscuit, when you consider what President Kennedy's successor did to Saddam.

He who knows not, and knows not that he knows not, is a fool. Shun him.
He who knows not, and knows that he knows not, is simple. Teach him.
He who knows, and knows not that he knows, is asleep. Wake him.
He who knows, and knows that he knows, is wise. Follow him.
Sir Richard Burton: Arabic proverb

Labour Relations

19th-century contacts between Britain and the Arabs were mostly of a political, commercial and military nature consonant with British policies and interests at that time. While this continued into the next century, the environment gradually changed and the discovery of oil dictated a much closer and more local involvement; and the delineation of frontiers of course. And the introduction of labour laws.

To put this subject into a local perspective it is perhaps best to start with an account of the pragmatic way in which the Arabians themselves have viewed the matter. In general Arabians eschew manual labour and, particularly in the northern Arabian lands, all the inhabitants have a burning desire to become or remain part of the government bureaucracy. Here they can take advantage of opportunities for social preferment and indulge in the pleasant occupation of earning a bit of extra cash by developing what might politely be described as extramural activities. They avidly join the endless ranks of Supervisors, Clerks, Inspectors and Ministerial Assistants so that they, too, can spend idle and profitable days stamping papers they never read.

This situation is beautifully described by the following tale. A eunuch once got a job in a government office. When he was appointed he asked his new boss when he should report for work. This eminent and kindly man thought for a moment and said, 'Well, we open the office at nine and all your colleagues come in and do nothing except play with their balls for three hours. You haven't got any balls, so why come early? Start at twelve'.

Much of the rest of the population in the Arabian Peninsula were the raggle-taggle gypsies fondly called Bedouin. Anything resembling manual labour was anathema to them. For centuries they had regarded towns not so much as centres of exchange as objects of pillage. This they had refined to an art. A Bedouin tribe would raid a town and, after some lackadaisical looting, would settle down and inform the merchant community that they quite understood that the merchants needed someone to look after them. At the risk of losing their freedom the traders would consent, reluctantly, to the Bedouin ruling over the town and themselves, while generously keeping other Bedouin away. Naturally, it would be piously explained, that would incur expenditure, and they therefore felt that the merchants would be only too willing to pay taxes to defray the costs involved.

A reader thinking that this was nothing more than a protection racket would be absolutely right. However, consider the Rulers of Bahrain, Saudi Arabia, Qatar, Kuwait and the United Arab Emirates – all Bedouin. Of course there are some Arabian countries where this principle doesn't hold true, but these are either the ones of anciently settled Arabia, where perhaps descendants of the Prophet himself or a local dynasty have retained the Rule; or modern Republics, whose gallant Presidents also seem to adopt the dynastic idea quite enthusiastically, as has been seen in recent years in Iraq, Syria, Egypt, Tunisia and Libya – and, of course, Yemen.

It was into a Bedouin environment where this kind of thinking was current that the oil companies plunged with reforming, if not missionary, gusto and developed splendid new labour laws. Throughout the region these are based mainly on American and British practice. However, the rules so propagated did not at first sit very easily on the locals, as may be imagined. In Oman oil was discovered in the tribal territory of the Duru', who had for at least a couple of hundred years lived in almost total isolation in the Northern Dhahira area of the interior, in a state of perpetual anarchy. They were extremely independent and their xenophobia was legendary in an area where that mindset was almost universal anyway. Sheikh Zayd of Abu Dhabi remarked that if one met a Duru'i and a snake in the desert it was advisable to shoot the Duru'i first!

Peter Brent repeats the 19th-century dictum of Arabian neighbours concerning the nearest centre of culture and civilisation to the Duru, namely the town of Ibri – that you should only go there armed to the teeth or as a beggar with a cloth, and that not of decent quality, round your waist. And these were the people among whom the innocent oil company proposed to drill their wells. It was a stroke of luck that the Duru' territory was close to the influence of the Omani Imamate. The destruction of this political edifice by Sultan Said, the ejection of the Saudis from Buraimi and the assistance given to these events by the oil company, persuaded the Duru' that their bread was best buttered by letting the company in. One of their sheikhs, Sulayman Bin Kharas, had earlier chased after Wilfred Thesiger, intent on cutting his throat and robbing him. When working as a guard for the company in later years he was asked why he had behaved like that. He answered that it had been said that the Christian was carrying bags of silver, so it was obviously entirely reasonable to rob him, and a bit of murder and brigandage was therefore perfectly all right, if not downright praiseworthy. The Personnel Department leapt in, perhaps not realising that the Duru', having been deprived of their previous targets for mayhem and pillage, now looked on the company with no little interest as providing a wonderful substitute.

There was one particular aspect of the modernising process that they took on particularly happily – they embraced the strike ethic with terrific enthusiasm. The company regulations initially covered two sides of A4 but developed over time to resemble a London telephone directory, providing lots of opportunities for the Duru' to amuse themselves, as well as the basis for the country's labour law. For instance, every employee was entitled to one pair of safety boots a year. However, when going on leave for the first time the young tribesman would proudly and naturally wear his boots home. His father would say what nice boots they were and the lad would respectfully hand them over as a gift. Returning to work bootless, he would ask for another pair. The company would refuse. The man would feel deeply wounded and his vociferous complaints would quickly attract a lot of sympathy, and there would quickly be a strike.

At this point the Personnel Department would call on help from a company representative, who would get in touch with a grandee from the tribe called the Duty Sheikh, and everyone would be gathered together at the oil rig where the strike was taking place. Rarely was it possible to persuade the workforce to go back to work pending discussions and mediation. It was much more usual for everyone to go to their tents to drink coffee and chat. The rig would provide a large lunch for the Duty Sheikh, who would actually spend most of his time taking advantage of the transport provided by the company, to scoop up as many rations as the cooks could steal for him. In the early days these cooks were actually appointed by the Duty Sheikh anyway. The company thought that this would assist in negotiations, while the Sheikh only saw this as an arrangement which allowed him to indulge in a sort of 20th-century theft fest. Progress indeed! This scene was complicated by the need to keep the whole tribe on side, so the Sultan had ordained that things should be shared out equitably. Accordingly there were appointed not one but three Duty Sheikhs. Get everyone of importance involved, but naturally divide and conquer too!

This was a lucrative, much sought-after post, and the soup of intrigue was thickened as two Sheikhs plotted in merry competition to blacken the face of the one in office. Each Sheikh officiated for three months. Sheikh One would conspire to denigrate Sheikh Two in the eyes of the company in an attempt to get him sacked. Sheikh Three would watch sympathetically from the sidelines looking for an opportunity to press for reward for his understanding and unswerving devotion to the company. It was all quite fun. Each Duty Sheikh was also responsible for providing labour. This enabled them to increase their personal influence amongst the tribesmen by getting jobs for their own people, and the changing of the Duty Sheikh always led to an appreciable changeover in the labour force. Later he would do his level best to get remaining supporters of the other two Sheikhs sacked. This made it rather difficult for things like training, which required that an employee be kept on for some time.

These proceedings did however provide some excuse for the Sheikhly ration-stealing. Tribesmen looking for work would travel to the Duty Sheikh's encampment and of course the Sheikh had to feed them. There was one interesting aspect to all this. Throughout the Sultanate not a single tribesman would accept work as a 'workman'. This was a very lower-class occupation, possibly suitable only for slaves. They all had to be called 'coolie', which word with its imperialistic and colonial overtones made it difficult for the company when its higher ranks had to attend international labour conferences. Why the Omani tribesmen insisted on it remains a mystery to this day.

The company's treatment of miscreants was of course just and meticulous, in western eyes. An infringement of the rules would lead to the issue of a warning letter. Three warning letters in a year meant the sack. One cause for getting a warning letter was refusal to accept the first one. No one in the company seemed to appreciate that their labour force was illiterate and in illiterate societies writing is looked upon as magic. A warning letter is clearly not good magic. The labourer only had one pocket in his *dishdasha* and this pocket was right next to his private parts. If he put the warning letter into this pocket he thought that his testicles would drop off, so he naturally refused the letter. The reader can easily understand what happened next, and the expensive strike that followed. It was also remarkable that every new regulation, written in English, was assiduously sent out to all company employees, none of whom could read their own language let alone English.

The labour force was given generous rations to use as picnic lunches. Amongst these was a packet of cream crackers, and it wasn't until too late that it was realised why the labourers always broke up into groups of three when taking their lunch. One day the brand that they were used to ran out and another brand was flown in from Bahrain. All hell was let loose and they skidded out on strike like greased lightning. Their usual brand had twenty-four biscuits in each packet – a number easily divided into threes, enabling the group to share out the biscuits, eight biscuits each being plenty, and so saving two packets at each meal to take home when they went on leave. The new brand had exactly the same weight of biscuits but they were packed in twenties!

The corned beef in these rations was also used as currency. Unused tins taken home by the labour force were used as barter in the market in the local town. When the company ran short of this commodity the company representative just went down to the market and bought back the tins from the merchants. After a while he began to mark the tins out of interest, and one tin was returned in this way seven times!

Sultan Said had also decreed that labour should be recruited from the tribe in whose area the work was to be carried out. This was fine as far as ordinary unskilled workers were concerned, but when men had been expensively trained it caused difficulties. The Sultan therefore agreed that trained personnel could be taken from one area to another. Naturally this helped to break up the tribal system a bit. As the Duru' had the longest experience of work for the company they naturally had the majority of skilled labour, but old habits die hard and old antipathies were often very close to the surface. When the company decided to put in a well in the Wadi Halfayn this was outside the Duru' area and in that of their old foes the Wahiba. Although their feud had technically been settled a while before, their inbred mutual hostility still simmered. The Wahiba supplied the coolies for the new location but the trained drivers were Duru'. Their initial boastful swaggering quickly changed, and these tough technical paragons were to be seen walking about in fours, nervously guarding each other's backs, as they passed the sneering glares of Wahiba coolies.

Later they had another problem when the company opened up the Dhofar Concession. The Duru' drivers, feeling very top dog, conceived the idea that the long distance from their home base warranted a substantial pay rise. This was refused, so they called a strike. Following the rules, the company called in the local Dhofari sheikh to mediate. This man, small of stature, was quite unused to things like internationally recognised personnel practice and he had no personal or tribal interest in the Duru' drivers. He was the Mahri sheikh, and standing in front of the drivers who were expecting to sit down, drink coffee and discuss things, he unslung his rifle from his shoulders and informed the astonished drivers that unless they went back to work at once he would shoot them. Deeply shocked, the Duru' drivers meekly and uncharacteristically capitulated at once.

As the company's operations increased and they were able to train the locals in a wide variety of skills, so did the scope of the personnel regulations, and the need for improvement in working and accommodation conditions. An improvement in the diet of the labour force was high on the list, as it not only made the lives of the workers more pleasant, but also enabled the company to get rid of the sheikhly-appointed cooks whose culinary skills fell far short of what was needed, but of course gave full rein to their acquisitive talents. A better diet involved the introduction of that old staple 'greens'. The Bedouin initially reckoned that the dried cabbage that was provided was poisonous, and they refused to eat it. The Personnel Department arranged that their man in the interior should take a plateful down to the labour camp and consume it with observable relish in front of everyone. The first mouthful convinced the man from Personnel that the labour force was probably correct in their assessment. However, he put on a magnificent show and his failure to drop dead convinced the men that, however unpleasant the greens might be, at least they weren't actually poisonous.

Having achieved the removal of the local cooks with a bit of arm twisting of the Duty Sheikhs, a replacement was needed. Down on the coast the company found a suitable chef who would provide better fare for the labour force, even though the dishes of the Batinah Coast were in fact just as foreign to the Bedouin coolies as the *haute cuisine* of Paris. Signals were sent to announce the arrival of the chef by a particular flight, and there was much expectancy in Fahud, the main camp in the interior. The plane arrived and down the gangway came a handsome vision in a pink *dishdasha* and a mauve turban, who looked distinctly alarmed at the sight of all the rough, hairy Bedouin. Coolies at the airstrip made a few rather unkind comments but the chef was whisked off to the labour camp, introduced to his kitchen, and told to get cooking.

All went well for about a week. Then one evening as the Personnel man was having a comforting drink in the Club he was startled, as was everyone else in the bar, when the door flew open and an Indian clerk, grey with fear, fell into the room and lay quivering on the floor. The poor man gasped, 'They're coming, they're coming'. The Personnel man went to the door at the top of the steps and found that the clerk was absolutely right. Every coolie in the place was advancing on the Club. Feeling a bit like Gordon of Khartoum in the famous picture of the final rush on the Residency, the man from Personnel leant over the railings and asked what was the matter. It transpired that the chef had found solace amongst the rough crowd into which he had been tipped – with the kitchen boy. However it was not the relationship that upset the labour force – it was that the chef was taking his pleasure with the lad under the table while at the same time doling out their rice. The chef was posted elsewhere the following day.

It is only fair to provide some balance to the previous story, so let me tell you about the Eid goats in Salala. Some hundred or so goats had been bought at no little cost, personally, by the Sultan, so that his soldiers in Dhofar could enjoy the feast at the end of Ramadan in a suitably generous fashion. The animals were corralled in an enclosure under the watchful eye of a Baluchi sentry. At about midnight a couple of days before the Eid festival was to be declared, the sentry was surprised to see a British soldier climb over the fence, lower his shorts and ravish one of the goats. No one knows why – perhaps he was overcome with admiration – but the sentry didn't report the matter until he came off duty in the morning. It was clear that the ravished and therefore impure goat would have to be removed. This proved impossible as the sentry was quite unable to identify which animal it was. Furthermore the sentry was unable to identify the soldier: he said that all the British soldiers looked alike to him. Consequently the whole flock had to be destroyed and replacements purchased.

There is another tale about another chef. An ex-Guards Catering Sergeant came out to Oman to work for the contractor running the Senior Staff Mess at Azayba on the coast. He was an excellent fellow, very tall, very military but perhaps lacking in tact. An extremely senior man from the company was visiting from Holland and, on being served at lunch, he said that he didn't like the look of the food. From behind him, a military voice responded that the visitor wasn't there to look at the food, but to eat it. Sadly that chef too lost his job.

The company was also compelled to employ guards from the local tribe. This was a way of giving some very old pensioners some cash, but also put any thefts onto the face of the tribe; or so the theory went. What it meant in reality was that the ancient and retired pillagers of yesteryear were put into a position to ensure that any thieving that went on was done by their own people and not outsiders. These old men were often a source of amusement to their own tribesmen as well as company officials.

One old gentleman employed to guard the catering contractor's office was wont to pass the nights away fast asleep under a Land Rover parked outside. While he was dreaming the dreams of the just, a couple of miscreants drove the Land Rover away at some point during the night. The following morning, when the office was being opened up, the manager noticed the old man still curled up fast asleep, and that his car was missing. He woke the man up and asked where his Land Rover was. The manager was then astonished to see the old fellow carefully uncurl and climb out from under a vehicle that wasn't there. The old dear hadn't noticed or heard a thing.

As a counterbalance to this it is only fair to repeat a story told by Glencairn Balfour-Paul. As our ambassador in Baghdad he met an ancient Englishman who had been a gunner in the British-Indian Expeditionary Force sent from India to invade Mesopotamia in 1915, and he had remained in Iraq ever since. The old soldier related how an inspecting General had asked to see him and his seven-man team demonstrate their firing drill. On the order to fire one of them instantly knelt with his right arm curled above his head. The General asked why on earth he was doing that and the man answered that they always did. It emerged that a month or two earlier the battery had had its mules replaced with trucks, but though the mules had gone the drill movement to prevent them bolting had not been changed.

Because there is usually half a gale blowing in deserts, the Bedouin have developed the habit of shouting in order to have a quiet conversation. One old guard went into the Personnel Office to cadge an extra blanket and yelled out his request at the top of his voice. At the time the man from Personnel was on the radio to the company offices on the coast some 250 miles distant. He politely asked the old man to keep quiet as he was talking to his boss on the coast. The old man roared out words to the effect that the man was a bare-faced liar because the coast was miles away and he hadn't even raised his voice. The Personnel man, realising that a conversation explaining all about the radio was not really going to get anywhere, resorted to a lie.

He told the old man that he was absolutely right. The truth was that he had a tame mouse who lived in the special little black house he was holding in his hand. The mouse's bedroom was at one end and his living room at the other. As the old man well knew, mice had very small voices and so it was necessary to keep quiet so that the mouse could be heard. The old guard believed every word and, rushing out of the office, told the young men outside that the Christian was barking mad. He kept a mouse in a little black box and spoke to it. The very progressive young men all fell about laughing at the poor old boy and teased him about it for days.

Paying off the guards at distant desert locations in the territory of the Harasis tribe was always a problem. The Harasis have their own language which only has numbers from one to ten. If a Harsusi wanted a number greater than this he would switch to Arabic. However the old Harsusi guards could only count up to ten anyway so they had no need to be numerically bilingual. With their pay the old men were given rations for the coming month. The rations were calculated on a daily basis – so many tins of corned beef, so many packets of tea and sugar, so many tins of tomato puree, and so on. It was almost plain sailing when there were thirty days in the month. The only trouble was that although the various tins could be arranged in three piles of ten, the old gentlemen continually lost count and everything had to be counted and recounted dozens of times until they were satisfied that they had got what they were entitled to. If there were thirty-one days in the month the extra day's rations could be proffered as a gift. February was always particularly hard because the old men would be convinced that they were being short-changed, and the company was stealing two days' rations from them. In order to keep the accountants quiet, a sensible Personnel man was advised to save up a couple of days' rations from the thirty-one-day months to hand out the following February!

Despite their rough and fierce reputation the Duru' showed a charming and innocent side of their natures when, shortly after the first European families arrived in the Sultanate, oil company wives were able to visit the oilfield at Fahud with their offspring. Shaggy bearded men, descendants of generations of cut-throats, wept to see the little blond children, tearfully saying they had never seen anything so beautiful. They said that they had always thought the Europeans didn't have children like them and that Europeans were surely made by machines! Another odd misunderstanding involved pilots. The Duru' initially believed that pilots were the strongest men in the world because, sitting behind them in a small aeroplane, you could see the pilot pull the plane up into the air by the joystick, with one hand!

Labour relations were not of course confined to the interaction between the oil company and the locals. There were the American contractors. Williams Brothers supplied the best welders in the world, but sometimes unexpected things cropped up. First of all, the local labour force was entranced to find 'Christians' who collected their pay in the same way as they did; namely with a thumb print. Secondly, their attitudes towards other people were, well, Texan. At their main camp, or 'spread' as they called it, at Izki, the young man employed by the Americans to clean out the bathrooms, and what the Americans quaintly call comfort stations, was from the servant class. He was affectionately known as the Shit House Nigger. The oil company man, at a meeting when there was not much on the agenda, thought that it would be better to get a rather more up-to-date job title for this post, as the man might one day discover the connotations involved. Accordingly the Shit House Nigger was relabelled as The Washroom Boy.

But this was not the end of the story. The American welders were heroic consumers of drink and one day the Washroom Boy got hold of some unfinished bottles. He wandered home for lunch, bouncing off the palm trees and singing at the top of his voice. The Governorate of Izki employed a policeman, who had been unable to effect an arrest during over twenty-five years in office. He leapt energetically at the opportunity that now presented itself. He arrested the Washroom Boy. When the welders returned from the pipeline in the evening there was no Washroom Boy. The Americans made enquiries and discovered that their man was in jail. In the finest tradition of the Wild West they got into a power wagon and drove down to the jail which, not surprisingly, was locked. The Americans simply attached a steel hawser to the jail door and pulled it right out of the building. Inside in the gloom they saw the Washroom Boy chained to the back wall, patently hungover. They put a hawser round him and pulled him clean out too. Despite the obvious disappointment of the policeman, the Governor agreed to settle for compensation and a brand new jail.

The Americans also found the Sultan's rule about changing labour at tribal boundaries rather irksome and every time a tribal boundary came up desperately tried to keep the workforce they were used to. Eventually at about the fourth tribal border the Englishman from the oil company told them that they really must obey the rule, and in any case if they didn't the tribe next in line would probably shoot them. He then drove off to lunch with the sheikh of the next tribe to discuss future labour requirements. After the meal the sheikh said how much he would like to see how the pipeline was getting on. Quite forgetting what he had said to the Americans earlier, the man from the oil company took the sheikh down to the line in his Land Rover. Naturally the sheikh's retainers piled into the back, picturesquely bedecked with daggers and rifles.

On arrival at the line the Americans were horrified and obviously thought that the Goddamned Limey had not only threatened what the next tribe up the road would do, but had brought them down to do it. The pipeliners fled into the desert, throwing themselves prone behind any cover they could find. The sheikh's interest was grabbed by this extraordinary spectacle and, sensing an opportunity, he asked the man from the oil company why the Americans were behaving in such a peculiar way. Fearful of the consequences should he just airily tell the sheikh that the Americans were frightened out of their wits, he thought he would risk a bit of a fib. The Americans, he said, were a different tribe to the English. Strange as it may seem, this was how they showed respect to important visitors like the sheikh.

🛕 🛕 🛕

Sultan Said Bin Taimur's grasp on what was regarded as reasonable in the field of workers' rights might also be considered as being somewhat 18th-century. He had a Goanese cook who slaved away in the Sultanic kitchen and, after about ten years, not unreasonably, asked for leave to go home and visit his family. Said was surprised but huffily agreed that the cook could go; he also told him that he need not return. The cook, a Mr Alvarez, did in fact come back to the area where he was given employment by Colonel Boustead, the British Resident in Mukalla, as his personal cook.

◌ ◌ ◌

In the 19th century, the Khedive of Egypt, Muhammad Ali, having resolved to invade the Arabian Peninsula and put an end to the troublesome followers of the House of Saud, raised a considerable force, and was then faced with the problem of who would command it in the field. He placed an apple in the middle of a huge carpet that covered the floor of his main reception hall. Calling all his councillors, courtiers and officers together he told them that the command of the army would be given to the man who could reach the apple without stepping on to the carpet.

In the event, even the tallest of the people present just couldn't stretch far enough to reach the apple. Last of all Ibrahim, one of the

Khedive's sons, came forward. It was difficult for the assembled company to stifle their mirth because Ibrahim was just about the shortest man in the room. Furthermore he was rather squat and plump. Ibrahim walked up to the edge of the carpet and just rolled it up until he could bend down and pick up the apple easily. His father gave him the command and Ibrahim successfully completed the mission, incidentally looting a large number of priceless Arabian horses, which his nephew Abbas used to found one of the most famous studs in the history of that beautiful breed.

****

The Qatari Minister of the Interior was a man of small stature and he had commissioned a carpet depicting his ancestry and that of his family, the Al Thani. It was to be hung between the two doors opening into the grand Council Chamber of his new palace. The designer obtained the necessary information, and when the design was approved the cartoon was sent to China for the carpet to be woven. All done, the beautiful thing came back to London for a final inspection before being sent out to Qatar to be installed. On arrival there, horror of horrors, the carpet was found to be six inches too wide to fit into the space prepared for it. The designer was attacked by a profound sinking feeling but cheered up a bit when it was discovered that it was the builders who were at fault, and they had put the doors too close together.

His Excellency the Minister was understandably furious. He carried a Sten gun, the safety catch of which was only too obviously missing, and he angrily and vehemently emphasised his displeasure by waiving the notoriously unreliable weapon about wildly. His Excellency suggested cutting the carpet to fit. The designer counter-suggested that perhaps the carpet could be put up elsewhere, cutting a work of art would be vandalism. His Excellency remained livid but decided to adjourn the meeting until the following morning. When the designer returned the following day, he was met by a smiling Excellency who proudly took him into the Council Chamber to show him the carpet happily and beautifully installed. He was naturally surprised and asked the Minister how this had been done. In reply the Minister said that the British didn't know everything. He had mulled over the problem the previous evening. At midnight he had found the answer. Accordingly he went down to the labour camp and woke everyone up. He ordered all the workmen to get down to the new palace at once, to take the end wall down, to build it up again with the doors six inches further apart, and all this to be done by ten o'clock the following morning to surprise the designer. His Excellency succeeded on all counts.

Justice and human rights

Arabian justice has, often with good reason, been regarded as being on the harsh side. For instance one of the earlier Emirs of Dhala in the Western Aden Protectorate was in the habit of chucking criminals over the battlements of his castle into the wadi several hundred feet below. This was a bit strong, even for the Brits – who got rid of him.

In Lahej the Sultans sometimes had a rather idiosyncratic view of justice. In the early part of the 20th century one of them used to throw sentences, fines and orders out of the window at people assembled below. He avoided the open window himself lest someone take a pot shot at him. In 1934 one of his successors even went so far as to have three slaves, found guilty of theft, crucified in the market place, and he is reported as being exceedingly miffed when the British authorities remonstrated. In the Sultanate of Oman in 1972 a desert Sheikh bemoaned his losing the power to punish people after the Sultan, Said Bin Taimur extended his own authority over the whole of the Interior in the 1950s. Up until then the Sheikh was wont to tie miscreants up into a bundle with string and have them tossed into the top of a thorn bush for a while. Further to the north, in the Trucial States the British pursued a purely advisory path, and on hearing of some draconian punishment being awarded would suggest to the Ruler concerned that perhaps the sentence could be ameliorated. Thus limb-lopping and the tying of criminals to cannon preparatory to a flogging rather died out.

It was however rather nice in a macabre sort of way that under the rule of the Imam Ahmad in Yemen it was the responsibility of the Minister of Health to organise legal amputations and executions! It is worthy of note too that the sword concerned was called 'Purity', which must have given the victims confidence that at least they would not die from blood poisoning. Such was the reputation of the Imam for the firmest application of the law that it used to be said that a naked teenage girl, loaded with gold and gems, could walk with impunity from the northern border with Saudi Arabia to the south of the Imamate. It was only when she entered the British Protectorate that she would be in danger of robbery and rape.

Otherwise Arabians, while maintaining for a lot longer than the West a habit of chaining people up, also demonstrated an unusually pragmatic view of things. A Wali of Izki in Oman was found to have serious difficulty with the official tax returns due to an inexplicable lack of arithmetical skills. He was thrown into jail. However, in order not to upset his quite important family, his son was installed as Wali in his place. Sadly, after a few years this son exhibited the same trouble with figures that had afflicted his father. But the two were re-united when the son joined his father in jail.

In 1980, when oil revenues were flooding into Dubai the splendid Hyatt Galleria hotel was built. A lavish opening was arranged and the Ruler, Sheikh Rashid, graciously performed the ceremony. The most wonderful buffet ever seen in the Gulf was put on, a band was specially imported from Germany, and there was dancing. Then it was discovered that the owner had indulged in mighty financial misbehaviour. But still, after a short period in prison ordered by Sheikh Rashid, he was able to return to a life of wealth and comfort.

◌ ◌ ◌

In the 1960s in Bayhan there had surprisingly not been a murder for about forty years and the jail only had ten inhabitants, who were exercised round the town every day. Though in leg irons and escorted by a single armed guard, they would clatter down to the souk to enjoy a cup of coffee and a chat with their friends. Sadly this amicable and really quite enlightened rehabilitation activity had to be curtailed if left-wing visitors were expected from London. When asked what crimes the prisoners had committed, the Sharif replied that nine were in for stealing camels and the tenth because he had made the Sharif suspicious.

****

It is often thrown at the Arabians that they have scant regard for what the liberal westerner feels about human rights. It is good therefore to have a story that underlines the need to take a step or two back to view things accurately. During the talks at the Colonial Office in London in 1963, this topic came up for discussion. The Secretary of State, Duncan Sandys, was adamant that safeguards should be built into the agreement over the Federal Constitution. Exhausting talks, drafting and redrafting, went on until about three o'clock in the morning. The Federal Minister of Defence, Sultan Salih Al Audhali, noticed an elderly secretary yawning for want of sleep and quickly asked Duncan Sandys if he really believed in human rights. Duncan Sandys replied that of course he did. 'Then why,' responded the Sultan, 'do you keep this unfortunate old lady sitting up all night'? It is reported that this remark was toned down a bit by the interpreter and one feels that possibly it shouldn't have been.

Robin Day came unstuck with Sheikh Yamani, the Saudi Oil Minister. Sheikh Yamani had the most wonderful smile, a characteristic which made every woman in the world fall in love with him. Day once attacked Yamani during a television interview by saying that Saudi Arabia was very backward, scarcely out of the Dark Ages. 'Why, they cut off people's hands for theft.' Sheikh Yamani gave Day the benefit of his very best smile and replied that they didn't have to do it very often.

****

One day Joha was acting as a Qadi and two petitioners came before him. The first one had his say and Joha said, 'I agree with you'. Then the second man stated his case. Joha said, 'You are correct, I agree with you'. Joha's wife was sitting in the court and she said, 'Joha, they can't both be right'. Joha replied, 'You are right also'.

The founder of the Kingdom, Abdulaziz Ibn Abdulrahman Al Saud, was by no means devoid of wit. A man picking dates in the oasis of Dara'iya slipped and fell out of the palm tree, right onto the head of a man walking by. In so doing he accidentally broke the walker's neck. The widow went to the King to claim justice. She eschewed the blood price, and demanded the man's life in exchange for that of her husband. The King said that certainly that was her right; however, it was up to her to carry out the sentence, and she would have to do it by climbing a palm tree and jumping out onto the head of the man who had inadvertently killed her husband. The lady withdrew her claim.

In 1925 Brigadier-General Sir Gilbert Clayton and a companion, both British envoys, were received by King Abdulaziz at Bahra, just outside Jeddah, to sort out some border questions. One evening the two, accompanied by an armed slave called Idris, took a stroll near the camp, and came across a Bedouin tent. Here they were met by two xenophobic and fanatical Arabians who cursed the Englishmen as dogs of Christians. The Englishmen walked on, trying to ignore the problem, but Idris began to remonstrate with the men and a crowd gathered. It looked as though there would be a brawl but things calmed down as the Englishmen put distance between themselves and the Arabians. However, Clayton thought it would be right to send a note to King Abdulaziz apologising for causing the difficulty by being where he perhaps should not have been. The King, far from reproving Clayton, immediately ordered the arrest of the two fanatics and had them brought before him. On entering the King's tent the men greeted their monarch with the customary formula, 'God greet you with prosperity'. King Abdulaziz roared at them in reply, 'God greet you with dung in your faces, you curs. Who are you to insult my guests?' He then ordered that each be given thirty lashes and taken at once to Makkah jail.

On another occasion when he was twitted with the criticism that Arabians are very lackadaisical in their attitude to time, Sheikh Yamani gently explained how matters stood, by referring to the word for tomorrow. 'In Spanish', he said, 'it's *mañana*, in Arabic it is *bukra*; the difference between the two being that *bukra* takes a lot longer than *mañana*.'

Time

After forty years the Bedu took his revenge, but then he was in a hurry.
Arabian Proverb

The invention of the watch has saddled the Westerner with the tyranny of time. One of the characteristics of this is a devotion to punctuality – not a quality much favoured in the Middle East until comparatively recently. One of the problems that surfaced was the way of reckoning the time. The Arabians had quite a different system – over much of the desert the Bedouin begin counting the hours from dawn.

In the settled ports of the Gulf, the Indian Political Service had left its own legacy over the matter of time. There were three systems. Arabic time reckoned from dawn, English time reckoned as usual and a third and wonderfully Arabian and Indian thing called just 'Taim'. This implied an obligation to be absolutely punctual and to arrive on the dot for an appointment. 'Taim' was much used by the Indian Political Service!

It was a matter of amusement to some that when Concorde made its first overseas flight it was to Bahrain – a destination inhabited by people who were unconcerned as to whether the plane arrived today or tomorrow, let alone a bit faster than the others.

Progress and change

Progress might have been all right once, but it has gone on too long.

Ogden Nash

It has always been a matter of some surprise that when the British run language courses they are so shy and prudish about lavatorial matters that the subject is never actually mentioned. How many readers have been taught the French or German for 'Where's the loo?' After the 1971 coup, a senior British officer seconded to the Sultan of Oman's Armed Forces was concerned to observe that after breakfast all the Omani soldiers under his command left the camp to squat on the mountainside to relieve themselves. Clearly this gave any enemy the chance to quite literally catch the Sultan's Army with its collective trousers down. Accordingly he ordered a little hut to be built over the water channel that ran beside the parade ground. Inside the hut was arranged a long seat with apertures at convenient intervals.

At the following parade the Adjutant informed the assembled men that in future they would use the new facility in the mornings and not pop out to the mountainside as hitherto. This was fine except that neither the Adjutant nor the CO were aware that for centuries Arabs had used small smooth pebbles instead of loo paper. The consequence was soon aromatically apparent as a small dam was built under each seat and a malodorous flood spread over the parade ground. The CO called his British officers together again and instructed them to tear up newspapers into conveniently-sized sheets which were then nailed up in fifties behind each seat. At the next parade the Adjutant told the men to use the paper. They did. And carefully wrapped each stone in a quarter of a sheet of the airmail edition of the *Daily Telegraph*. The consequence of this of course was the construction of bigger and better dams, and hence a bigger disaster than before. At this point the CO gave up.

A young Dutch civil engineer in the oil company had a similar experience when he tried to introduce the Bedouin to the delights of the S-bend!

Comments on progress can be salutary, as this story about Sheikh Ma'ayuf of the Duru' shows. He was entertaining a man from the oil company to an evening meal. During the course of the meal the oil man looked up into the wonderful Arabian sky and amongst the millions of stars he noticed a satellite crossing the heavens. He pointed this out to the sheikh, saying that the Christians could even make stars nowadays; that was real progress wasn't it? Sheikh Ma'ayuf watched the satellite for a little while and then said it wasn't really any good at all. One couldn't possibly steer by something moving so fast. It would be better to stick with the stars made by God.

*****

Just after the takeover by Sultan Qaboos in 1971, the citizens of Muscat were rather put out by the effects of progress on one of their mosques. The dear old gentleman who for many years had painfully climbed up the stairs of the minaret to call the faithful to prayer had always paused at the top before he began in order to get his breath back and clear his throat. Then progress struck. A loudspeaker was installed and unthinkingly turned on by a switch at the bottom of the stairs. Consequently when the old man reached the top of the stairs the microphone was already live and the city was treated to a cacophony of coughs, wheezes and spitting noises, often lasting for nearly five minutes.

There is another salutary if sad story about the collision between one culture and another consequent on the inexorable march of progress. After the succession of Sultan Qaboos, a humble and small Baluch merchant in Muttrah souk obtained the contract to clean the splendid new Ministry of Defence building. The complexities of modern business administration rather eluded the merchant and after a few years he hired a retiring British sergeant to run his little office for him. The sergeant set to work and, in attempting to get some sort of order into the muddled and dusty piles of paper, discovered that his employer had never collected payment from the ministry. When he asked the merchant about it the little man shamefacedly told him that he was such a small and insignificant person that he had not dared to approach the great ministry for his money. Scooping up the relevant papers, the sergeant went round to the ministry on his shy employer's behalf. He returned with a cheque for a huge sum of money. The merchant was delighted and diffidently told the sergeant that this sum would allow him to realise a lifetime's ambition – to start a shipping line.

At this time the Sultanate did not have its own Shipping Register, so the merchant couldn't buy a boat registered for the Sultanate of Oman. He would have to register his ship elsewhere; and this would mean travelling to London to arrange matters through a firm of marine lawyers there. The merchant arrived in the old-fashioned offices of a very traditional legal firm, all mahogany and frosted glass partitions. Here it was explained to him, by a young man in black coat and striped trousers, that he would have to register a company in Panama and that, while this company would be owned by him, the company would own the ship.

The merchant couldn't understand this arrangement at all. The little man despairingly said that this would mean he would not own the ship that he had set his heart on possessing; he had known all along that his ship would be stolen from him, and no further explanations would budge him from this belief. Nevertheless he finally acquiesced, and signed the necessary papers, even though he really thought everything he treasured would be taken from him. He then repaired to Marks & Spencer in Oxford Street to buy presents for his family. He was so upset that he forgot what sizes might be appropriate for his family and was forced to buy one of everything to make sure that everyone would get clothes that fitted them.

When asked how the rushing changes of the second half of the 20th century had affected him, the head of a prominent merchant family in Jeddah wryly remarked with smiling eyes, that nowadays 'one had to pay the slaves'. Another, on first meeting an English businessman, asked him if he minded being called Jack. By way of explanation the Arabian, smiling broadly, said that he liked to call all Englishmen by that name because they all looked alike (*pace* the English colonial canard that all natives looked the same).

This factor is rubbed in by the tale of the Gulf sheikh who had all his considerable amount of jewellery stolen from his London hotel suite. The thief had arrived at the suite pretending to be a window cleaner, and was admitted by a maidservant who got a good sight of him. After the man had left the theft was discovered and the police had high hopes of getting a good description of the miscreant. However, when shown a large book of photographs of possible culprits, the maid confidently identified every single one of them as the guilty man because they all looked alike to her. There is at least one other version of this story which actually refers to Sheikh Khalid of Abu Dhabi, a brother of the late Sheikh Zayd. In this second version the British police are said to have paraded suspects in front of the maid rather than showing her photographs. The result was the same. However, it was additionally related that this event made Sheikh Khalid give up his habit of keeping all his money and jewellery in an old tin box.

Politics and democracy

Let's Have an Election

Edited by Sir Donald Hawley, there is a wonderful compendium of stories from the Sudan in which Donald Weir contributes a most topical tale. Today the West is pushing democracy with all the energetic fervour a Victorian missionary put into getting the natives into school, church and trousers. However, ways, means and results are not always what one expects.

This story refers to a time over half a century ago.

The Bani Hanzal are a Bedouin tribe of the Sudan who had but one settlement in their tribal range. This consisted of a very few mud huts, mud shops and a brackish water well, all surrounded by miles of desert. It rejoiced in the name of Umm Bakheet, or Mother of Melons, a name more optimistic than accurate, as melons hadn't grown there for years. So, when the Government called an election it was only natural that the polling should take place in Umm Bakheet, and the General Electoral Supervisory Board duly sent their representative there to arrange everything. Now, Bedouin have very loose ideas as to precise timing and punctuality. A week or two here or there doesn't make any real difference to them. The Board, having had bitter experience of the consequences of this failing, instructed their man to ensure that the Bani Hanzal were made fully aware of their public duty, to ensure support for their democratic rights, and to turn up to vote between 9 a.m. and 5 p.m. on election day. An additional factor creating mayhem over time was also the universal way that the Bedouin throughout Arabia calculated the time of day themselves. You start at dawn and so one o'clock is one hour after dawn, say six o'clock GMT. The Bani Hanzal would therefore have perhaps understood this timetable better if they had been asked to come between 3.00 and 11.00. If the reader is interested in knowing the time in the old desert, all he has to do is turn his watch upside down.

For countless generations the Bani Hanzal had had their lives successfully guided and guarded by their own tribal chief, the Kaid. They were therefore at a loss to understand why they needed an election at all. Understanding this, the Man on the Spot arranged for the Kaid himself to be nominated and pay the ten pound fee. This sum somehow got deducted from the Kaid's tax assessment, which only seemed just. The Man on the Spot was quietly confident that everything had been suitably and properly arranged.

However, on the very morning of the closing date for nominations two lorries appeared in Umm Bakheet carrying two dishevelled merchants from a nearby town, whose reputations were less than savoury. Disaster struck as they both presented their own nominations.

The first consequence was that the Kaid demanded his money back, but on being told that this wasn't possible he seemed to accept the situation with equanimity. Then the two new candidates set about organising hustings to gather support for their political parties. The Bani Hanzal viewed these activities with disdain, but the settled community of Umm Bakheet became very excited and it wasn't long before rumours of bribery emerged.

This meant that the actual polling had to proceed in complete secrecy to ensure that the purchase of votes would profit no one. Accordingly a large palm leaf hut was built in the middle of an animal pound. It had a single entrance and a single exit. It was arranged that only two electoral clerks would be allowed into the pound and they would sit in the open in full view of everyone outside the hut. The electors would be let in one by one to have their credentials checked. They would then be given a token stamped with the Government Seal and, all by themselves, would enter the hut and drop their token into one of three iron boxes each marked with the symbol of one candidate, and then leave.

The Man on the Spot was nevertheless a bit uneasy, a feeling exacerbated by the arrival of a further instruction from the General Electoral Supervisory Board. This said that following representations the presence of officials at the polling station would be regarded as direct interference with the freedom of the election. So the Man on the Spot had to absent himself and appoint his Police Sergeant to oversee events.

Surprisingly, on polling day the Bani Hanzal streamed into town on time to vote. Clearly something was afoot. Only money could have engendered such interest.

The count took place in the evening at about 8 p.m. and a silent crowd had gathered round the animal pound. Suddenly there was a roar, swords were drawn and rifles discharged. Alarmed, the Man on the Spot called for his escort and stumbled out of his office into the arms of a smiling Kaid who said, 'My people are happy at my election, I had ordered a sheep to be killed and brought to you in thanksgiving, but your Sergeant said that even such a paltry gift might be misconstrued in some quarters, so I rescinded the order'.

The following morning Umm Bakheet returned to its customary torpor and the Bani Hanzal had disappeared back to their desert. The Man on the Spot set off on his camel, accompanied by his Police Sergeant. After a while the Sergeant said, 'Sir, I have been thinking about this election thing because I too am a voter and the Government says it is a duty to vote. I am also a policeman and must do my duty. So this is what I did.

'You know that my brothers of the Bani Hanzal are not interested in elections, since the Kaid is their representative in all things for all time. You would know also that they would forget that if they did not vote for the Kaid they might find themselves with a representative for the Government's Parliament whom they had never before dreamt of as a leader among them.

'Because you knew this and you suspected the two nominees from the town, you built a good voting booth in the compound to make sure that everything would be fair.

'I was very surprised to see so many of the Bani Hanzal coming in to vote and felt it my duty to see that with a fair election the Kaid was elected. After all he had paid the Government ten pounds to get elected.

'I discovered that these two men from the town had told the Bani Hanzal that they would pay five shillings for them to cast their votes as they wished. When I first heard of this I thought that the arrangements for the voting would make this pointless, and the Bani Hanzal would vote for the Kaid anyway. This was what the Bani Hanzal thought too, and that was why they all came in to vote. To get the money. But the townsmen were not stupid and they told the Bani Hanzal to enter the booth as instructed but not to place their tokens into any of the boxes, but to hide them about their persons and bring them out and exchange them for five shillings each with one of the townsmen, though one of these men was paying more to ensure getting elected himself. Then the townsmen would go to vote just before the polling station closed and tip the tokens into their own box. When I thought about this it seemed obvious that very few votes would go to the Kaid. But I soon found out where the townsmen were collecting the tokens. I didn't interfere at once because the Bani Hanzal were making good money and they have had a bad year.

'Late in the afternoon I covered my uniform with a cloak and went to where one of the men was collecting tokens. I told him who I was and that the Government would send him to prison for ten years. He was very afraid and offered me a pound. Naturally I refused and, telling him the Court would need the tokens as evidence, I swept them all up into a bag. He nearly burst into tears, and asked me who had given me my information. I told him it was his colleague, the other townsman. Then I went to where the second man was buying tokens and, telling him about the prison that awaited, him I swept up his tokens as well, telling him that the first man had told me what he was up to.

'Then I went to the polling station to cast my own vote and after putting it into the Kaid's box I then filled the box up with the tokens I had collected, leaving some for the townsmen's box because some people would have voted for them.'

The General Electoral Supervisory Board were very pleased with the way they thought the election had been carried out, and congratulated all concerned. They were happy, too, to confirm the election of the Kaid to represent the Bani Hanzal.

****

When Sultan Said Bin Taimur ascended the throne of Muscat and Oman in 1932 on the abdication of his father, he was interviewed by a journalist. It being rather warm in Muscat, this reporter turned up to interview the Sultan without wearing a tie. Sultan Said was horrified that the man should have the effrontery to appear before him improperly dressed and, taking this as the way all members of the press behaved, he steadfastly refused to see another journalist until 1968. In this year his advisers succeeded in persuading him that, for the good of his country, he really should try and join just a little bit with the modern age and the rest of the world. Reluctantly Said agreed and a suitable journalist was found. However, remembering the effect that the first journalist had had on the Sultan, the advisers impressed on the new one the need to dress properly, and wear a tie. So keen were they on the sartorial aspect of the event that they completely forgot to give the poor man any other briefing at all. So when asked to put a question to Sultan Said the journalist politely enquired as to what political parties Said had in his Sultanate. Said was clearly a bit put out by this question and replied, somewhat testily, that as neither he nor his subjects had any politics there was no need at all for political parties, so they didn't have any. The journalist next asked Said what he and his people felt about the Palestinian situation. Said crossly and peremptorily snapped that that was a political question and that, as he had just stated, he and his people didn't have any politics. And that was the end of the interview.

It can be difficult for Westerners to understand how politics works in Saudi Arabia. There are no political parties, and only recently is a rudimentary voting system being put into place. Politics in Saudi Arabia are all about the relationship between one prince and another, and the overlapping of their spheres of influence. In the West we are perfectly happy, really, with the idea that we pay taxes to the government. Is it unreasonable then, when the government is made up of princes, that we should complain if the princes get paid? After all, in both systems some of the money eventually gets paid back to the citizenry. This has been much misunderstood in the West and has created fertile ground for misunderstandings all round. Keeping it in the family has its uses.

****

When His Majesty King Idris Al Sanusi of Libya liberated his country from the Italians after the Second World War, his grip on the principles of democracy might have appeared a little vague – that is, until the world became accustomed to those of his successor, Colonel Mu'ammar Gaddafi. Gaddafi's successful coup aptly illustrates the Arabian propensity mentioned earlier for jumping out of the frying pan into the fire.

King Idris took a keen interest in the Government and would instruct his Prime Minister as to which way votes needed to go when debates were held in the Parliament. Frequently the decision arrived at would be contrary to the wishes of His Majesty, who would then politely suggest to the Prime Minister that it would be best to debate the matter a second time. Meanwhile, the King said he would keep open a vacancy he had for an assistant in his Tobruk library, so that if the decision went the wrong way a second time the Prime Minister would have another job to go to.

The Legislative Assembly in Bahrain disappeared in the 1970s but later events created a need to provide an explanation for this. What happened was as follows. In the time of the benign Amir, Sheikh Issa Al Khalifa, it was thought, rightly or wrongly, that the Emirate needed a leaflet to boost its public image. Accordingly a PR Consultant was hired in London and he flew to the island. There he made appointments to see various Ministers to get an idea of how the Government worked. This was fine as far as the first meeting, with the Minister of Power, was concerned. The Minister was extremely friendly and His Excellency gave all the right kind of information, and lots of detail about the splendours of Bahraini electricity. As he was leaving the Minister asked the PR chap where he was going next. The PR man told him he was going to see the Minister of Health.

'You poor man,' said the Minister of Power. 'My Ministerial colleague is at best a congenital liar. You can't believe a word he says.'

Feeling a little apprehensive, the PR man jumped into a taxi and was taken to the Health Ministry. There the Minister of Health beamed an effusive welcome and asked the PR man whom he had interviewed so far.

'The Minister of Power, Your Excellency.' answered the PR man.

'Good Heavens,' responded the Minister. 'That man is an absolute rogue. The very word "corruption" was coined with him in mind.' And so it continued throughout the PR man's interviews.

However, it also emerged that there were two years missing in Bahrain's history and it became clear to the PR man that the only person who could resolve the matter was the Ruler himself. The matter concerned the complete disappearance of the Bahraini Legislative Assembly.

The Emir proved to be as charming as he was reputed to be, and quite understood the position when it was explained that if the leaflet had been about a person, such a gap would lead everyone to suppose that the person concerned had been in prison for those two missing years. In answer to the PR man's question as to what had happened, the Emir replied that actually it was all the fault of the British. For years they had nagged him and his brother, the Prime Minister, to have an elected Legislative Assembly, and the two of them had finally agreed. Accordingly a huge sum of money was spent – and with an English company to boot – and an appropriate building was erected. It nearly fell down later, but that is another story. The Emir went on to tell of the expensive Italian leather furniture that was installed and the election that followed. All the elected members had arrived and sat down comfortably on the costly furniture and began to debate things.

The Emir explained that two years later he woke up one day wondering what the Legislative Assembly had achieved. He told the PR man that he must by now have realised that Arabians are great talkers, and that is just what the Assembly had done. For two years they had talked and talked and talked, and had achieved precisely nothing for the people of Bahrain.

'What happened next?' asked the PR man.

'I conferred with the Prime Minister and then issued a Decree cancelling the Assembly,' replied the Emir, rather smugly. 'Then I had a cup of coffee and issued another Decree which gave my people a Health Service; then I had another coffee and issued a second Decree which gave my people free education. Another coffee later, poor Bahrainis had housing. By midday I had issued so many decrees that I felt a bit tired so I had lunch and then a siesta.' The PR man thanked His Highness and promised he would tell the story in the leaflet in such a way that liberal Western opinion would not be outraged. It is however reported that the Prime Minister had rather forced the Emir's hand.

****

Once a salesman called on a prince who worked in the Saudi Ministry of Education to find out what opportunities there were for selling school furniture. The prince was seated in a large room at a tiny school desk, and all round the walls were seated people with business to lay before His Royal Highness. As each person saw the prince everyone moved up one chair closer to him. Just in front of the salesman there was a young student, and the salesman couldn't escape overhearing what transpired when the young man had his turn. Apparently the lad was at Riyadh University and came from a very poor family in the Asir region of the Kingdom bordering the Red Sea. Studying in Riyadh meant that he could no longer support his parents, and he had taken a job so that he could send them money. This was forbidden, as students were supposed to study and not waste time in employment. Accordingly the Rector of the university had expelled the young man.

The prince looked sympathetic but began by saying that the Rector was quite right. However, he continued, 'My cousin is the

Governor of the Asir and I will telephone him and ask him to provide your old parents with enough money for them to live comfortably'. The prince made the call then and there. When he put the phone down he said to the student, 'Now take this letter to the Rector and he will reinstate you, but you must get a letter from your employer stating that you have left your job and bring it to me so that after reading it I can forward it to the Rector of the university as well'.

If only things like this could be dealt with so simply in the West.

Censorship and bureaucracy frequently tie things into incongruous knots. Officialdom, even in the nicest places and with the nicest governments, can often get things into a complex muddle. Nothing is sacred. In Bahrain, even the commemoration of the Martyrdom of the Imam Hussein as long ago as the seventh century created difficulties one year. In order to ensure that everything would go off peacefully at the commemoration ceremony the police carefully briefed a young religious Sheikh as to what he should say in his sermon to mark this very important festival. He was forbidden to mention that it was the Ummayads of Syria who killed Hussein, as this would upset the Syrians. He was told that he mustn't mention either the Sunnis or the Shi'a, as this would weaken national unity and inflame relations with Iraq. He must refrain from mentioning the Christians lest that seem discriminatory. He must not mention the Jews lest this be seen as being anti-Semitic. He was even forbidden to say how the Imam died. In despair the young man asked sarcastically if he could just say that the Imam Hussein touched an electric cable and killed himself. This was turned down in case it upset the Iranians!

****

The expression 'Keeny Meeny' is mainly used in South Arabia and is defined as political intrigue or manoeuvring. It is difficult to know who started it, but it has probably been going on since before the Queen of Sheba tried it on with King Solomon. Certainly by the days of the Imam Yahya everyone spied on everyone else. All of the Imam's sons did it, all the sheikhs did it, and all their tribesmen did it. Every merchant, soldier and sailor did it. Every Sultan, Emir and Sharif did it. It is the chess game that is the life and soul of South Arabia. It is a game that the British took up with no little enthusiasm, but the home teams usually won most of the matches and, after the British withdrawal, the locals have continued to play it with unabated delight. No cricketer ever honed his skills in the nets as finely as a South Arabian his talent for Keeny Meeny.

One of the main tools in this merry-go-round as far as the British were concerned was the supply of arms. Treaty Chiefs were 'paid' with varying numbers of rifles and the requisite ammunition. This may seem a kind and avuncular thing to do, as the guns were quite obviously what the Rulers needed, given the warlike and rebellious nature of their devoted subjects. As it turned out, the rifles had another quite unexpected effect. They made the pursuit of the blood feud much more efficient. Instead of having to actually get to grips with your enemy and stab him with a dagger, you could achieve the same result sitting comfortably behind a rock a hundred yards away.

Of course the guns also served to provide a firm basis for a thriving commercial activity, which was given a tremendous boost by some enterprises in London's Tottenham Court Road. There a First World War .303 rifle could be bought for ten pounds. Delivered to a purchaser in the Western Aden Protectorate, the weapon could then be sent on to the Eastern Aden Protectorate, where they were forbidden, and sold for a hundred pounds. This was quite a useful cash flow, which of itself purchased much influence as well as plenty more guns.

The 1967 Six-Day War

At the start of the Six-Day War of 1967 there was a tremendous surge of solidarity with the Palestinians throughout the Arab World. The Qataris naturally felt the same way as everyone else and hundreds of them demanded to go to join in the war. Their Ruler prudently and generously agreed and even offered to pay for their air tickets. Apparently it wasn't until these enthusiastic would-be warriors arrived in Jordan that they realised that all their tickets were one way only.

Saudi Arabia was the only country in the Middle East from which British citizens were not evacuated during the Six-Day War. However, the British valiantly made plans for such an event and created a list of British expatriate nationals who could be appointed as wardens to look after the others. The Embassy staff were very loath to leave their compound. Britons were told to stay indoors and under no circumstances to go to the Market. Due to the lack of telephones very few of the people appointed as wardens ever found out about their appointment.

One suggestion to overcome this was that such people who were contacted should be asked to get in touch with their fellows by bicycle. But it sadly transpired that not only were there no bicycles available, but neither could anyone ride one. This eventuality was a deep disappointment to a Mrs Barbara Wood, the wife of one of the English teachers. She was also a classical cellist of considerable talent and had spent most of her overseas allowance in getting her cello to Saudi Arabia. After the arrival of her instrument it was discovered that there was little or no call for cello concerts in the Kingdom. However, when she heard that a British warship would come to rescue everyone she perked up considerably, and looked forward to entertaining the Captain and his gallant crew to a recital as they sailed away down the Red Sea. Even this forlorn hope had to be abandoned during the course of subsequent events.

The Six-Day War broke out just as the Yemeni Civil War between Egyptian-backed republicans and Saudi-backed Royalists reached its apogee. The Royalists were being pressed hard by the Egyptians, who had begun to bomb not only Yemeni targets, but also parts of southern Saudi Arabia such as Najran. This caused concern amongst the British in Jeddah who had friends in the south, and further worry arose as it was expected that the Egyptians would also bomb Jeddah. The Saudi authorities accordingly ordered a blackout. Car headlights were painted out, street lighting was switched off and business premises and private houses turned off their lights. The police did their level best to enforce the rules but they were frustrated in their efforts because in many areas, especially around the airport, they found it impossible to get members of the Royal Family to join in, and most palaces remained brilliantly illuminated.

Actually, no Egyptian bombs fell. With the advent of the Six-Day War, it was quickly announced that the hitherto hated Egyptians were really valiant brothers in the struggle against the Israelis; and, instead of bombing Jeddah they were actually going to land and refuel there. This underlines the very real talent that the Arabians have of not only being on every side at once, but also of being able to change sides in the twinkling of an eye. This talent mystifies the average Briton, who is used to supporting either Liverpool or Manchester United, but not both. When the first Egyptian planes landed in Jeddah the crews were taken for a rest to the Kandara Palace Hotel where they were greeted by Prince Sultan, the Minister of Defence.

This *volte face* did not go down well with many of the British and some members of the diplomatic community. Remembering how their Yemeni Royalist friends had suffered at the hands of the Egyptians, a number of them arranged to meet at the Kandara Palace, and reserved tables for lunch. When the Saudi dignitaries arrived escorting the Egyptian Air Force people this party, to make their feelings felt, just stood up and walked out.

During the Six-Day War, feelings were running high among Saudi youth and the student body and it was difficult to keep them in the classrooms. In at least one school the boys wanted to commandeer buses and taxis and drive northwards to the battlefield to join the fight. They were only stopped by a personal appeal from their headmaster. He succeeded in convincing them that in the long run attendance at their physics and chemistry lessons would prove a better way of conquering the Israelis.

The hatred for the State of Israel is a very real thing throughout the region. But the Arabian ability to exclude personal relationships from this most deeply-entrenched antagonism is nicely expressed by the feelings held by dozens of medical staff in Saudi Arabia. They were all taught in the USA, very often by Jewish doctors at the medical schools there. Young Arabian doctors and surgeons are very grateful to their American Jewish teachers and frequently contribute to funds needed by their mentors for research and charitable activities. This does not at all prevent them expressing the most virulent hatred for Jews in general.

This is a good place to repeat a comment of Khalid Kishtainy (described in his novel *By the Rivers of Babylon* as 'an old fatwa from a thick volume of sharia edicts'): 'Eat with the Jews and sleep with the Christians'.

Arabian Attitudes to History

In the light of the events of 2011 and the use of the expression 'Arab Spring', there are a couple of things that it may be apposite to mention. History can often come up with unpalatable truths. The Arabian answer to the possible embarrassment that historical revelations might produce is simply to ignore them. Thus in Saudi Arabia the profligacy of King Saud Bin Abdulaziz's reign is just never mentioned: it wasn't his fault but as Monarch he was responsible, and now his portrait just doesn't appear alongside those of his brothers who succeeded him on the throne. In 2010, however, there were signs that Saud was being rehabilitated a bit. In Oman the person of the Sultan Said bin Taimur has been expunged from the historical page. In Bahrain the subject of the disappearance of the Legislative Assembly was never mentioned, and remained a mystery for quite a while, as explained elsewhere.

Animals

The beetle is a beauty in the eyes of its mother.
Egyptian proverb

The trouble with the younger generation is that, by God, they can't even ride a camel.
Elderly Bedouin taxi driver in Jeddah, 1976

Saudi Arabia is the last country in the world to have been united by people on horseback, which should endear it to a British public hooked on horse racing. Another connection with horses that most people seem to have missed relates to the birth of children in the Royal Family. No one puts up a notice on the palace gate to announce the arrival of a new little prince. Instead the Riyadh papers will report a runner in a horse race to be owned by a prince not previously known. The horse is the gift of a proud new father!

It is perhaps unkind to mention that, in order to maintain the purity of the breed in the Kingdom, it is forbidden to import horses from outside the country. On one occasion the Greek agent of one of the princes working from Cairo approached an Englishman with the idea that he should buy small English racehorses; runts, in fact. These would look small enough to pass as Arab steeds and, smuggled into Saudi Arabia, could be passed off as Saudi-bred. Anyone who has bet on the horses will see the fallacy of this reasoning, but the Royal Highness concerned was persuaded by his Greek agent that this would enable him to win all the races in Riyadh.

This idea was, however, not new. During the 19th century it was quite common for unscrupulous dealers to cross mares of inferior breeding with purebred Arabian stallions. The mares would then be sent out to the desert to foal and then their offspring would be brought back to be proudly presented as desert-bred, and sold for racing in India, Egypt and Syria.

It would be absurd not to mention camels somewhere. They have been variously described, but the definition of a camel as being a horse designed by a committee is pretty close to the mark. The European reader will doubtless like to know that camels come in red, green, blue and yellow, as well as white and black. To such a reader, they all look to be a sort of tan grey brown, but that is not what an Arabian sees.

Camels have fabulous eyes, and eyelashes to die for. Everything else looks quite remarkably ungainly. When away from home they get lonely, especially when camped at night, though once hobbled and folded up they manage to jerk themselves along on their elbows to get as close as possible to their human companions. This can be embarrassing, particularly if their companion is a European confined to a sleeping bag, which prevents him from getting out of the way. Being knelt on by a lonely camel in the middle of the night can be fatal. When falling in love, male camels inflate a large pink blubbery balloon out of the side of their mouths. This inflation is accompanied by an appalling blubbery noise which unaccountably female camels think is the love song to beat all love songs.

A male camel has tushes up to ten inches long completely hidden inside his soft upper lip. With these he can bite your leg off. The characteristic of the male camel that causes the most amusement, however, is the fact that he pees backwards. It is a delight for Arabians to get pompous Westerners to walk behind a male camel and then frighten the beast at the crucial moment. It is then that the Arabian headdress fulfills another of its many purposes. It can be deftly wrapped around the face to conceal the gales of laughter provoked by the sight of the discomforted Westerner dripping with camel pee.

****

In the last quarter of the 19th century, Lady Anne and Wilfrid Blunt bought Arabian horses when passing through Aleppo. They were not the first to do this and the locals may well have been alerted to the market potential that Europeans represented. In addition, the Blunts appointed the British Consul in Aleppo as their agent. This man, James Henry Skene, had been resident in Aleppo for twenty years and was familiar with the Arabic language and tribal customs. He had bought horses for others from England, and these purchases had already caused a price rise. Skene seems to have had all the instincts of a second-hand car dealer. Wilfrid Blunt was suspicious of him from the start, finding his qualifications suspect. Lady Anne, ever anxious to please her husband, quickly realised that Skene did not know Arab horses were bred in the desert (as opposed to how it was done in the towns of the Levant). At that time so impressed were the Europeans with pedigrees that these were merrily forged by helpful horse dealers, and documents firmly following the patrilineal lines of human pedigrees in the *Almanach de Gotha* and *Debrett's* were produced, complete with suitable seals and calligraphy. In fact, the real Bedouin breeders were mostly illiterate and passed the ancestry of their strains of the purebred Arabian down by oral tradition – the name of the strain being passed down through the female line rather than that of the stallion, the so-called Tail Female Line. Eventually Mr Skene accumulated debts of some £2,000, and our man in the Constantinople Embassy instituted legal proceedings against him, and demanded his arrest. His wife had to sell her jewellery to get him out of trouble. These events throw not inconsiderable doubt on the veracity of some famous pedigrees today.

The English think that they are the only people in the world who know how to look after animals and, despite the clear announcement in Genesis that God made animals in the first place to fulfil no other purpose than to serve Mankind, which had absolute dominion over them, feel that all foreigners treat their animals abominably. This deeply-held belief led the wife of a senior official in the Western Aden Protectorate to march down to the souk in Crater a couple of days before the British left. She was armed with two wicker hampers, which in earlier and happier days had been used to accommodate picnic requisites. To the great surprise of the onlookers, the lady then caught at least a couple of dozen feral cats and stuffed them into the baskets. Rightly, she thought that the National Liberation Front, communists to a man, would be quite incapable of looking after them; not that anyone had previously done so under the British administration either. But that wasn't the point. The question of what the cats might have thought about it never arose of course, and so they weren't consulted.

In the end, they landed up in Sardinia where they settled to a life of unparalleled feline luxury. Not having to waste any time looking for food, they could devote all their energies to breeding, which they did with incomparable enthusiasm. The consequence was a population explosion of nuclear proportions. The lady's husband suggested euthanasia but this was fiercely turned down by his outraged spouse, so he had to wait for her to go on a shopping trip back to London.

While she was away he planned to collect the cats in batches and take them down to the vet for neutering. However his grasp of Arabian tribes was much better than his expertise in basic zoology, and he had no idea how to tell the difference between a tomcat and a female. Having returned home with the first batch, he released them and tried to catch another lot. This proved impossible, however, because he could not distinguish which cats had been seen to and which had not. Despairingly, he contemplated his life ending by being drowned in a feline ocean. Then an idea came to mind. He sauntered down to the local fishing village and during, the course of a glass or two of wine in the taverna, let slip that cat meat was the most effective aphrodisiac known to man. The cats thereafter rapidly disappeared, but it is not recorded whether or not their flesh passed on to their eaters their talent for procreation.

It isn't easy, in the interests of being even handed, to find tales of Arabians behaving in the same kind of way, but there is the odd anecdote that perhaps fits the bill. Due to the increase in wealth following the discovery of oil, the amount of rubbish created by households in the Eastern Province of Saudi Arabia escalated dramatically. This meant that the pye-dogs bred at a ferocious rate, demonstrating that a Saudi pye-dog was certainly the equal of an Adeni cat in this respect. The Saudi authorities became very alarmed and wondered what to do; shooting the dogs would not go down well with the large British community. Then the Saudis discovered to their delight that Koreans ate dogs. They were also astute enough to see a business opportunity, so they approached a couple of Korean companies involved in building oil refineries and desalination plants. The Saudi authorities sold them licences to catch the pye-dogs and dispose of them. In only a couple of months there was not a pye-dog to be seen, and hitherto rather slim Koreans had clearly put on quite a bit of weight.

A Story to Gladden the English Heart

Once upon a time there was a King in Arabia who had been very successful in conquering many of the tribes in the desert. During the course of his campaigns he had made quite a few enemies. One night, while the King slept in his castle, some of these enemies climbed over the town wall intent on killing him. However, the town dogs barked their heads off at the intruders, waking the King and his bodyguards, who were able to repel the attack and chase the enemy back into the desert. In gratitude for the warning they had given him, the king ordered that henceforth, in distinction to the previous way things had been done, it was forbidden to kill any of the dogs and, furthermore, his chamberlain was authorised to provide the dogs with rations of meat and rice.

This created a problem because the dogs bred and their numbers increased enormously. The inhabitants of the town hit on an ingenious solution that enabled them to both control the numbers of the dogs and obey the King's command. Every so often they rounded up some of the dogs and sent them in lorries to other towns. There the strange dogs were largely disposed of by the indigenous dog population who at once attacked the interlopers.

The name of the king was Abdulaziz Ibn Abdulrahman Al Saud and the town where he lived was Riyadh.

◊ ◊ ◊

There is a rather nice story about a fatwa that was supposedly issued especially to help the Royalists at one juncture in the Civil War. A fatwa is an opinion as to what the Prophet Muhammad would have said had he been asked about a new situation. It is also something that has acquired some notoriety in the West.

The Egyptians had established an ammunition dump in the desert in the east of the country and the Royalists thought it would be a splendid idea to blow it up. Sadly, inside the barbed wire the makings of a first class firework display were guarded by police dogs. The Royalist tribesmen felt they could not run the risk of being bitten by unclean dogs, and Egyptian ones at that. A British adviser lightened the ensuing gloom and disappointment by telling the Yemenis that all they had to do was get hold of a pye-dog bitch in season and tie her up to one side of the ammunition dump compound. Then all the Egyptian police dogs would rush over to that side and the Yemenis could, without endangering their immortal souls, climb over the other side and do the business. The tribesmen were entranced with the idea of using sex to trap the police dogs but suddenly realised that a pye-dog bitch, albeit a Yemeni one, was also unclean and being in season made her doubly so. With heavy hearts and the deepest reluctance they therefore declined to go through with this idea.

The Adviser took the problem to a Qadi immensely famed for his great knowledge, wisdom and holiness. The old judge came up with the perfect solution. He gave it as his considered opinion in a fatwa that if a Christian were to wipe the backside of a pye-dog bitch with a piece of cloth and tie this to a string fifteen feet long, then a Muslim could pick up the other end of the string with impunity, and run about with it outside the wire. The relief amongst the tribesmen was huge and in no time a suitable bitch, Christian and length of string were collected together, and that very night one of their number danced up to the wire. Every police dog in the place raced to that side of the compound. The Yemenis climbed over the other side and in no time there was an enormous and wholly satisfying explosion which was heard and seen for miles around.

The Pye Dog's Tale

In a drain beside the old airfield in Tobruk there lived a scruffy, scarred, smelly and toothless old white pye-dog. Mr Pie, for that was his name, fell in love with a beautiful German Shepherd bitch called Lady. Whenever Lady went for a walk, Mr Pie followed adoringly some twenty yards behind, and Lady ignored him completely. The reason Mr Pie had no teeth was because his only enjoyment in life, apart from dreaming about Lady, was to lie in wait for any unsuspecting Arab on a bicycle. As the cyclist passed, Mr Pie would jump out and grab the back wheel of the bicycle, toppling the rider in an undignified heap on the ground. This wasn't good for Mr Pie's teeth, which were all eventually wrenched out by the spokes. Nevertheless Mr Pie continued the game and whenever he succeeded he would sit in the road laughing his head off.

One day, thus paralysed with mirth he was unable to dodge the rock hurled at him by an aggrieved Libyan cyclist. He yelped in pain as the stone hit his side. Lady heard, turned, and raced back to Mr Pie's rescue, and leapt for the throat of his attacker. Luckily, her front paws hit the man's chest and pushed him backwards so that her jaws snapped shut on thin air just under his chin. Mr Pie was delighted that Lady had clearly been aware of him all the time!

❖ ❖ ❖

There is plenty of hypocrisy in the West, but Western hypocrisy is actually more than a little wishy-washy compared to the Arabian variety. In Arabia, hypocrisy is almost elevated to an art form. Dogs are abhorred as being unclean but there is huge honour in owning and breeding Salukis. It is quite simple – these lovely dogs aren't dogs at all! They are Salukis, and so not subject to any kind of ban. This thinking can apply to other breeds too; but in special circumstances. I owned a German Shepherd dog in Aden and she was thoroughly spoilt at Arabian meals, being plied with haunches of sheep and so on. It was explained that she was in reality an English sheep, and this obvious lie happily let everyone off the hook – the Arabians naturally making lots of jokes about an English sheep eating Arabian sheep.

The Arabian Oryx that used to roam the peninsula in large herds was approaching extinction in the late 1960s. In this last decade before it was eventually rescued by the Government of Oman, one of the Qatari Sheikhs attracted a huge amount of opprobrium because he was widely reported to be hunting the few animals that remained. When he announced that he wanted to present the World Wildlife Fund with a very large cheque, they were in something of a quandary. However, they swallowed their principles and sent a representative to the Gulf to pick up the cash. The representative was put up in a luxurious guest palace and, the morning after his arrival, a servant appeared in his room to draw the curtains. The large windows opened onto a spacious park-like garden in which a large group of Arabian Oryx were grazing contentedly. It thus emerged that the Sheikh had in fact been rescuing the Oryx rather than shooting them. He was awarded Life Membership of the Fund.

His Majesty Sultan Qaboos, who is a devoted animal lover, has been very keen to conserve the natural wildlife in his Sultanate, and appointed a former colonial officer to organise the project. Oman is the last place in Arabia where a number of important animals survive. One of these is the mountain goat and the story goes that the brother of the late Shah of Iran was a fanatic collector of hunting trophies. The one animal missing from his collection was the mountain goat of Oman. Accordingly he approached Sultan Qaboos and obtained permission to hunt down and shoot one of these animals. Sultan Qaboos was very shame-faced about this in confessing to his wildlife officer what he had agreed, but explained that in the cause of international relations he had had no option.

In the event, the officer in charge of wildlife was able to find an ancient wild goat that was at death's door. It was arranged that the wretched old beast be propped up just long enough so that the Shah's brother could jump into his helicopter and fly out to the Sultanate, shoot it and obtain his trophy. Thus were both the objectives of conservation and the needs of international relations achieved.

In Saudi Arabia in 2011 much mirth was created by the capture of a vulture carrying an Israeli tracking device. This was taken overly seriously by some sections of the government who, knowing nothing of modern ornithological techniques used for tracking avian journeys, thought the matter to be very sinister indeed. Israeli vultures spying on us!

Sport

The Eid Horse Race at Ibri

This is a story about differing ideas of sportsmanship. At the end of the fasting month of Ramadan, part of the celebrations in the town of Ibri in the Dhahirah region of the Omani interior was the staging of a horse-race. Every year this was won by the Ghafiri sheikh, mainly because he owned all the horses. However, in the year in question a Baluchi corporal from the Army Garrison entered the race, which created considerable mockery as he clearly didn't stand a chance. The rules, if there were any, didn't say anything that would enable this intrusive entry to be declared null and void, so the feeling was that, as the Ghafiri sheikh had about fifteen horses entered in the race, the corporal's chances were so slim that the usual result could be confidently expected. All the inhabitants and the Governor, a distant cousin of the Sultan himself, dressed in their best, and duly lined the wadi outside the town to watch the finish.

Encouraging shouts were heard out towards the gap in the mountains, from which the wadi flowed, to announce the rapid approach of the runners. Then a gasp of horrified amazement – leading by a good twenty lengths was the Baluchi corporal. He maintained and increased his lead and triumphantly flashed past the winning post in front of the Governor, a clear winner. As he dismounted and approached the Governor to collect the prize, a comfortable sum of money, there were hasty consultations. It was announced to general approval that the corporal could not possibly claim the prize because he wasn't dressed as an Arab, but had ridden in the baggy trousers and shirt worn by the Baluch. Naturally the lad looked rather crestfallen, but seemed to accept the decision.

However, a visiting Englishman working for the oil company was outraged, and raised the matter quite strongly with the Governor, explaining how disqualifying the corporal was absolutely unsporting. The Governor, not wishing to upset a guest, or for that matter the oil company, but nevertheless remaining totally uncomprehending of the Englishman's position, decided that a compromise was called for. Consequently, following further discussion it was decided that the corporal could have half the prize money provided he changed into Arab clothes to receive it.

Football Clubs

It will always be something of a surprise that it is possible to get eleven Arabians together on the same side for long enough to make up a football team! Nevertheless. this is frequently achieved with astonishing success.

However, there is a sting in the tail. Throughout the region these clubs have often been banned – not by rival and perhaps richer sporting adversaries, but because the Football Club as an institution is almost always a hotbed of political intrigue, usually of a violently revolutionary character. This is actually quite a clever idea if you are a revolutionary politician. Football clubs have large fan bases and so their political clout can be much amplified quite quickly.

Arabians and the Rest of the World

King Saud Bin Abdulaziz Al Saud

During the short reign of King Saud Ibn Abdulaziz, a man much cheated by his own Saudi advisers, who kept him in almost complete ignorance of financial affairs, there were many events which gave rise to stories which in retrospect give cause for amusement.

The King found a Turkish doctor in Germany called Dr Kemal who, despite being hired as a dentist, purported to have a wonderful diet that would solve His Majesty's health problems. This consisted of a rigorous menu for the King's breakfast – one carrot, one apple, one celery root, one spoon of honey and one English walnut. In announcing himself in the main reception room to the Palace Steward, who was an American sent from Aramco to look after the King, Dr Kemal confided that he himself was living proof of the diet's efficacy. 'I am sixty-eight years old,' he said archly, 'and am nevertheless the waltz king of Europe'. With that, and humming to the tune of The Blue Danube, he proceeded to pirouette around the room. The watching Bedouin were stunned. Halting in front of the Steward, Dr Kemal announced that His Majesty, following assiduous attention to the diet, would be doing the same thing in no time. Perhaps sadly for its potential for humour Dr Kemal didn't last very long in his appointment.

The State Visit of King Saud to the United States

King Saud's state visit to the USA occasioned several amusing culture clashes. Aboard the ship on the way over, a very attractive young blonde American lady passenger caught the eye of one of the King's coffee boys. Indeed, the boy breathlessly described her as a

Goddess. Apparently he had been watching the stars in the night sky, standing beside her on the deck when the lady expressed her appreciation of his coffee pots. Of course the lad promptly gave them to her, confident that, as is the Arabian way, one gift deserves another, and he would surely get a favour in return. But going back to her cabin full of expectation he was appalled when she just said goodnight to him at the door, and taking the pots with her, shut the door in his face. In the end, following suitable explanations, the pots were returned to him.

Later, after the Saudi party had arrived at their hotel, the hapless Steward was suddenly summoned to the reception desk by an outraged female receptionist. Another of the King's coffee boys was running about the hotel lobby, dressed only in his underpants, a sight that caused no little comment from the other guests. On being returned to his room it transpired that the trunk containing the boy's ceremonial clothes was missing, and he needed them urgently to wait on the King. Upstairs the boy was persuaded to put on the long white costume usually worn by Saudi men and to return to the reception desk to look for his luggage. The receptionist looked at the lad and complained that he had first turned up in his pants, now he was wearing a nightdress, even if it did have cufflinks. The Steward explained that this was perfectly usual attire but the receptionist would have none of it, and threatened to call the house detective. This was explained to the coffee boy, who rushed back to his room to find more clothing.

He quickly reappeared with a smart broad black leather belt around his waist. From the belt hung a revolver. The receptionist took one look at this and fled. Though creating no small impression on the other hotel guests, the Steward and the coffee boy managed to find the missing luggage, a large colourfully decorated tin trunk. The hotel staff would not however allow the coffee boy to carry the trunk into the passenger lift and insisted it be taken up in the luggage lift. The coffee boy refused to be parted from his trunk, and putting it down, sat on it. Eventually he was persuaded that actually all would be well if his trunk was taken to his room for him. He and the Steward then got into the passenger lift up to their floor. On getting out they were met by the house detective who had been summoned by the receptionist. It took a little while for the Steward to explain to the detective and the distraught receptionist that the gun had no bullets in it and everything was all right.

Meanwhile the coffee boy had returned to his room, and had had time to change into his official uniform. He suddenly re-emerged in a red velvet cloak trimmed with silver embroidery, yellow shoes, and a violet, blue and orange headdress. Swinging below his cloak, his golden sword almost dragged on the floor. In his hands he flourished a golden incense burner billowing smoke like a steam train. This apparition tore off down the hallway to attend the King. The receptionist who had recovered a bit asked somewhat contemptuously, 'Just what do you have him do for an encore; bring on his genie with the light brown hair and burn down the hotel?'

His Excellency the Ambassador of the United Arab Emirates

Mahdi Al-Tajir was a Bahraini by birth and, having attended Millfield School in England, returned to his home island where he obtained work with the British. Apparently he then upset the Governor, Sir William Luce, who posted him away down the Gulf to Dubai, without telling his compatriots there what had transpired in Bahrain. The British in the Trucial States at that time were thrilled to get a bright young Arabian who could speak such perfect English, and promptly put him in charge of Customs. This post provided the young Mahdi with a regular income, which, combined with going into business on his own account, permitted him to accumulate a very considerable fortune. However, as far as the British are concerned it proved to be not altogether disadvantageous. Eventually, after the United Arab Emirates was created, Mahdi was appointed the country's first Ambassador to the Court of St James's in London where he spent vast sums of money. For instance he purchased, to the great benefit of the British economy, several large country mansions. Interviewed on television by Robin Day, Mahdi was asked why it was that he needed so many huge houses. Mahdi quietly replied that he had to have somewhere to hang all his pictures, didn't he?

PART TWO

THE BRITISH AND ARABIA

Lines on the Map: Strategy

Had a Committee been assembled from the padded chambers of Bedlam, they could hardly have devised anything more extravagant in its madness or more mischievous in its operation.

Lord Curzon commenting on early British government in India

With Britain as a friend, you don't need enemies.

Unattributed

It is better to be England's enemy than her friend, for in the former case you have a good chance of being bought but in the latter only the certainty of being sold.

Sharif Hussein of Bayhan

Sharif Hussein was a devoted smoker of Gauloises cigarettes. When asked why he had chosen this brand he replied that it was because they made guests from the Labour Party cough! In fact the Sharif was one of the staunchest allies the British had and the remark above exemplifies the deep sense of betrayal that the eventual British withdrawal from Aden caused.

I like the English. They have the most rigid code of immorality in the world.

Malcolm Bradbury

*In England they ring little bells to bring rain, unlike with us whose loudest
shouted prayers are carried away by the wind and not heard.*

Sharif Awadh of Bayhan

*Joha announced in a loud voice, 'Friends, I have discovered the cause for all the
problems'. Everyone sat up and paid attention. 'It's people providing solutions',
added Joha.*

A Generous Gift

In 1854 the then Sultan of Muscat presented Queen Victoria with
the Kuria Muria Islands. These scarcely inhabited guano-covered
islets lie off the coast of Dhofar, and were almost never visited by
anyone. However, it can be conjectured that this fact in itself exerted
a curiously soporific effect on the powers that be. Consequently,
they didn't wake up to their responsibilities with respect to the Kuria
Muria Islands for a hundred years. It wasn't until 1959 that they
leapt into belated action, grandly and imperially issued an Order
in Council. This decreed, rather incongruously, that the islands
should be governed by the Governor of Aden while their day-to-day
affairs would be looked after by the Political Resident in Bahrain,
who was given the extra and dignified title of Commissioner of the
Kuria Muria Islands. Accordingly Sir William Luce in his capacity
as Governor of Aden and Sir George Middleton, Political Resident
in the Gulf, organised a visit in 1960, using Royal Naval transport,
in order to sort out their respective responsibilities. Foremost among
these was naturally a somewhat pressing need to inform the island's
inhabitants, if there were any, of these arrangements.

On arrival, the dignitaries aboard the Royal Naval ship were met
by appalling weather, and had to wade ashore from a launch, which
had its roof torn off as it was put into the water due to a faulty derrick.

A proper drill had naturally been designed for the occasion, involving the Royal Marines and bugles; and, of course it had been arranged that a flagpole would be erected, not only embellished by a flag, but also by a brass plaque, especially engraved with a suitable text to commemorate the historic event. As it had been impossible to let the Kuria Murians – if there were any – know about the impending visit, it is not surprising that not a single inhabitant witnessed these impressive events. Nevertheless the expedition continued undaunted and the ship sailed round to the other side of the island to see if there was anyone there instead. A solitary man was seen through binoculars, and his attention was gained by dint of vigorous use of the ship's hooter. The man leapt to his feet, waved, and raced away across the beach and over the cliffs presumably to collect his friends. The Governor and the Commissioner decided to go ashore once more, and collected together a parcel of welfare goods to give to the inhabitants.

The second landing was even more difficult than the first, and the launch had to get in backwards due to the way the wind was blowing. This dangerous manouevre elicited a terse response when a naval rating on the launch was asked by the ship's Captain over the radio how things were progressing. The man replied that his next of kin was his mother! Despite all these unpromising goings-on, the party eventually landed in one piece, and were much buoyed up by the thought that they were about to meet some real Kuria Murians. When they finally met up with the inhabitants they were mortified to discover that the Kuria Murians were less than pleased to see them: they thought the gifts paltry, and complained bitterly that there were no cigarettes, though they did like some buckets that were offered. What was really interesting was that they asked the visitors if they had had permission from the Sultan of Muscat for the visit. It crossed the minds of the august visitors that it was likely that no one had ever bothered to tell the Kuria Murians that they had been given to Queen

Victoria a century previously. It was now time to leave and the party nearly drowned getting back to the ship.

As a footnote to this story it is fun to see how the communist Peoples Democratic Republic of Yemen (PDRY) viewed these islands. As the British left Aden they had given the Kuria Muria Islands back to Oman in 1967. The PDRY, good Marxists to a man, were furious about this and energetically laid claim to the islands, even incorporating a little blue triangle into the design of their flag to represent these overseas possessions.

◎ ◎ ◎

Ian Skeet, who was Shell Representative in Qatar in 1959 and afterwards in Oman, and whose father had been Governor of Khartoum and Sudanese Equatoria, has given us this anecdote.

At the bottom of the Gulf – it is tactful today to refrain from saying which one, Persian or Arabian – there is a wonderfully mountainous and rocky peninsular called Musandam. Inhabited by an ancient and special people called the Shihuh (who have the entertaining habit of howling like lost dogs by way of saying thank you for a meal), it was also the locus of the short-lived (1864–1869) station for the Gulf Telegraph Cable. This was erected on a little island hidden deep in a vast cleft in the mountains formed by what the British called the Elphinstone Inlet. It was quickly found to be quite impossible for a European to live there, and the site was abandoned, but not before it had been christened Telegraph Island.

A bit later, in 1904, the place attracted the attention of the great Viceroy of India, Lord Curzon. He became convinced of the area's crucial importance in the defence of the Empire against the Russian Threat. It was therefore of great importance that flagpoles be erected as symbols of defiance. Lord Curzon had proposed this idea in 1901 but now returned to the matter with renewed vigour, and sent letters to London. There, the inventors of the bureaucracy that has paralysed half the world leapt into action and the files bulged with memos from the India Office to the Treasury and the Foreign Office, the Admiralty and the Committee for Imperial Defence, and the Cabinet Office. The latter, of course, brought the Prime Minister himself into the picture. After a while, it emerged that the Foreign Office and the India Office had obtained everyone's agreement to the Viceroy's proposals, and accordingly instructions were issued for the erection of no fewer than three flagpoles. We were, after all, an Imperial Power and anything less would appear flippant, and derogate seriously from what was expected of an Empire.

However, as no decision had been taken as to what should be flown, no flags accompanied the flagpoles. The question of the flags was a tricky one, and nobody in London had been able to find the answer. To start with, it was unclear who actually owned the territory: if it was the Shihuh, they didn't have a flag anyway; it certainly wasn't the British, so the Union Flag was out of the question (such modesty). The Foreign Office somewhat hesitantly suggested the Blue Ensign of the Royal Indian Marine, but this was turned down flat by an outraged Admiralty who were, at that stage in the proceedings, unaware that any flagpoles had been erected. They also stated forcefully that any flag that was flown would need to be defended. This idea, on being minuted to the Committee for Imperial Defence, was strongly rejected as they could in no way countenance defending the poles, Russian Threat or no Russian Threat. Instructions were therefore issued that the poles be taken down.

In the event, only two were removed and the third was allowed to remain on Telegraph Island. The logic ran that there had been a British connection to the place for quite a while, and the lack of any flag would imply that HMG was not seriously committed to it. There were sighs of relief that no dangerous precedent had been set. What escaped everyone's notice was the simple fact that, situated deep in the bowels of the Elphinstone Inlet, it was quite impossible to see one, three or even a hundred flagpoles from the open sea.

Let's Have a Revolt

A foolish consistency is the hobgoblin of little minds.
Ralph Waldo Emerson

We lived many lives in those whirling campaigns, never sparing ourselves: yet when we achieved and the new world dawned, the old men came out again and took our victory to re-make in the likeness of the former world they knew. Youth could win, but had not learned to keep: and was pitiably weak against age. We stammered that we had worked for a new heaven and a new earth, and they thanked us kindly and made their peace.
T.E. Lawrence, *Seven Pillars of Wisdom*

It was, of course, a wizard wheeze in 1914 to flummox the Turks by encouraging the Arabians to come out in rebellion. The Arab Revolt was the consequence.

Naturally a Revolt requires control, and the British leapt at the opportunity this presented. There stepped forward any number of agencies and personalities, all with their own contradictory ideas and conflicting policies. The British High Commissioner in Egypt, the Commander-in-Chief of the British Expeditionary Force, the Arab Bureau in Cairo, Military Intelligence in Ismailia, halfway between Port Said and Suez; the War Office, the Foreign Office, and the Colonial Office in London; the Government of India in Delhi; the Governor-General of the Sudan in Khartoum, included because the shortest route for the supply of materiel to the Arabians chosen to revolt was between Jeddah and Port Sudan, across the Red

Sea. Our Man in Jeddah was a Colonel Wilson, the representative of the magnificent General Sir Reginald Wingate Pasha, GCB, GCVO, GBE, KCMG, DSO, a man of bellicose and inflammable temperament. The High Commissioner in Egypt was Sir Henry McMahon who was advised by the diplomat Storrs. Brigadier Gilbert Clayton was the head of Military Intelligence, and he did not have much confidence in Storrs, whom he regarded as a mere civil servant, relying more on the opinions of T.E. Lawrence.

Back in London nearly all the older members of the War Cabinet had been or were strongly Turcophile. After all, support for the Ottoman Empire had been the cornerstone of British policy in the area for some two hundred years. It was the buffer between us and the Russian Threat. They naturally felt disconcerted that bumbling diplomacy had brought us out in 1914 against the Turks and on the same side as the Russians. This is why support for an Arab Revolt was always a bit lukewarm in London. In Delhi there was actual and fierce opposition to the whole idea: it was feared that encouraging a Revolt of the Arabs against the Turks would unleash a rebellion amongst the large Muslim population of the sub-continent. It would be best to just annex Arabia into the Raj! All these factors provided the ingredients for a first-class British muddle. It is something of a miracle that they didn't produce the chaos one would have expected, and that the Arab Revolt was as much of a success as it was. Nevertheless, it encouraged the British in their belief that everything would be all right on the day – a belief that has been an important part of British behaviour on the world stage for some while. The awful thought occurs that this is usually true.

Let's Make a Kingdom

Do not get too close to the Arabs, or they will break your heart.
John Bagot Glubb

The detailed historical accuracy of the following account is more than a little dubious, but the spirit is somehow not inaccurate. This all concerns the Sharifian family of Makkah who provided so many of the cast for the film Lawrence of Arabia! After the end of the First World War, when the Arabians were getting used to the consequences of the Sykes–Picot Agreement and the contradictory recommendations of Sir Henry McMahon of the Arab Bureau in Cairo, it transpired that despite promises, only one of Sharif Hussein's sons had been given a Kingdom. This was the Emir Faisal, who was set up, under the French, with Syria and Damascus. His father ended up in exile in Cyprus where the Greeks killed his beloved horses and it is said, ate them. However, Faisal didn't get on with the French terribly well – it seems they were even more possessive than the English, and really wanted a malleable Republic. So, the British awarded Faisal Iraq as a consolation prize. Faisal's brother, the Emir Abdullah, had got nothing. The third brother, the Emir Ali, remained in Makkah in succession to his father. There he stayed for a year or two until kicked out by King Abdulaziz Al Saud.

Now, the British had taken up the League of Nations mandate to exercise authority in Jerusalem and Palestine, and naturally had their Man on the Spot. He was a tall Scot by the name of Sir Alec Kirkbride and, taking a little time off from the exasperating squabbles by which his position was surrounded, he crossed the river Jordan to do a bit of relaxing grouse shooting, to the eastward from Jerusalem. Those readers possessed of some classical education will at once see the importance of this last sentence, because Sir Alec clearly moved into territory accurately described as Transjordan! Here, at a halt beside a stretch of railway track, part of the Hejaz Railway that hadn't been blown up by T.E. Lawrence, he found a small person accompanied by a large black man in a scarlet outfit carrying a carpet bag and a sword. Sir Alec looked down at the little fellow and asked him who he was. 'We are the Amir Abdullah bin Hussein,' replied the wee fellow. 'And I have come to claim the Kingdom I was promised by the British'. Sir Alec said words to the effect of 'Laddie, all the best bits have been taken really, so you might as well have this little bit here where we are'. And that's what happened! As he became King, Abdullah built his Kingdom using the great Bedouin tribes of the area riding their famous horses, thus making Jordan the very last Kingdom on Earth to be created on horseback. Incidentally, the halt by the railway line was called Amman, which became the capital of the Hashemite Kingdom of Jordan.

****

In 1840 the then British Political Officer in Aden, Captain Haines, had to put up with the intrigues of firstly the Sultan of Lahej, who regretted selling Aden to the British in the first place; and then of the Fadhli Sultan, who saw an opportunity for advancement. On the other hand, Haines was much hampered by the authorities in India, who seemed to have a problem sorting out who was responsible for what, and who should tell who about really anything at all.

In this year, with the Arabians about to gang up on him, the military control of the Colony was taken from Haines for a crucial month simply because the military in India couldn't bear the thought of a naval man in a civilian post being in charge of what they fondly thought of as an Army Fort, rather than what it was, a Colony. This led inexorably to a serious misunderstanding on the ground between Captain Haines and Colonel Capon, the garrison commander. In the event all ended well, but it was a close-run thing as the outcome of the actual battle was further bedevilled by rivalry between the army and the navy on the ground. On reading the history of the times one is seriously grateful that there was no Royal Air Force to add a further complication to events.

It should be said that the story of British military expertise in the Middle East presents a picture not entirely made up of glorious successes and immense and world-shaking victories along the lines of Waterloo. During the First World War, while further north Allenby and Lawrence laid down the script for a splendid film, and the betrayal of the Arabs' desires for independence, in the south things were a little different. In 1915 the Turkish Forces in the Yemen were under the command of a Circassian called Ali Said Pasha. They advanced southwards towards the Sultanate of Lahej just north of Aden.

On their way they were joined more than enthusiastically by Protectorate tribesmen scenting loot. The British response was remarkable if only for its torpidity. However, a force was eventually assembled to counter the threat, and after endless delays it set off across the desert to defend Lahej – at the hottest time of the year, July! Off they all went under the blazing sun, and no sooner had they left the township of Sheikh Othman just to the north of Aden than the camels carrying their water ran away. Whether this was due to the cowardice of their drivers or treachery is not known. Many of the soldiers died of heat stroke, and casualties would have been much higher if the British civilian population had not bought up the Colony's entire commercial supply of ice, and taken it after the troops in their private cars.

When the survivors reached Lahej they hastily set about building defences. It was at this point that the weather took a bizarre hand in events. It poured with rain. In their thin uniforms the troops who had been roasted by the sun now found themselves freezing as they stumbled through the mud. At daybreak they reached the northern edges of the Sultanate looking out for the expected arrival of the

Turks. There they were met by the Sultan of Lahej himself, riding back with news of the enemy. This meeting was not a success. The British mistook the Sultan for the Turks and promptly shot him. At that time he was the only Ruler friendly towards the British in the entire Protectorate. All this was a bit disheartening to say the least, and the British Force retired back to Aden. They were naturally followed by the Turks who couldn't believe their luck and who effortlessly occupied Lahej, Sheikh Othman, the peninsula of Little Aden and the north shore of the harbour.

There followed an amazing series of events. By 1917, when nothing further of significance had happened, the great Sir Ronald Storrs arrived. During what proved to be a very short visit (he had much more important matters to attend to in Cairo), he discovered that General Stewart was at loggerheads with his political adviser, Colonel Jacobs. This antipathy between the Military and Political Advisers was sadly not uncommon, and has often taken place throughout the region over the years. The good Colonel advised strongly that the Turks should be turfed out, but for some reason the General disagreed. Sir Ronald left without resolving the stalemate, which would have continued into 1918 if it had not been for an intervention by the Khormaksar Golf Club. The members strongly urged military action because the golf course was within range of the Turkish rifles and this seriously impeded play. Following a visit by a delegation from the Club committee, which vehemently put their case, the General relented and flung the Turks out of Sheikh Othman.

After this energetic exertion the front remained stable and quiescent. Camel trains passed amicably between the two sets of lines. The Turks were able to profit by levying tolls on caravans going in both directions: the British could send supplies to such friends as they still had in the Protectorate, who could maintain their exports through Aden Port. So everyone was happy until the Armistice, when the War came to a halt anyway.

So it is said, but God alone knows if it is true.
An Arabian storyteller's saying

*I have a Government in possession of 15,000 rifles to rule over a
people in possession of 120,000 rifles.*
King Faisal I of Iraq

The reader may be under the general impression that British rule was
really quite simple to understand, at least from a territorial standpoint.
Wherever they went, the British strove to introduce some order into
what they perceived as an Arabian chaos; and borders tended to be
neatly drawn on maps, to the subsequent great advantage of those
defining oil concessions.

The Arabians, however, knew where their territories were and
happily quarreled over them all the time. Their problem, if a problem
it really was, was that a large proportion of their populations were
nomads. As Arabian Rulers rule over people rather than real estate,
it stood to reason that their frontiers were a bit fluid as their gypsy
subjects walked about all over the peninsula, hither and yon, as grazing
and raiding dictated. But the South of Arabia is cause for at least some
further uncertainty due to British administrative arrangements.

The word 'uncertainty' is used here as an example of British
understatement. To start with, under the Queen Empress Victoria,
and until 1947, Aden and the Gulf fell under the control of the
Indian Empire and were ruled from Bombay by the External Affairs
Department of the Government of India. Consequently posts in the
area were filled from the Indian Political Service and their incumbents
'advised' Kuwait, Qatar, Bahrain and Oman – and also the United
Arab Emirates, which were of course the Sheikhdoms, destined due
to the inflation of titles to become Emirates, of Abu Dhabi, Ras Al-
Khaimah, Fujairah, Sharjah, Ajman, Dubai and Umm Al-Quwain,
with at least four other bits which were later to become defunct

(Hamriya in 1922, Heera in 1942, Dibba in 1951 and Kalba in 1952). All the other Arabians, that is to say the Egyptians, Iraqis, Jordanians, Syrians and Palestinians, were thought to be controlled from Cairo when not directly under the thumb of London, and its relations with the Sublime Porte in Turkey, that is to say control by the Foreign Office.

After the Second World War and the demise of the Raj in India, in August 1947 the Gulf passed into the hands of the Foreign Office and the Western and Eastern Aden Protectorates came under the Colonial Office. Before the redistribution of responsibilities, there had been considerable changes to the naming of Omani Territory. The Sultanate of Oman used to be the Sultanate of Muscat and Oman, and before that just the Sultanate of Muscat. This was because the interior of what is now known as Oman was an almost wholly independent entity called the Imamate of Oman. And to make it more complicated, the whole of the bottom right hand corner of Arabia was collectively known as Oman by the rest of Arabia. Thus, if you travelled at that time overland from Qatar to Muscat people would tell you that you were gong to Oman as soon as you crossed the Qatari frontier into what was the Trucial States and is now the United Arab Emirates. And to emphasise the point, when you arrived in Muscat people there would tell you that you had just come from Oman. Now that the geography is crystal clear, we can continue…

The western border of this Omani Sultanate, much to the interest of the Foreign Office, which had inherited Lord Curzon's perceived duty of repelling the Russian menace, edged onto a tiny oasis called Habarut. This oasis is situated at what was the easternmost end of the Eastern Aden Protectorate in the Sultanate of Mahra and Socotra. Apart from some water it contained only a few extraordinarily scruffy, shrunken and totally unappetising wild palms.

The Mahri Sultan, lord and master of Habarut, lived on the island of Socotra, many hundreds of miles distant from the bulk of his so-called subjects who, while acknowledging his right to the Sultanate, steadfastly refused to accept that he had any right whatsoever to order them about. Indeed, when persuaded by his British Advisers to visit his loyal and loving subjects, the Mahri Sultan was greeted with a hail of lead. This was not in the form of the traditional welcome given to authority in this part of the world, where fusillades are fired pretty close over the visitor's head in order to express a jolly and enthusiastically explosive 'Hello'. This fire was intended to assassinate. The Sultan prudently refrained from visiting them ever again, and retired to his ancestral island to sign passports and sultanic instructions, using the base of a little coffee cup as a stamp.

At this time the Colonial Office was naturally loath to give up the smallest piece of its territory to the Foreign Office, despite the fact that only Aden itself was actually a Colony. The Colonial Office's position in the two Protectorates was purely advisery, but it was with the Sultan of Mahra and Socotra that Great Britain had signed the original Treaty, and he was therefore the only person who could officially resist the claims to the oasis of Habarut by the Sultan of Muscat, who was backed up by the Foreign Office. This administrative nightmare looked set to produce an interesting international conflict, with two great offices of the British state on opposite sides of the argument. In addition there was the further complication on the ground that there were about four different tribes who also had claims on Habarut. This provided a subtext which involved at least two other Sultans, the Kathiri and Qu'aiti.

It was also possible that Saudi Arabia could get involved due to parties of mooching Bedouin who, when asked, might say that the Saudi monarch might have a claim to rule over them, if he had recently doled out a bit of cash in their direction. It is hoped that this explanation makes the matter crystal clear.

As a footnote to the foregoing, and to add further clarity, it should be noted that a Border Commission was set up in 1966. Their work was actually quite simple from a political point of view. The British were, after all, as mentioned above, on both sides of wherever the border would turn out to be! However, with their deliberations complete, it was a shock to hear that, on a cruise off his southern coast of Dhofar, Sultan Said Bin Taimur of Oman suddenly leapt to his feet, saying 'There is the split rock, there is my border'. The rock was about two miles to the East of where the Commission had decided the border to be. Not unexpectedly, no one seems able to recall the consequence, if any, of the Sultan's remark.

❁ ❁ ❁

King Idris of Libya was very friendly towards the British, and bravely loyal to that friendship. During anti-British riots in Tobruk in the late '50s, the yelling crowds noticed a growing pile of suitcases outside the palace gates. They paused to ask what was happening and the reply emerged that it was the British who had created the Kingdom of Libya, and without them the country would not exist. The King did not like the idea of ruling over ungrateful people and so was leaving. The riots stopped instantly, and the suitcases were taken back into the palace.

The Suez Crisis of 1956

Before the main story here on this somewhat vexed subject, it is probably good to muse on what might have been if lots of circumstances had been different.

The British will have to go, but I wish, personally, that they could stay. Whatever their faults, the British produce a sense of security. And we Egyptians are an insecure people.
Colonel Jamal Nasser to John Laffin, Australian military historian,
April 1956

The English are easy to deceive, but when you have deceived them they give you a terrific kick in the backside.
An Egyptian to Jeremy Paxman, 2011

In this land no one ever keeps their promises.
Anonymous Bedouin in the Sinai Desert, 2011

The final chapter in British relations with Egypt followed their seventy-year occupation of the country. Throughout this period the British strongly denied that their presence amounted to anything more than a Protectorate, and perish the thought that anyone could possibly think of it as an occupation. For a lot of this time the man in charge was Sir Evelyn Baring, who though technically only a Consul-General behaved rather like a reincarnation of the Pharaoh Rameses the Great – hence his nickname Sir Over-Baring. However, this wasn't a waste of time because of course the Canal was defended: and, as Jeremy Paxman discovered in his BBC programme Empire, the British taught the Egyptians how to play croquet. The game is still played, at the time of writing, by the exalted members of the Gezirah Club in Cairo, none of whose present members would have been allowed into the Club during the time of the British presence.

Suez truly was a crisis but, nothing daunted, the British staunchly maintained their reputation for duplicitous incompetence at this difficult time. No one in the Middle East forgets the McMahon Agreement or the Sykes-Picot Agreement at the end of the First World War! And they set a standard that surely had not only to be lived up to but improved upon. It needs to be said that the Arabians should not have been surprised, because the behaviour of the British government in the Middle East from the middle of the 1800s onwards was constantly beset by fibs of increasing complexity.

On the occasion of the Suez debacle, diplomatic relations with the Saudi Kingdom were broken off, as they were with many other countries in the region. But they were restored in the summer of 1964 when an English teacher arrived to take up his post just before the new ambassador arrived in Jeddah. The teacher and his four colleagues were the first to be employed in Saudi Arabia. There had been a few American teachers but these had proved unsuitable. Unlike the delegation accompanying Lord Bowden described below, these teachers were given a briefing. The Foreign Office told them in magisterial tones that while in Saudi Arabia it would be unwise to discuss politics, religion or sex. (Incidentally this is the 'rule' in Officers' Messes throughout the Services, and seems officially to be a safe bit of advice to give to just about everyone.) However, on arrival the teachers discovered that their students never talked about anything other than politics, religion or sex – particularly the last item. Rather like Officers' Messes.

On one occasion an interesting question put to one teacher with no little glee went as follows. 'Sir! When the British bombed Cairo, why did they hit the Children's Hospital and the Old People's Home and not President Nasser's Office?' The teacher answered that the British bombing was not as accurate as the student evidently hoped. (At that time Air Traffic Control at Cairo Airport talked the British bombers onto their targets.) It is also important to relate how supportive ordinary Egyptians were of British citizens caught in Egypt while all this was going on. One, the wife of an Oxford professor, was staying with an Egyptian family in Cairo. Some while elapsed before official evacuation was possible, so the family let her sleep on the top floor of their house, arming her with a can of kerosene to light and throw down the stairs if the authorities sent anyone to arrest her. This would doubtless lead to the house burning down, but that was of no importance to the owners. Knowing how their own police behaved, they told her that this drastic course would prevent her being dishonoured.

Yes, we have broken our promises but it is our custom.
Adeni Arabs to Haines, circa 1840

Just over a hundred and twenty years after that encouraging remark made by the locals, Harold Wilson, when Leader of the Opposition, promised the Rulers and Ministers of the Federation that, should he win the election, he would keep the promises made to them by the Tory government. He won the election and promptly broke his word! This penchant for breaking promises is sadly not confined to the British. President Truman ignored a promise made by his predecessor President Roosevelt to King Abdulaziz Al Saud, that the Americans would not provide assistance to the Jews. It is notable that, in contrast to the behaviour of British and American political leaders, the Adeni Arabs cheerfully admit to their mendacity.

A Cautionary Story

Harold Wilson had so many Foreign Secretaries in his government that it was difficult for people in the Middle East to keep up. The nadir of these appointments as far as the Arabs were concerned was the appearance of George Brown, the third appointee. The Saudis, including young students, not understanding how the British government worked, could not comprehend how it was that the Queen should put a man manifestly devoid of tact, sensitivity and dignity in such a position. He drank too much, as well. Finally, having mulled over the question for a while they came up with an answer. Clearly George Brown was either Jewish himself or had a Jewish mother; and must be a part of the international Jewish conspiracy. In vain was it pointed out that the Queen had nothing to do with his appointment and that Brown was scarcely a Jewish name, either.

The Civil War in the Yemen

As a somewhat prophetic curtain raiser to the sad events outlined below, the War following the Egyptian invasion of the Yemen demonstrates the difficulty British politicians had in following any kind of cohesive policy in the region. While Aden and the Protectorates staggered towards their thoroughly nasty fate, strange events were taking place to the north of them. In September 1962 the Revolution broke out in Sana'a and the Imam Badr, escaping from his palace by crawling down the long drop loo, fled for his life to the northern mountains. This again demonstrated the Arabian talent for jumping enthusiastically out of the frying pan into the fire. The establishment of a regime so blood-soaked that it made the cruelties of the Imam Ahmad's government look almost benign, if not quaint, by comparison, was to pose an immediate problem for the British government. This was due, once again, to conflicting policies in the Foreign Office and the Colonial Office.

The Foreign Office wanted to recognise the Republican government because the Americans had already done so, and the British wanted to make amends for upsetting the USA in 1956 over Suez. Meanwhile, the Colonial Office, who surely had the most reason to dislike the Imamic regime and had good cause to rejoice at its downfall, actually took quite the contrary view and strongly opposed recognition. However, the Foreign Secretary of the time actually supported the Colonial Office, in total contradiction with his own department! This meant that British policy, if it could have been said to exist at all, was characterised by monumental dithering. In deciding what action to take, Prime Minister Macmillan was poetically defeatist, saying that the conflict reminded him of the story of Bonnie Prince Charlie: while the Highlanders were the more attractive, the Lowlanders would win in the end. He was much assailed in other directions as well. The Profumo scandal broke at this time and the amatory exploits of Christine Keeler were all over the press. Just to add to his difficulties the Duchess of Argyll, having reportedly slept with eighty-two men, was understandably being divorced by the Duke. One rumour flying about was that one of the eighty-two was no less a figure than the Colonial Secretary himself, Duncan Sandys.

It therefore became clear that, for one reason or another, HMG could not overtly support the Royalists, and a covert operation was put in place. This was enthusiastically manned by a very few heroes of earlier Balkan derring-do, and men of a similar frame of mind. HMG kept its distance and actually the enterprise got more useful support from the Saudi Government and the Israeli Secret Service Mossad, with the latter organising parachuted supplies of arms, medicines and food into Royalist-held areas. This was because the more Colonel Nasser could be tied down in the Yemen, the less danger his forces would pose to Israel and indeed to Saudi Arabia.

These events are graphically described by Duff Hart-Davis, who disproves a rumour circulating at the time, that because it was necessary to supply the Royalists with weapons from the Communist bloc so that it could be pleaded that they had captured them from the Egyptians (who were supplied from that source), the following arrangement was put in place. Arms were purchased in Yugoslavia and flown by Yugoslav UN pilots to Addis Ababa. Here the Yugoslavs ran out of flying time and were replaced by Norwegian UN pilots, who happily flew out over the Yemen and dropped their cargoes. Sqawks from the Egyptian and Republican authorities that HMG was infringing their airspace could then be honestly denied. It does make quite a good story.

The British involved led an adventurous and dangerous life but in 1965 managed to recognise Christmas in style. Christmas Eve saw a celebratory fusillade of such generous proportions that it was reported as a Republican attack. Meanwhile an Englishman was entertained to dinner by French colleagues, who told their guest that they had fattened up five desert partridges. The Englishman told his hosts that their birds had a much stronger taste than English ones. The Frenchmen then admitted that their partridges had actually been eaten by a feral cat and in revenge they had cooked the cat!

Following the 1966 election, which Harold Wilson won, the somewhat erratic George Brown took over as Foreign Secretary. That year President Sallal, returning from a sojourn in Cairo, took over the Yemeni government and promptly decided on a purge, almost certainly on the orders of Colonel Nasser. At the time it was part of the Aden gossip that actually the Brits had been able to 'buy' the Republican government. But before use could be made of this triumph George Brown, as Foreign Secretary, had had to be asked to give his approval. It was said that he telephoned his fellow socialist, Colonel Nasser, to ask his advice. Arrests followed immediately. Apparently, George Brown frequently phoned the Colonel in Cairo but what else they chatted about is not yet known.

Conspiracy theory

Prince Abdullah Bin Faisal Al Saud, after serving as Minister of Education, gave up all political activity to turn his attention entirely to commercial and sporting activities. In the course of the latter he sponsored football clubs in particular. He was also a tremendous fan of Umm Kulthum, probably one of the most successful singers anywhere. It was for this Egyptian lady that the Middle East would close down completely on a Thursday night while everyone listened to her broadcast from Cairo. The prince's devotion to business is exemplified by a report that, when meeting Sir Kennedy Trevaskis, he remarked that if a day passed when he made no money he didn't count it as a day of his life.

There is a strange account that in 1964 word reached Prince

Abdullah that the Wilson government in Britain was considering putting him forward to take over the South Arabian Federation as a Republican President. Prince Abdullah was a bit worried, as he had eschewed all political ambitions long before. The account continues that the British idea was that Prince Abdullah would then succeed his father as king of Saudi Arabia, thus uniting almost the whole peninsula under one head, a Republican one at that! Like the curate's egg, some parts of this could well have been quite a good idea, though it is lamentable that HMG at that time seems to have had no idea as to the rules governing the inheritance of the Saudi throne, which are that the succession goes down the line of the sons of King Abdulaziz before going into the next generation. (The idea of creating a Republic of the Arabian Peninsula had been aired previously in 1962 by that noted and lovable democrat, President Sallal of the Yemen.)

A borrowed cloak does not keep one warm.

Egyptian proverb

During those tragic years before the final withdrawal of the British from South Arabia there was much to-ing and fro-ing between Aden and London, while HMG tried to persuade the many Treaty Chiefs of the two Protectorates, and the Colony of Aden itself, that unity under a Federal Government would provide the best future for all concerned. The Arabians suffered from mutual jealousies and everyone was suspicious of everyone else. These things combined were a fertile source of stories as well as political mayhem.

To start with it was perhaps symptomatic that only in Bayhan was the universally-recognised distress signal of a three-star red Very Pistol cartridge not applicable. All pilots had to be warned. The reason was that an aged inhabitant with a deep dislike of the British had, some time previously, stolen a box of Three Star Reds and a Very pistol from the Federal Regular Army. Whenever an aircraft flew over Bayhan the old man, convinced that it could only be a British plane, tried to shoot it down with his Very pistol.

The Great Betrayal: British Withdrawal from South Arabia 1967

The feelings of local Arabians about the British withdrawal were cogently made known in the words of two leaders at the time.

> *For many years we have borne the abuse and vilification of most of the Arab World because we believed that the British Government was our true friend and that, until we were able to defend ourselves, it would protect us against the consequences of our unwavering support.*
>
> **Sultan Salih Al Audhali**

> *… we cannot believe that it is your wish that we shall be sacrificed just because, after many years of repeated promises to the contrary, the British Government finds that it suits its own self-interest to desert friends and leave them in the lurch.*
>
> **The Sharif of Bayhan**

While the deep seriousness and sadness of many Middle Eastern events cannot be denied, a recital of some of them provides occasion for continued surprise that the Arabians talk to us at all. Even laughter can become bitter. Some stories highlight the dichotomy between the devoted behaviour of the British on the ground and that of a sadly mendacious government at home. It is in hindsight that some things can become amusing.

For example, while the British were preparing to withdraw from South Arabia, the RAF married quarters at Khormaksar in Aden were being readied for the handover to the National Liberation Front.

If there was so much as a scratch on one of the refrigerators it was replaced with a new one, doubtless to the despair of British taxpayers, had they ever found out that they were effectively making sure that the East German Secret Police would be comfortable.

Tales about what happened in the Protectorate after the National Liberation Front took over are not only few in number but also usually doom-laden. At the time of the Revolution the High Commissioner, Sir Humphrey Trevelyan, told the Rulers from the Eastern Arabian Protectorate, the Qu'aiti, Kathiri and Mahri Sultans, to go to Geneva to present their people's case to a sub-committee of the United Nations Decolonisation Committee. The Mahri arrived first and waited for his two colleagues. When they too arrived they were told that the British Residency in the Qu'aiti capital of Mukalla had been closed forty days before the scheduled date, and the staff had been withdrawn four days before that. Getting this calamitous news and sensing that the UN were giving them the runaround, the Sultans decided to return to their States. However, having asked that they be taken on to their States on an RAF plane, they were told that due to the deteriorating security situation in the Eastern Arabian Protectorates they could not be taken home.

This news was delivered just as they were about to board a Middle East Airlines plane back to Aden from Beirut, via Jeddah. They decided nevertheless to get on the plane but disembarked on arrival in Jeddah. There they could have met Lord Shackleton, Minister without Portfolio in the Labour government, who was also in the Kingdom to see an infuriated King Faisal. However, His Lordship refused to speak to any of them. There now followed a period of dilly dallying. Sultan Ghalib, the Qu'aiti Ruler, asked the Saudis to fly them back or alternatively to provide transport by land, so that all three Sultans could get home before independence was declared, as it looked as though this too would be brought forward. The Saudis rejected the air option because they would need to ask permission from the British in Aden. Travelling by land also posed problems. The Kathiri Sultan sensed treachery awaited them in the guise of the British-commanded and -financed Hadrami Bedouin Legion (HBL), who occupied the important frontier post at Al Abr. He therefore favoured the only option left, the sea route. So they all decided to return to Mukalla by sea.

Luckily, there lived in Jeddah a loyal Hadrami shipowner, Muhammad Bakhashab, who had been ennobled by Sultan Ghalib's grandfather, the Sultan Salih. Muhammad kindly put at the Sultans' disposal one of his ships which was going to Berbera. Having accepted this generous offer the Sultans set sail for Mukalla. On arrival at the port in the early morning Sultan Ghalib was surprised at the absence of any activity in what was normally a very busy place at that time. The Customs wharf was also silent. It transpired that this was due to the imposition of a curfew. Distress signals were sent out and the shipping agent came alongside – accompanied by a party of armed revolutionaries. These at first pleaded with Sultan Ghalib to abdicate and then became threatening when he courageously refused to do so, saying he had already committed to the UN to hold a referendum under its auspices to enable his people to choose their own political future.

The revolutionaries were from the Popular Democratic Front, secretly a proxy for the communist National Liberation Front of Aden, and Sultan Ghalib told them that as they only had a membership of sixty they could scarcely claim to represent the people. The PDF spokesman had no reply to this but asked the Sultan if he had any message for his people. Sultan Ghalib wrote a few lines asking that there should be no bloodshed and that they should look for solutions to their problems in a peaceful way. He also warned the revolutionary party that they should not join or follow blindly whatever was happening in Aden and elsewhere in the Federation, but should keep open the possibility for an alternative course of action that would enable Hadramaut to go it alone and look after its own interests, should events turn out that were not to their liking. The revolutionaries successfully prevented the Sultan from landing, although failing to secure his abdication, despite threatening that 'he sign and deliver within half an hour or else'. After further spurious inducements had also failed, the ship sailed on to Berbera to take on cargo before returning to Jeddah.

Later the Sultan discovered that the revolutionaries had tried to forge his abdication by adding at the end of his letter to his people the phrase, 'and I have abdicated'. They also looted the Treasury and these funds were used for yet more internecine mayhem and helped the NLF in their fight with the Egyptian-backed Front for the Liberation of South Yemen (FLOSY).

Soon afterwards the British would order the bombing, on some four occasions, of tribes loyal to their treaty relationship with the Qu'aiti Sultan, who were laying siege to three HBL-occupied forts on the Saudi frontier at Al Abr, Zamalkh and Minwakh. This treaty relationship was said to be perpetual. The tribes' action against these forts had been taken by them in an effort to secure a route for the return of Sultan Ghalib by land. Their motive was not entirely without an element of self-interest as they were perfectly aware of the possibilities emanating from any coming tussle between the NLF and the Sultan. The example of the flow of Saudi gold and arms to the Royalists in next-door Yemen was much in their minds. Sultan Ghalib's protests over the airstrikes were made to both Harold Wilson and Sir Alec Douglas-Home (Wilson's predecessor) but fell on deaf ears. In addition, an appeal to the UN Secretary General U Thant was fobbed off by the United Kingdom representative Lord Caradon, who denied that the tribes concerned owed allegiance to Sultan Ghalib, and the air attacks were not only carried out in the interests of law and order but also in support of forces still under the command of, and being paid by, the United Kingdom.

It was a strange interpretation of the facts. The only access that the British had to the area was as the result of the Treaty they themselves had with the Sultan. It was odd, then, that the RAF should bomb loyal people, subjects of a Sultan with a valid Protectorate Treaty with the UK and whose interests they were supposed to protect and to represent both before the UN and the world at large. In addition the UK at this time had already claimed to have withdrawn from the area, which had been the reason given for refusing to convey the Sultan back to Mukalla.

The foregoing detailed account includes information which amazingly, only came to the notice of the Sultan following declassification of the relevant Foreign and Commonwealth some decades later.

After the arrival of the NLF in Mukalla and the Sultan's attempt to return, it was a day or two before the not very brave revolutionaries dared to enter the palace, and a couple more days before they attempted to enter the private apartments. At first the palace staff made themselves scarce but, after getting hold of some Dutch courage, the revolutionaries summoned the head cook and ordered him to prepare a meal for them. Too frightened to disobey, he returned to the kitchen and discussed what to do with his colleagues. Everyone decided that the revolutionaries should get the welcome they deserved and accordingly contaminated the food before serving it.

This story, most probably apocryphal in part, maintains that after the meal the revolutionaries slept off the food and booze and on awakening noticed the Sultan's State flag still flying from a flagpole on a nearby public building. It was found that the lanyard holding the flag in place had been cut, making it impossible to lower it in the usual way. They called on a boy to climb onto the roof to lower it. The boy did as he was told, but then decided to wrap the flag around his body to make the descent easier. Then something happened. Some say he slipped, others that he threw himself down to his death.

British Officialdom in Arabia

The colony of Aden was in reality the most important of all the British 'bus stops'. and extended its influence into the southern part of the Red Sea with the pinching of the island of Kamaran after the fall of the Ottoman Empire at the end of the First World War. The 'K' of Kamaran is a 'Q' in Arabic and the name means two moons, but see below.

This little island lies off the coast of northern Yemen. It is likely that the following accounts owe their provenance to wishful thinking, if not downright fibbing, but they go a long way to explaining the dogged way that the British coped with the discomforts of Empire, and the resourcefulness they like to think they possessed. The veracity of the two following anecdotes is in doubt, mainly because they are very inaccurate with regard to the size of the island of Kamaran, which is quite a bit bigger than indicated by the story. It is most likely that in the telling the raconteur has confused Kamaran with Perim island, further to the south, and situated at the very entrance to the Red Sea.

At first it was a year's posting for Our Man on Kamaran, who was accommodated in a small bungalow with a drive some fifty yards long to the jetty. One of the unfortunate incumbents was reported to have taken solace in gin, and had lined both sides of the drive with green Gordon's bottles by the time his year of duty was up– a total distance of a hundred yards filled with gin bottles. At three bottles a foot, this works out at nine hundred bottles and a consumption of seventeen bottles a week. A little fanciful, one feels, particularly as there appears to be no record of a funeral.) His successor apparently took the landscaping as a challenge and, having pulled up all the Gordon's bottles, replaced them with Angostura bottles.

However this heroic activity and the conditions on the island did not impress another appointee to the post of Resident. It is related that he never took up residence at all, but remained in London; simply writing twelve monthly reports and sending them to his clerk on the island with instructions to send one back to London each month. All went well for a while but then our Resident in Kamaran went for dinner in his London club. Sadly the Colonial Secretary of the day chose the same night to have dinner at the same club. And the whole story emerged with unpleasant consequences for the rapidly-created ex-Resident.

This tale resonates closely with another related by Donald Foster that concerns the island of Perim, south of Kamaran at the entrance to the Red Sea. This other tale is indeed so close in its theme that the two may well be different versions of the same story. This tale, which may be the original, concerns a young subaltern stationed with his detachment on this godforsaken rock who is reported to have become so brassed off with his duty that he persuaded the skipper of a passing ship to take him to England for a spot of unauthorised leave. Everything went well until, for a young man clearly exercising his officer qualities and initiative a bit inappropriately, he entered the area of St James's which was stiff with senior officers visiting their clubs. There he came face to face with the very Colonel from Aden who had sent him to Perim in the first place, some weeks previously. There was no chance of escape, but the young man's fate is not recorded.

Though Kamaran was a distant outpost of Empire, standards were of the highest in later years, and it is reliably recorded that Retreat was played on a bugle every night as the Union Jack was lowered from its flagpole, the bugler stoutly blasting out the notes towards the Yemen shore. The last Commissioner (there is some uncertainty in the accounts as to whether he was a Commissioner or a Resident) was in post for an astonishing seventeen years. It may be that he was slightly eccentric, but he was clearly keen that the benefits of an organised and civilised society should be imposed on his tiny domain. He put up road signs to bring a proper air of order into things. 'Halt at Major Road Ahead' alerted the driver of the only vehicle on the island to possible hazards on the track between three cottages and nothing else. There were signposts, one indicating the way to Windermere, as well as milestones. Carefully laid out, exactly twenty-two-foot wide carriageways led from nowhere in particular to, well, nowhere in particular. The high point of the signage was, however, kept for the airstrip where the only terminal facilities were provided by a small hut built out of white coral. Beside it was a large notice board. This information was recorded by Donald Foster but, as he himself says, it is worth recording in full.

Established 1882

YOUR QUESTIONS ANSWERED
1. Land of Two Moons. Kamar=Moon; Kamaran=Two Moons
> *Standing on the highest point observe:*
> > *Moon proper rising in the East and*
> > *Moon reflected in sea on West.*
> > *So they say. We haven't tried.*
2. Yes, it is very hot in Summer. Humidity high.
3. Yes, it rains sometimes
4. Yes, plenty of water, 200 brackish wells. We drink distilled water and / prefer it.
5. Europeans? Normally just one. Quite Normal
6. Lonely? No.
7. Fishing? Marvellous, not of expanding variety.

8. Cinema? Yes, but no films.

9. Trees: How many? Both are flourishing thank you

10. Name three people we would take with us to a desert island? Can't say.
    Don't know what a desert island looks like

11. You are standing fifty-one feet above sea level. On the level.

Later, an inspection of the files led to the discovery of an indent, dated 1939, for twenty-four Belisha Beacons.

Stephen Day adds a revealing postscript. The Kamaran post was eventually scrapped by a Whitehall bean counter, but the Secretariat in Aden took a different view when it produced a new administrative structure for the Federal Government which was taking over British responsibilities. Aden was full of the most extraordinary eccentrics, and one, Archie by name, saw a chance to find a quiet retreat where he could relax and drink. Accordingly he wrote into the new structure a fresh post in Kamaran. This alteration passed by everyone unnoticed and, having secured the job, Archie went off to Kamaran, accompanied by a small contingent of police, to drink himself to death. Archie's sole job on the island, it seems, was to raise and lower the flag. One night as Archie sat, stupefied, on his veranda, all hell broke loose. It appeared that the island was under attack from a party landing on the beach. The police jumped into their defensive sangars and returned fire at the unknown assailants. Eventually English voices were heard and a ceasefire arranged. It transpired that a party of British Marines had carried out a practice assault on an island which they thought to be deserted and uninhabited.

In the end, Archie was pensioned off when Aden achieved independence. His tall and distinguished figure, set off by a flowing moustache, enabled him to get a job as a male model. He frequently appeared on television in an advertisement for some alcoholic beverage or other under the by-line, 'The Ambassador Loves Pink Gin', or some such.

While the contribution to the welfare of the Eastern Aden Protectorate made by both Colonel Hugh Boustead, Resident in Mukalla, and Harold Ingrams should not be belittled, many extant accounts do rather ignore the strenuous efforts made by other people as well. Colonel Boustead also, perhaps in the spirit of this compilation, remarked that as we get older we remember more than actually happened. It is reported that Colonel Boustead stoutly refused to believe that anything made in Britain could ever go wrong. Consequently he drove about the Wadi Hadramawt in a Rolls-Royce on its rims, as it was clearly impossible for the vehicle to have a puncture!

One of the Colonel's undoubted triumphs was the control of the flood waters of the Great Wadi itself. Previous attempts to construct dams had all been swept away by the ferocity of the periodic floods. It was Colonel Boustead who arranged for the naval anti-submarine nets stored at Pondicherry to be brought to South Arabia, and installed across the Wadi. There they successfully caught the boulders and soil being washed down and effective dams were created. On official visits, Colonel Boustead also controlled the traffic with fierce blasts on a police whistle which efficiently cleared the road, while doubtless surprising the local inhabitants.

Colonel Boustead had a memorable career serving in the Sudan, Hadramaut and the Trucial States. When he eventually retired he was summoned back from the UK to take charge of Sheikh Zayed's horses at Al Ain in Abu Dhabi. Having taken up this appointment the Colonel assiduously handed out medicines to all and sundry without prescription. He used his own diagnoses and queues of people lined up after afternoon prayers for their cures.

The ignorance about Arabian matters to be found in the exalted circles of the upper echelons of Whitehall is cogently revealed by the thoughtful provision of Travel Warrants for British troops, to be used in obtaining tickets for the train journey between Aden and Kuwait. This occurred during the first Kuwait crisis in 1961. However, while this story is risible enough in itself, it may in fact betray a distant memory hoarily preserved in an ancient file.

At the beginning of the Second World War an Italian bomber was shot down close to Aden; the plane fell into the sea but the crew were all rescued. It was then discovered that they had a passenger, an Italian Colonel who was flying over the target area to see what damage they had been able to inflict. Having seen craters in the Ma'alla area he was reported to have remarked that at least they had been able to destroy the railway before they had been shot down. This shows that the Italian maps were a trifle out of date as, while there had been a very short length of railway at Ma'alla connecting the Colony with the State of Lahej to the north, this had been taken up and abandoned some twenty years previously, all the rails and sleepers being sold. One wonders if the memory of this rather small bit of railway still hung in the air in the corridors of power in the Whitehall of 1961, and led to the issue of the Railway Warrants.

Mind you, the British always had an obsession with building railways and for decades none of them were brought up without toy trains to play with. To this day old model trains command huge prices at auction. The following story rather nicely illustrates British attitudes at the beginning of the 20th century. Aubrey Herbert was an MP, Turkish expert, and diplomat, who in 1915 would accompany a twenty-eight-year-old T.E. Lawrence in a failed attempt to bribe the Turkish Commander, Khalil Pasha, to lift the siege of Kut Al Amara in Iraq. In 1905, having casually met his friend Leland Buxton in the House of Commons Lobby, they decided, perhaps eccentrically, to go and have a look at Sana'a. Where else would one meet a possible companion with whom to travel to Yemen? They arrived at a time when the country had been ravaged by starvation, consequent on a war of liberation from the Turks involving a nasty siege. On observing the frightful privations of the populace, Herbert at once decided that the only salvation for the country lay with the Empire and railways. On his return he wrote:

Those were the days when the majority of our countrymen were full of imperialist ambitions, and I confess I left the Yemen looking forward to the day when it should be controlled and its extraordinary resources be developed, by Great Britain, when a British railway would run from Hodeidah to Sana'a and from Sana'a to Aden.

This Imperial attitude conferred an air of supreme confidence on the employees of the Colonial Office. After all, they had enormous backing and garrisons to fall back on. In South Arabia in the opening years of the 20th century, a fine exemplar of this was one G. Wyman Bury. Peter Brent describes his sporting joviality and undoubted affection for the people of Yemen, and his undying belief in the righteousness of his mission to bring order to the place. Of the Yemen Bury, ever the British gentleman with a military background, whose thoughts never strayed far from his firearms or their use, writes

From a sportsman's point of view Yamen [sic] *is disappointing. It may be divided broadly into districts where game goes and you can't, and districts where you can go and game won't.*

****

Abu Dhabi on the Trucial Coast shares ownership of the Buraimi oasis with the Sultanate of Oman. The oasis was the scene of a notable disagreement between the United Kingdom and the Kingdom of Saudi Arabia, and by obvious extension the oil company Aramco, and so the United States of America. The Saudi Arabians tried to annex the oasis in a move to encroach further on the territories of the little Sheikhdoms comprising the Trucial States on the Gulf coast. It is an open secret that the USA and the UK have actually been in enthusiastic and often quite lively rivalry in the area, if not actually at war. The oasis was defended by a mud fort that was manned by the Trucial Oman Scouts. Their Commanding Officer was once asked by a journalist what it was that frightened him most. The officer replied that he rather thought it would be an adversary armed with a water pistol.

Sheikh Shakhbut, Ruler of Abu Dhabi, was the elder brother of Sheikh Zayed, who became the first President of the United Arab Emirates. But in those now somewhat distant days Abu Dhabi had no oil and was just a rather hot little fishing village. Shakhbut, or 'Jackpot' as he was irreverently but perhaps not inaccurately nicknamed, was the first Ruler to succeed to the throne of his forefathers without murdering his predecessor for several generations, and he had an annual income of about £250 which, paid in equivalent rupee notes, he carefully shared out amongst his large and greedy family, rupee by rupee. A rupee was worth about fifteen pence in modern day British currency. Being perpetually broke throughout his reign before the discovery of oil inculcated in Shakhbut a limpet-like addiction to parsimony, which is not a characteristic associated with oil Sheikhs today.

In the disbursement of these meagre state funds Shakhbut was assisted and advised by a Man from the Foreign Office, who was supplied by Her Majesty's Government with a Land Rover. However, the Sheikh was responsible for the repair and fuelling of this vehicle. Naturally with the paucity of available funds for this purpose the wretched Land Rover sat in the sand, devoid of petrol, and with four flat tyres. Then the miracle took place and oil was found. The Man from the Foreign Office talked often and gently to the Sheikh about what benefits this would bring, and as the day approached for the first tanker to be filled up, he told Shakhbut that he ought to hire a man to read the meter, so that he would know just how much oil had been taken. Shakhbut looked at his little pile of rupees and decided that tomorrow would be a good time to hire someone.

This went on for a while until the first tanker actually docked at the terminal. As the Sheikh had failed to hire a meter reader, the Man from the Foreign Office had to go down to the port himself; as the Land Rover was out of action, he took a taxi. He carefully wrote down the figures and returned to Sheikh Shakhbut to inform him that he no longer had an income of £250 a year but £80,000,000 or so. At least that was what it was to start with! The Sheikh remained calm and simply asked, 'How much was the taxi?'

With the arrival of this huge sum of money, which Shakhbut insisted be paid in cash, there was the obvious problem of what to do with it. Initially it was stored under his bed and unkind Europeans took bets on whether or not the rats would eat the banknotes before the Sheikhly bed reached the ceiling. This habit of clinging onto the money was not uncommon amongst Arabian Rulers. The great King Abdulaziz of Saudi Arabia kept his cash in tin trunks which accompanied him everywhere on camelback, and the Fadhli Sultan in South Arabia kept his Treasury in a brown tin box which he took out every five minutes, or so it seemed, to count the cash.

But back in Abu Dhabi the nice Man from the Foreign Office eventually persuaded Shakhbut that it would be best to put the money into the bank, despite the Sheikh's worry that this was just a way to enable the bank, and possibly other malignant people, to steal it. However, having deposited the money with some reluctance, Shakhbut, who was quite unable to shake off his suspicions, went down to the bank a couple of weeks later, and demanded to see his money. A beaming bank manager showed Shakhbut his statement. Consternation! 'This is a just a piece of paper', said Shakhbut, his darkest suspicions apparently confirmed. He therefore decided that the bank should be given the chance to get the money back at once, and to make sure they did, he surrounded the bank with guards, telling the manager that no one could leave until the 'stolen' money was returned. Luckily the phone line remained intact. Frantic messages were sent out and a day or two later a plane arrived in Abu Dhabi loaded with gold bullion. Shakhbut counted the bars carefully on the airstrip, and now trusting in the bank's ability to at least produce what they said he had, agreed to the release of the bank staff and the return of the gold to London.

This story seems to be the much embellished shell of a smaller nut, and the truth of the matter is certainly as told by Sir Donald Hawley. He recounts that Sheikh Shakhbut, ever suspicious of new ways, once told him that the British Bank of the Middle East had stolen ten lakhs of rupees from him (a lakh is one hundred thousand). The bank had been unable to produce the actual money when the Sheikh made an unexpected visit to see that his money was safe. Sir Donald also casts doubt on the story that Sheikh Shakhbut kept his cash under his bed!

****

The stories about Sheikh Shakhbut are numerous and it really is a pity that his Rule was curtailed by the British because of his difficult and reactionary behaviour. One of the British Agents reporting to London in a telegram was moved to remark that 'the peace that had reigned in Abu Dhabi for the last month was rudely shattered by the return of the Ruler from holiday this week'. Shakhbut was really a very nice and well-disposed person who cared deeply what wealth would do to his people. Some of his more distant relatives did in fact try to get rid of him but his brothers had all been sworn to an oath of loyalty by their indomitable mother. Without him life must have been rather dull.

When Abu Dhabi was given its own Political Agent independent of the one in Dubai, relations with Shakhbut improved markedly.

The previous position was, he felt, demeaning to him and his tribe, a branch of the Bani Yas, whose other branch ruled in Dubai. But things did take a nasty turn over negotiations about the ownership of the island of Halul. This was claimed both by Abu Dhabi and by Qatar. The Ruler of the latter was loathed by Shakhbut, who took the line that the island was clearly his and that there was no need at all to go to the expense of providing any evidence of this fact. The Qatari Sheikh took the opposite view and hired a very astute Egyptian lawyer to present his case.

The background to this squabble went back to the 19th century, to a time when none of the Gulf Sheikhdoms laid claim to Halul. It was a small, waterless islet that provided shelter to fishing and pearling vessels in stormy weather, and people from Qatar visited it in season to collect terns' eggs. But in 1869 an event of international importance took place. A buoy from the harbour at Basra, miles away to the north, got adrift and washed up on the shores of Halul. The British authorities, clinging uncharacteristically to the policy of doing the right thing, decided that they couldn't just turn up and retrieve their buoy: they had to ask permission. However they immediately came up against a difficulty. From whom should they seek permission? No one seemed to know who owned Halul Island.

The dilemma was swiftly solved when the British assigned the island to Abu Dhabi. The reason for this arbitrary decision is now completely lost. Anyway, having made this magisterial decision the assistant to the British Political Agent in the Gulf duly wrote a letter to the then Sheikh of Abu Dhabi asking for their buoy back. Doubtless this polite request came as a surprise to the Sheikh, but he was not averse to having the island added to his territory. Ever afterwards the British regarded the Ruler of Abu Dhabi as overlord and master of Halul.

All proceeded smoothly until the discovery of oil. This precipitated the dispute between Qatar and Abu Dhabi. Sheikh Ali Bin Abdullah

Al Thani of Qatar forcefully claimed the island because of the tern egg collection, the use of the island as a refuge for Qatari fishermen and the fact that his father had visited Halul on several occasions. Neither Sheikh Shakhbut of Abu Dhabi nor any of his ancestors had ever been anywhere near the place. The two Rulers agreed to British arbitration however, but while the history of the buoy initially persuaded the British to favour the claims of Abu Dhabi, in 1962 sovereignty over Halul was awarded to Qatar. Sheikh Shakhbut was furious and blamed the British for not taking his side, and relations between them became very frosty. Though later there was some improvement, it seems clear that this event led to such a loss of trust that HMG finally decided to remove Shakhbut from power. It must be said that this was accomplished with great tact and gentleness on the part of the British Agent who managed with consummate skill to maintain the Sheikh's dignity to the end.

The advent of oil, and the enormous income that accompanied it, attracted the commercial world, which flocked to the Sheikhdom like iron filings to a magnet. On one occasion a very eminent banker obtained an audience with Sheikh Shakhbut in order to obtain a license to operate in Abu Dhabi. During the course of the meeting he extolled the talents of his chairman, who was a lord. This last bit of information immediately caught Shakhbut's attention, as his interest in the peerage had been aroused some years earlier when he had been tickled pink to entertain Lord Jellicoe in Buraimi. He enquired closely as to what sort of lord the bank's chairman was, and where he stood in the order of precedence. Then Shakhbut turned to the British Agent and asked him if he had any peers in his family: sadly there were none. Despite this distraction, everything was going splendidly, and the banker's Lebanese interpreter was on his knees in front of the Sheikh praising him for his charm, wisdom and generosity. At this point it seemed that the licence was in the bag and the banker began to draw the paper out of his suit pocket. This terrified Sheikh Shakhbut, who was much afraid of bits of paper which might force him to part with money. The Lebanese interpreter was still on his knees looking like a praying mantis and the Ruler was paralysed with apprehension on the sofa. The British Agent vainly tried to signal to the banker to put the paper away but he didn't get the message. In the event the Sheikh resolutely refused to sign.

A Political Officer's Story

In describing life in Dhala during the final years of British rule in South Arabia, James Nash graphically demonstrates the qualities that made our Men on the Spot so special – naturally without knowing he was doing so.

It seems he had accumulated a collection of antique silver as a young man and brought it to Arabia with him because it was less likely to be stolen there, than if it had been left at home in Chelsea or Kensington, where its value would have been recognised. The collection comprised a William and Mary tankard, a pair of candlesticks and some silver wine goblets. While this action may at first seem a bit daft, there was good sense in it. China and glass are far too fragile to survive being carted about in a Gendarmerie truck, while the silverware would easily come through intact.

James lived in the Political Officer's house in Dhala during 1964 and 1965. At this time the house wasn't a very comfortable home because the dissident tribesmen, later to become Heroes of the Revolution, used it for target practice. This eventually reached a crescendo of three attacks a week, with rifles, machine guns and bazookas being brought into play. James decided to bring what he described as cowboymanship into the equation.

His plan was to throw a rather grand dinner party with all the silver on the table, a great menu, and good wines. During the course of this feast the regular cacophony of an attack would start up outside. James would then apologise to his guests, and having blown out the candles would pick up his own Bren gun from behind the curtains and, throwing open the shutters, blaze away in the direction of the dissidents. This done, he would repeat his apologies and, putting away his Bren, continue with the party.

Sadly, it never really worked out as planned. To start with, nobody really wanted to come and join in being target practice for the dissidents; and James only had one guest bedroom. However, one day an unfortunate soldier appeared. James supposed him to be a Field Intelligence Officer and althought the reason for the visit escapes him, he does remember that it was at the end of the month and his rations were running low. Consequently, and due to the short notice, his cook could only rustle up some very tough beef olives made from an elderly bullock hanging in Dhala market that morning. So when the shooting started both James and his guest were happy to abandon the beef olives and seize their firearms. Getting up onto the roof they joined in the affray. It was now that the real hero of the night appeared. James's cook, Said, followed the pair up to the roof and, rifle on shoulder, grinning from ear to ear, demonstrated that he had not lost an ounce of sangfroid, carefully placing their puddings beside them on the battlements.

Meanwhile up in the Gulf, at a time when only Land Rovers could navigate the roadless wastes of the Trucial States, the Political Resident in Bahrain descended on the hapless Sheikhdoms, having sent his saloon car down in advance. Naturally this grandee was wearing full official kit –Summer Uniform, which included a spectacular spiked helmet, and sword. Seated in his unsuitable car he was bounced around the territory until the car went over a particularly vicious bump. The Political Resident was catapulted upwards and the spike on the top of his helmet was driven through the roof of the vehicle. Suspended by his chin strap the great man was almost strangled, and only survived because his quick-thinking ADC stopped the car, and climbing onto the roof unscrewed the spike from the helmet. One simply can't beat Sandhurst training.

****

The British Political Agent in Bahrain and his wife were invited by a prominent Arabian to dinner. After the British couple arrived the Agent told his wife to be careful what she ate because he was sure the plates were dirty. Foolishly he had assumed that no one else spoke English. However, the host's schoolboy son did. The boy told his father what had been said, and after that the conversation rather languished.

Naturally the British inspired trust, loyalty and affection wherever they went. So much so that the somewhat feckless Sultan of the Fadhlis, Ahmad Bin Abdullah, Minister of Agriculture in the Federal Government, realised that the British wouldn't lift a finger to help the Treaty Chiefs and so, returning from a trip to London, he defected to Egypt. From there he sent instructions to his people to throw the British out of the Sultanate. Both of them. There were only two, the Political Officer and the Agricultural Adviser. The PO did a deal with the now ex-Sultan's brother Nasir Bin Abdullah, promising him support. At which Sultan Nasir smilingly remarked that he had studied the history of the British Government in the Middle East and knew that it had never kept a single promise.

'However, I expect you to keep this one.' He added, jabbing the young PO in the chest, 'I will trust YOU'. They were to remain in regular contact until the Sultan died in 2008.

Soon after the installation of the new Sultan he was appointed Minister of Justice in the Federal Government – a post he chose, remarking that, since there was no justice in South Arabia, he had no need to waste more than a morning a month in the Federal capital, and would concentrate on running his Sultanate, which he did with great skill until the eve of independence.

One day the PO was instructed by his own boss to reprimand Sultan Nasir for marrying too often. The reader may find this stretching the scope of official advice rather further than was intended in a Protectorate Treaty, but there you are. The Colonial regime clearly felt that excessive polygamy was inappropriate to the office of Minister of Justice. The young PO appealed that someone older and wiser than he should perform this task. He was after all unmarried himself, and wondered if indeed the moral position chimed with the Advisery Treaty, which only provided for authority in the fields of foreign affairs, security and good governance. Nevertheless he was told to get on with it. So, plucking up his courage one day he tackled the amorous Ruler. Sultan Nasir reacted most unexpectedly and poured out his heart to the PO. He explained that the love of his life had died young. Since then he had tried in vain to find a satisfactory replacement and wondered if the British Government could offer a solution.

This story, which has sad undertones, does however have a happier outcome. Some two years later the PO himself got married and Sultan Nasir threw a large tribal party for him which was attended by all the tribes in the Sultanate. The Sultan congratulated the young man on his wise choice and asked if someone similar could be found for himself. Years later the two met up again in London. It transpired that the Sultan was still looking and he asked the PO if he could get hold of an Australian bride for him. 'Why an Australian?' asked the PO. Sultan Nasir explained that he had read that Australian women were tough and so assumed that they would be particularly good at looking after the sheep!

At the last meeting between the two men, shortly before he died, the Sultan was living in his ancestral fort surrounded by sheep and goats, as well as the latest of his numerous offspring, who was only two months old. Sultan Nasir had married into all the tribes in his area and, producing in all some thirty-five children, could with truth be called the father of his people.

****

In the 1960s, as the time for British withdrawal came closer, the Foreign Office took over more control. This also gave cause for a laugh at bureaucracy. While under the Colonial Office one of the Political Officers drew a horse allowance – in fact he was the last man to benefit from this Imperial relic. He had been given three horses by the Fadhlis. Under Colonial Office rules this allowance was not accountable, and so the PO was financed to take his staff to the Shalimar cinema in Aden once a year, the show to be followed by a slap-up meal. Under the Foreign Office it was accountable, and the FO and Treasury were at a loss to understand why the PO needed this allowance as he had a Land Rover. Protestations that the horses could go anywhere, and the Land Rover could not, were huffily rebuffed by the Rover Company who had been asked for their opinion by the FO, so that they could justify cessation of the payment. Correspondence was lengthily exchanged. In the end the PO did manage to keep the allowance, as he explained to the Treasury that, should it cease, he would be forced to have the horses put down; or they would just starve, and this would not do the reputation of the United Kingdom any good at all. Quite the reverse.

Half a century before this the Foreign Office and the Arab Bureau in Cairo had staunchly supported the Sharif Hussein in the Hejaz, whose telephone number was Makkah 1, as you would expect. On the other hand the Colonial Office and the Government of India, just as staunchly supported Ibn Saud, who at this date had no telephone. So the British taxpayer paid for both sides in the struggle for control of the Hejaz. Arabian readers will doubtless question the use of the phrase 'staunch support' given by any British organisation in respect of their affairs. However, the writer does suggest that this is an example of fiendish cunning. After all, this meant that whoever won the British could proudly take their place on the winning side. Not that this did them much good in the long run.

In November 1964, the Ruling Family Council met and approved the removal of King Saud from the throne. Three days later, after the appointment of his brother Faisal as King, he was amicably sent into exile in Europe, where he continued to be visited by his family until his death.

Prime Minister Harold Wilson was most gratified to hear from our Embassy in Jeddah that the transition had been carried out smoothly, and thought that a Parliamentary delegation should be sent out to Saudi Arabia at the start of the new king's reign. The delegation was headed by Lord Bertram Bowden, a socialist life peer in his fifties, who before his elevation in 1963 had pursued a middle-of-the-road career as Head of the College of Technology in Manchester. It would seem that the British Labour Government, taking an incongruously imperialistic attitude to the visit, thought that no preparation or briefing as to how the delegation members should behave was required. British socialists didn't need to accommodate the natives that far! At this time the best schools in Saudi Arabia were anxious to promote scientific education and they hoped that Lord Bowden would be able to give them some helpful ideas and useful contacts. In the event the noble lord sadly caught a cold on the aeroplane out, and this condition was not improved by the air-conditioning in the delegation's hotel. Lord Bowden became obsessed with his illness and was quite unable to concentrate or think about anything else.

When he arrived at 'The Eton of the Hijaz', The Al Thagh School, which had been created as a centre of excellence by King Faisal himself, he was met by the Principal, his British Oxford-educated Head of English, and officials from the Ministry of Education. Everyone at once realised that the eminent visitor from England was incapable of taking anything in and his delegation was likewise completely disinterested as they all trooped around the multi-million pound facilities on show, including the chemistry and physics labs, the photographic studios and sound theatres. It wasn't until they all reached the new laundry that any animation appeared. To the astonishment of the Saudis, the delegation seized on a pile of headdresses and, apparently thinking that they were being friendly in the familiar fashion of modern English schoolteachers, proceeded to clown about with them. The Saudis were naturally appalled as they were used to treating teachers with the deepest reverence. The visit was a disaster.

At tea in the Headmaster's room afterwards, the English teacher sought to rescue the situation as best he could. He realised that serious discussion would be impossible and so he asked Lord Bowden if he had met the King yet. Lord Bowden frowned, looked confused, and then turned to one of his sidekicks and asked if it was the King they had had tea with the day before. However, things did take a turn for the better subsequently because the English teacher, perhaps mischievously, had noticed a resemblance between Lord Bowden and some of Enid Blyton's characters – Big Ears and Noddy in particular. Consequently, Lord Bowden was nicknamed Lord

Blyton. The name stuck and in Saudi Arabia Lord B. became known by this name ever afterwards.

****

In the course of events it sometimes becomes necessary to ask people questions, but you don't always get the sort of answer you expect. In Aden, in the early sixties, British troops caught a terrorist. Naturally they were very proud of this achievement and, having shot the unfortunate man in the backside, hauled him off to hospital. The need to question their captive now cropped up, and accordingly an Arabist was called in to make the necessary enquiries. When the Arabist arrived at the hospital he was somewhat surprised to see that so excited were the military by their prowess that they had completely forgotten to search or disarm their prize. After having tactfully removed a Kalashnikov, a bandolier of ammunition, a dagger and three or four hand grenades from the wounded man, the Arabist set about the interrogation.

In that situation it is part of the technique to belittle the subject so that he feels small and diminished, and is thus made compliant and amenable to questioning, or so runs the theory. On opening a pouch on the man's belt the Arabist found a single shoelace. This was clearly a terrific opportunity and, seizing his chance, the Arabist with heavy sarcasm praised the recumbent terrorist, telling him how progressive he was. He had one shoelace and maybe soon he would get the other one and perhaps also the shoes to go with them. 'Oh no', responded the terrorist, 'Tie that round it and you won't get any babies!'

Some months later an Egyptian pilot misread his altimeter and inadvertently landed his Ilyushin, marked with Yemeni Republican insignia, at Lodar in the Audhali Sultanate of the South Arabian Federation. A quick-thinking British army officer drove his Land Rover in front of the plane before it could take off again. The crew and passengers were then arrested and taken to the Naib's Fort. There the Arabist was sent to question them, and one of the most bizarre interrogations took place. It was 'chaired' (everyone was sitting on the floor) by the Naib himself who, following Arabian custom, entertained the Arabist and each prisoner as he was led in, with coffee, dates and slices of water melon. The Arabist was unaware at this stage that the Naib had a trick involving no little skill with regard to this last item. When eating the water melon, the Naib was able to store the black seeds of the fruit in his cheek, like a hamster. When the cheek was full the Naib would spit them out like machine gun bullets.

Each prisoner was greeted in the usual way with enquiries as to his health and that of his family. This formality completed, the Naib let out an explosive and accusing series of sentences at the prisoner. He asked the man why he had had the audacity to land without permission, and accused him of treachery towards the great causes of Arabian Nationalism and Liberty, and of having betrayed Muslim principles. He then ordered him to answer the questions he would get from the Naib's friend and brother, the British officer, a man who represented all that was honourable between staunch and loyal allies. The Arabist was then able to seek identification and make enquiries as to the purpose of the flight, where it had come from, and where it was going to, and so on. The replies having been noted down, the Naib would clear his cheek of water melon seeds once more, and with deadly accuracy spit them into the middle of the mat around which everyone was sitting. This done, he would address the Arabist. 'There you are,' he would say. 'Our valiant and dearly beloved Arab Brother has answered your imperialist and impertinent questions as any honest Son of Arabia would, so what have you to say to that?' Another volley of seeds would be fired at the mat and the Arabist would ask for the next prisoner to brought in. The whole performance was then repeated.

The irony of this event was that the passengers were all senior Egyptian intelligence officers and, for some unknown reason, the British Powers That Be did not seize what seemed to be a golden opportunity to suggest to Colonel Nasser's government that, in order to get their important people back, the Egyptians would have to ask the Federal Government to send them home – thus recognising the Federal Government. Col. Nasser had steadfastly refused to accord this recognition and this occasion might have been a way to force the issue a bit. However, in the event, the passengers were taken down to Aden and sent back to Cairo by BOAC, First Class. It has not been recorded whether or not they ever expressed any gratitude for this wonderful example of British altruism.

On one occasion when accompanying Sir Kennedy Trevaskis to London, the Sharif Hussein of Bayhan wept when Sir Kennedy sent his children off to boarding school. He could not comprehend how Sir Kennedy could bear to be parted from them. This from a man who, in his capacity as Minister of the Interior, was with the Government party for the periodic meetings on the frontier with the officials from the Imamate of Yemen. These meetings took place when cross-border raiding reached a crescendo and it was necessary to calm things down a bit. The British flew up to Mukayras in the Audhali Sultanate, and the Yemeni party were already on the airstrip waiting for them. The official plane, a de Havilland Dove, carrying the Governor and the Commander-in-Chief, as well as the Minister of the Interior and other notables, demonstrated the awesome power of the British by obligingly crashing while landing. The eminent members of the British delegation emerged from the aeroplane somewhat shaken but unhurt. However, one person was missing. There was no sign of the Sharif.

The Awadhi Sheikh from the Yemeni side was heard to remark rather loudly and unkindly that God should be praised, as the old fox of Bayhan had copped it. The words were no sooner out of his mouth than the Sharif, a bit singed, emerged from the back of the plane. Two weeks later news was brought to the Sharif in his Aden office that an unknown assailant had shot the Awadhi Sheikh stone dead. The Sharif merely said, with a smile, 'That'll teach him to mind his manners'.

◎ ◎ ◎

God gives nuts to those without teeth

Arabian Proverb

The original British Embassy in Saudi Arabia occupied a central position in old Jeddah between the old Red Sea Hotel and the start of the Main Street, opposite the Ministry of Foreign Affairs. It was memorably said in a guidebook that the Embassy was well worth visiting if only for its architecture.

At the inception of one of the crises that have beset Anglo-Saudi relations down the years, the Embassy hastily improvised a burning-room to enable them to destroy secret documents. On one occasion when it was felt that the political situation had deteriorated sufficiently to warrant it the burning-room was brought into use, and incineration began. However, the room became very hot and rapidly filled with smoke and fumes. Accordingly the windows were opened to the breeze blowing in off the Red Sea. At once, partially burnt and singed secret documents were blown out of the building. Small boys avidly collected them and, having retrieved the bits, brazenly approached the Embassy to sell them back.

It is mportant to explain that at this time all embassies were in Jeddah rather than the capital at Riyadh, the reason being that the Saudis, possibly with good reason, regarded foreigners with deep suspicion, and they were usually an ungodly lot as well. It was therefore safer for all concerned if they were kept up on the Red Sea coast, where the locals were used to dealing with such people. Should the Saudis need to talk to one of these foreigners, they could be whistled for as required.

****

While the absorption of Egypt into the British Sphere of Influence during the 19th century, weaning it away from its Ottoman suzerains, was indeed accompanied by perhaps necessary political shenanigans, it did enable us to get a firm grip on the defence of the Suez Canal and so protect our sea route to the India of the Raj. This was developed before and after the First World War, when what has been characterised as British duplicity peaked with the encouragement of the Arab Revolt, and the subsequent rather lame creation of Kingdoms as a reward for the Arabians.

It may therefore be seen by the cynical as being entirely appropriate that a one-time First Secretary at our Cairo Embassy should bring to Egypt a circus from England. This may be viewed by some to have been just the right sort of thing to epitomise British activities there over the previous century or so. The First Secretary was reported at the time, 1973, to have made this commercial gesture in preparation for his own retirement, when he would continue his travelling mode of life following the Circus Americano. While on leave, he had met the owners – Count Andre Maximilian Lazard, of Bulgarian descent, and his 'brother' William – encamped on Penistone Moor near Sheffield, and had negotiated a share in the business. This fulfilled a childhood dream which had endured through both Army and Foreign Office service.

The Circus was a great success and received a good spread in the famed Al Ahram newspaper, where the main headline announced that a very young girl member of the cast 'was only nine and forbidden to show fear'. In one act she had a fourteen-foot python draped round her neck, and later a blindfolded seventeen-year-old boy standing on one leg on a high wire threw knives around her. During the week's performance, which was carried out jointly with the Egyptian State Circus, the Union Jack and the Egyptian flag were flown side by side over the Big Top at Zamalek – probably the first occasion on which this had happened since the Suez Crisis. The opening joint performance was attended by the British Ambassador and his wife sitting on a ringside seat next to the Egyptian Deputy Prime Minister as well as the Minister of Culture.

Eventually the Circus folded when Count Andre died of cancer and his 'brother' had a nasty accident involving a crocodile.

One wonders if anything should be made of it, but it needs to be mentioned here also that during the late 19th century the French Naval Attaché in Cairo, while *en poste*, performed a series of daring acts on a trapeze.

Official Letter Writing

The British have maintained, particularly in the Armed Services, a system of official letter writing which has several categories, used according both to the importance of the recipient and the content. Amongst other things this prevents the lower ranks from addressing their superiors in an overly familiar way. For instance, a private deeply admiring of Field Marshal Montgomery would be stopped from addressing the hero of Alamein as Darling Monty. When this system passes through the hands of an Indian typist writing, while sitting on the pavement, on behalf of an illiterate Yemeni soldier, the effect changes from the mundanely bizarre to the truly fantastic.

ADEN COLONY
21st January 1963
The Hon'ble, The Commanding Officer,
Federal Regular Army,
Seedasar Line, Khor Maksar,
Aden.

Honoured:-
I beg respectfully invite reference to my last two Applications of January,
63, and address your distinguished honour upon the subject, which is to the
utmost important to my dignity, integrity, and exigence, as follows:-

In my capacity as disciplined soldier rank Pte. No. 4109 and automobile
driver, have carried on my service under your noble control for the past
period of 12 and 8 years respectively, aggregating twenty years. During
which, performed my duties with great fidelity, guiltlessly, actively, gallantly,
prosperously, regularly, abidingly, and satisfactorily, as splendidly recorded in
the concerned depts. and exhibited in the bonafide Testimonial issued to me.

In view of the accomplishment of my service contract, my engagement
has been terminated on 9th Jan 63. while my bonus, gratuity, privileges
entitlements, are still due and outstanding to me by this glorious Force.

In consideration of the abovementioned multitude of my service period, with
excellent results, your honour will find to have become materially, longivally
and qualifically entitled to the approbation of my above Applications for the
extension of my service for one year, bestow of a rifle medal, and grant of a
succour of one rifle indiscriminatingly and assimilatingly to those who served
for a period below the above enumerated years of my service.

In the pursuance of the system, usage, custom and practice prevailing in this
splendid Force, I have every confidence in your magnanimous characteristic

that you will entertain my above applications and more particularly narrated above, so that I may not be deprived of the concessions and assimilations derived by me under the meritorious performance of my duties in the above service.

Therefore I earnestly pray that the necessary significant action will be exercised for the approval of my above request and for which I shall ever remain grateful.

Wishing Your Honour and This Magnificent Force
Glorious and Victorious Luck.

Your most obedt. servt.
Nasser Haddi Azani
Seedasar Line
Federal Regular Army,
K/Maksar, Aden.

This is not the only example of the way this genre has impressed itself on Arabia. As reported by Khalid Kishtainy the great Egyptian politician, Saad Zaghlul, was more than a little tickled when he was arrested by a British officer who showed him the warrant. It was signed by General Allenby under the superscription, 'Your Most Obedient Servant'. Saad said, 'It was typical of the hypocrisy of an Englishman! He grabs you by the scruff of the neck, nearly strangles you and then tells you he is your obedient servant.' So many successful national Presidents, Prime Ministers, and Rulers in the area have been imprisoned by the British that it seems to have almost been a qualification for the job.

As a balance to this, perhaps, critical comment on the way British letter writing can be perceived, here is a splendid balance quoted by Michael Korda in his biography of Lawrence of Arabia. In addressing the Sharif Hussein of Makkah, Sir Henry McMahon was constrained by Arabian custom to address the Sharif in the following terms.

> *To the excellent and well born Sayyed, the descendant of Sharifs, the Crown of the Proud, Scion of Muhammad's Tree and Branch of the Quraishite Trunk, him of the Exalted Presence and of the Lofty Rank, Sayyed son of Sayyed, Sharif son of Sharif, the Venerable, Honoured Sayyed, his Exellency the Sharif Hussein, Lord of the Many, Amir of Mecca the Blessed, the lodestar of the Faithful, and the cynosure of all devout Believers, may his blessing descend upon the people in their multitudes.*

Game, set and match to the Arabians!

Matters Sartorial

Very close to this British desire for written formality and correctness is their passion for being in the right dress for any particular occasion – uniform, dress or otherwise, white tie or black tie and so on. They stick to this set of rules like limpets and they have carried them around the world throughout which they steadfastly refuse to wear local costume, even though this has been evolved by the natives to provide both splendour and above all comfort. It is striking how Arabians faithfully don morning dress in the Royal Enclosure at Ascot, but the British stick to formal suiting while attending the races in Riyadh. There have been attempts at mingling in the past but these have not always been terribly successful. During the First World War some British officers reduced their Arabian colleagues to helpless mirth by putting Arabian headdress over the top of their solar topees. When the officer concerned then mounted a camel and bobbed up and down as the animal walked along, the Arabians' amusement changed to hysteria. This fun caused by sartorial mixing is not one-sided. The dignified arrival of the Sharif Abdullah in Jeddah to meet Sir Ronald Storrs was the occasion for some merriment. The Sharif was attired in a magnificent yellow silk headcloth, a white silk shirt and a camelhair cloak, sitting astride a magnificent white Arabian mare. The whole ensemble was set off by his rather ugly Turkish elastic-sided boots. Half a century later, wonderfully costumed and gold-bedaggered chieftains in South Arabia would turn up at Government House. Their orange and green Day-Glow socks spoiled it all. Particularly as they didn't appear to realise that socks went in pairs, and so they frequently wore one of each colour.

The British love to keep up appearances and, although things like dress codes are not much in vogue at the start of the 21st century, there was a time when they were the very core of existence. The British company Gellatly Hankey and Co. had dominated the Basra trade in Iraq for years until thrown out by the Baathist regime. It was discovered that in 1901 the six British employees then resident in Basra regularly sent their laundry to be done back at home in England. The laundry was packed into wicker baskets and sent across the river to Persia to get to a rail head. It then rushed on the train to the Edgware Road in London. Three weeks later it was back in Basra, wrapped in tissue paper and smelling of lavender.

Glencairn Balfour-Paul, who tells this story, was so tickled by it that on returning to his Embassy in Baghdad he told the Polish Ambassador about it expecting him to be surprised. Not at all. The Polish Ambassador said that before the Second World War all Polish officers sent their laundry to London. It was the only place where they could get their boiled evening shirts ironed properly. Later Balfour-Paul was in Aden where, despite the Communist government's ban on talking to foreigners under pain of arrest and interrogation, his taxi driver expressed the wish that the British would return. On being asked why, he replied that anything good in Aden they had from the

British. When asked what kind of things, the man answered 'things like walking on the pavement as opposed to the middle of the road, and ironing our trousers'. Empire and its legacy!

The Military

At RAF El Adem in Libya, eighteen miles inland from the coast, there happened to be a very, very bored airman in the Equipment Section. To relieve the tedium he idly filled in a requisition for a Lighthouse, and hid it in a pile of similar forms, secure in the knowledge that it had a good chance of getting through because his superior officer never read all the forms, just signed them as quickly as he could and scooted back to the bar. So, off everything went to London, where one can imagine the powers-that-be frantically checking a Philip's School Atlas. After all, it would be taxpayers' money that paid for the lighthouse, and its putative location must surely be marked on the atlas. A thoughtful person could have placed a dot by Tobruk and labelled it El Adem: right by the sea it clearly looked to be. This seemed to be the only feasible explanation. Accordingly, everything was arranged and a signal sent to RAF El Adem asking whether the Station Commander had prepared the site, as his lighthouse was ready for shipment.

The telephone lines from Tobruk to El Adem crossed the road at about the halfway mark. This, while making an interesting 'bridge' for helicopter pilots to fly under, was actually the work of an enterprising Royal Engineers officer. When instructed to erect the telegraph poles, he felt his men would respond to a bit of healthy competition that would make the work proceed more speedily, so he divided the men into two teams. One team would start in Tobruk and the other would set out towards the coast from El Adem. With military precision both teams were told to put the poles up on the left side of the road. It was not until they met (or didn't!) in the middle that they discovered what this actually meant in practice!

There is another anecdote concerning British military skill in the area. The Royal Air Force Regiment decided to test their navigation skills and two Land Rovers were needed for the exercise. One set out from Benghazi travelling eastwards and south of the Cyrenaican Mountains. The other set out from Tobruk in the opposite direction. So riveted were the two parties on their sun compasses, that even after traversing several hundred miles of desert, they managed to have a head-on collision.

****

A notably tense moment in Anglo-American relations once occurred in the Mediterranean. The American Sixth Fleet paid a courtesy call on Tobruk, and their Commodore and his Officers were entertained by the RAF at El Adem. The dining-in night in the Officers' Mess went well until about halfway through the meal, when the imbibing of strong drink brought to the surface feelings hitherto well under control, even unsuspected. It transpired that the one thing that got under the skin of the American Commodore was the sight of an Englishman, or Dot Dot Dash Limey as he himself might have put it. Simultaneously, it was discovered that the thing that really infuriated the Group Captain, an Australian, was the very mention of the United States. These two worthies were naturally sitting next to each other. This arrangement created a critical mass that suddenly exploded, and to the astonishment of all present the two men rose to their feet bellowing with rage and set to with a will. Assorted American and British junior officers leapt upon their superiors, and having parted them, sent the Group Captain back to his quarters and the Commodore back to his ship. Peace restored, dinner was successfully concluded and the remainder of the evening pleasantly and riotously completed with an exchange of mess games.

The British have an unrivalled reputation for doing things properly but, as Leslie McLoughlin reports, they too have had problems with flags. During the visit of the the head of the Iraqi Army, Taha Yassin Ramadan, to the UK in 1983 the Iraqi party was entertained at Sandhurst, where a number of Iraqi students were in training. The Vice-President was visibly impressed by the magnificence of the architecture and deeply affected by the sight of the Deputy Commander, who was wearing a kilt. However, on entering the dining room it was obvious that the flags on the top table were not those of Iraq. Leslie McLoughlin was able to gently point this out. With great steadiness, as it were, under fire, the Deputy Commander passed the information to the Mess Steward and the party was diverted to look at the portraits on the wall. By the time the party got to the table the Iraqi flags were correctly in place.

In 2011, the West still doggedly pursued a course beset with futility, failure and endless fatalities on all sides. Nevertheless, some incidents that took place contain a humorous element in the midst of the horrors of war.

As related by Frank Ledwidge in his book *Losing Small Wars*, in 2006 British troops in Basra embarked on Operation Sinbad. This was designed to regain control of parts of the city from the Shi'a insurgents of the Jaysh Al Mahdi, or Army of the Mahdi, who had largely taken over the city as well as the local police. This was to be done by 'pulsing' out for just forty-eight hours at a time from their defensive positions, and then constructing something useful with a view to influencing public opinion, before withdrawing to their positions. On one occasion it was thought that making a school playground would be just the thing to make the locals love the British. Accordingly the troops, in battalion strength, fought their way out of their own position, and in the short time available built a playground complete with swings and slides. The troops then fought their way back to their base.

During the night the playground was dismantled by the Jaysh Al Mahdi. That is, everything with the exception of the slides, which the Jaysh used as launch pads for their rockets to attack the British base! The humour of the situation was not lost on the British soldiers who, with typical black humour, renamed the operation Operation Spinbad. The final irony connected to this incident, and indeed to the rather less than glorious occupation of Basra, is that when the British troops did eventually withdraw to their base away from the city they were actually escorted out by the Jaysh Al Mahdi!

British Expatriates

I don't think I'll bother to go ashore, thanks. It doesn't look much of a place.
Donald Foster on Aden

Everyone in Cairo is so nice and friendly that we'll have to be nicer too. Do Arabs not only write backwards but think backwards too?
Hamish Balfour-Paul, aged 8

The Oddness of the British

Originally Aden Colony had been controlled by the Raj Government in India and the Brits working and living in the Colony developed a way of thought and living that reflected this. The ferocity of social protocols is exemplified by Lady Anne Blunt's account of events taking place when she and her husband boarded the British India ship *Ghoorka* at Suez in 1883. The other passengers were mostly Anglo-Indian tea planters and the aristocratic Lady Blunt was struck by the way these people constantly shouted 'Boy, Boy!' when they required attention. On their first day in the Red Sea she and her husband Wilfrid first sat sipping tea on deck, enjoying the early morning breeze. Later they went into lunch, Lady Anne wearing a fetching hat. She was handed a note by a servant which caused her no little amusement. It read, 'Madam you are requested not to appear at your meals in your hat and ladies are not allowed on deck before 8 o'clock. A compliance with the above rules is desired'.

In the thirties Evelyn Waugh visited and gave a most favourable report. He praised Aden above the African imperial possessions, but pointed out some pleasant incongruities. For instance the Aden Boy Scouts was a thriving organisation, but the Aden Arabs would not serve in the same patrol as the Aden Jews. However both attended the same events and would sit happily on opposite sides of the camp fire singing their own songs in turn. Amicably, they would frequently nevertheless join in with each other's choruses.

The social life in the colony was peaceful. It seems that the main event of interest during the week was a film show on a Thursday evening. Everyone entertained friends to dinner before the show, which was attended by the Resident who arrived in an official car, complete with pennant. He and his party took their places in the front row of wicker chairs arranged on the roof of the Seamen's Institute. Naturally everyone was in evening dress. The films shown were scarcely up to date: a Pathé News of the King Emperor going to Bognor Regis some twenty months previously, and an old running of the Grand National. The main film was a rather ancient comedy. However no one saw it as everyone fell fast asleep. Waugh comments that it was impossible in the Aden climate to remain both immobile and conscious. The evening's programme concluded with the playing of the National Anthem on a piano, which briskly woke everyone up. The audience then repaired to the club for beer, oysters and bridge. The great man betrayed perhaps his own views on things by expressing pleasant surprise that the Colony was bereft of what he considered to be the usual accompaniments of Empire – Mission Schools, Japanese and German salesmen, clinics, Prevention of Cruelty to Animals Inspectors and Fabian women collecting statistics.

The changeover of control to the Colonial Office in 1927 presaged the eventual demise of the Raj after the Second World War and initially made little difference to British attitudes. But the Resident did become a Governor. Despite the fact that the change meant that Aden lost its original *raison d'être*, it got a new lease of life as a bastion against the Soviet Union in the Cold War that then ensued. So, a visitor landing at the Prince of Wales Pier and turning to his right could have wandered for hours without seeing a single Arabian. The hills were dotted with the residences of senior military people, flaunting Union Jacks. The Victorian Gothic church only made concession to local geography by having slowly-whirling electric fans where its fellows in the UK had electric heating. Nearby be-shorted supporters cheered their football teams and the sound of bat on ball came from the matted cricket pitch.

It was to this part of the Colony that the annual Queen's Birthday Parade had been relocated for security reasons, to be less provocative to the locals. This event, starting in the cool of the early morning, attracted a gathering of the British Establishment. The ladies would be wearing their very best hats and gloves and Government officials would be arranged on their seats strictly in accordance with the Order of Precedence. Senior officers vied with the Roman Catholic bishop in splendour, the former in full dress uniform and swords, the latter in a white *soutane* set off by a fetchingly brilliant magenta silk sash. Colonial officials were no less splendidly accoutred. White drill uniforms with gold lace at the throat set off the white gloves, the medals, the buckskin shoes, and the sword. The whole outfit gorgeously, if ridiculously to our eyes nowadays, capped by a huge sun helmet.

In Aden there was one factor which tended to lend levity to the occasion. This was the fact that the climate meant that much of the finery tended to get nibbled by white ants and so on. One official had the tip of his scabbard fall off, leaving his calf open to being stabbed by the exposure of the naked blade within, not to mention the danger to his wife's dress. He solved the problem by impaling the point of his sword on a champagne cork.

The parade itself would have gladdened the heart of any film producer. Red turbaned policemen, green turbaned camel-borne lancers, black turbaned Federal Guardsmen all swept magnificently past the saluting base. There they saluted the Governor, with his hat bedecked with red and white cock's feathers. It is reported that this garish ornament was introduced when the Colonial Office discovered that these feathers were a powerful spell in Darkest Africa. The whole parade was moved encouragingly along by an Arabian band manfully playing *Sussex by the Sea* as loudly as they could. It was a tune played on every single official occasion giving rise to the unkind thought that they knew no other.

It goes without saying that due to the close involvement with the Indian Raj there was one institution in Aden that simply had to exist – the Union Club. As the days of British rule drew slowly to a close no other institution demonstrated the decay of Imperial power better than the Union Club. Wooden screens bleached by the sun hid the Bombay finials and Malabar tiles of the interior behind a sagging veranda. It was a prime example of a British club in the tropics, and would have been much admired by Somerset Maugham. A trellised entrance led to a creaking stair up the sides of which hung shabby unpainted noticeboards covered in tatty green baize. These displayed rather grubby notices, held in place with rusting drawing pins, that tiredly announced the details of recently-acquired library books, the dates of gymkhanas and polo matches, pleas from the British Legion for poppy sellers and the Women's Voluntary Service for volunteers to distribute milk powder to Arabian mothers, recommendations for nursemaids and the times of lessons in Scottish dancing in preparation for the Burns Night dinner. This fixation with Scottish dancing in fact outlasted the demise of Aden and eventually became a feature of British diplomatic life throughout the Middle East. Joining in the Eightsome Reel became a routine and dangerous cost of getting a drink at the Embassy.

At the Union Club in Aden a long veranda stretched from the top of the stairs and there was a wonderful view of the busy harbour through the iron balustrade that edged it. Behind the veranda was the dance floor and a run-down bar where the air conditioning didn't work. Everything about it was dowdy, but here met the British business community, the administrators from Government House and occasional military men. Here were held the St Andrew's Night bash, the Yacht Club dinner, and the Christmas Party, with Father Christmas arriving on anything from a camel to a fire engine.

Imperial splendour lingered too in the faded atmosphere of the Crescent Hotel. This verandaed hostelry was named after the Crescent in which it was built in 1932. This sort of half-moon of a bit of street was itself called Prince of Wales Crescent in commemoration of the visit of the future King Emperor, Edward VII, in 1875. On that auspicious occasion, as Prince of Wales, he was doubtless deeply gratified to be presented with no fewer than three ostriches. Sadly it is not recorded what became of these birds.

During the days of the fading grandeur of the Club and Aden's colonial life there were odd events which lightened life a bit. At one New Year's Eve fancy dress party the wife of the British Agent, Sir Kennedy Trevaskis, appeared dressed as a Belle of the South Seas. A now anonymous reveller set fire to her grass skirt.

A remnant of Raj-like society lingered too, in the form of the Khormaksar races, usually attended by the Sultan of Lahej and, of course, with the band playing *Sussex by the Sea*. And the whole rodomontade was fuelled by the little jealous competitions for Government House invitations, the catty put-downs, the one-upmanship of who went to which cocktail party, and all the gossip.

◇ ◇ ◇

The influence of Scotland also endured in the Gulf where, for some extraordinary reason, the Political Agent in Dubai had a bagpiper on his staff. Why this was so no one seems to know but Glencairn Balfour-Paul reports that during his term of office the piper, who came from Pakistan and played excruciatingly badly – and only a Scotsman could have been an accurate judge of that – would march up and down outside his bungalow, playing fit to burst. He accompanied his master on trek, and on one occasion when the tents and all comfort and dignity had been blown away by a tempest, the piper alone bestrode the beach at Khor Fakkan playing a Highland lament. Sadly Balfour-Paul's successor disestablished the piper. However, pipe bands are still favoured in the lower Gulf and though small Arabian soldiers with thin twinkling brown legs, kilts and bagpipes look almost risibly incongruous to Western eyes, they perform bravely on official occasions. It does seem that the music of the bagpipe resonates happily with the Arabian ear. In the Yemen they actually play very similar music.

> *You'll have to watch the Yemenis. They're very fly, you know.*
> **Margaret Thatcher**

◇ ◇ ◇

Perhaps the greatest British figure in Libya at the time of King Idris was the redoubtable Miss Britain, who lived in the Cyrenaican mountains in a house decorated internally with military murals painted by members of Rommel's army. Miss Britain looked after the King's bees, and had the reputation for being a fierce guardian of her charges and their produce. When Colonel Gaddafi ousted the monarch and the Libyans jumped from the frying pan to the fire, the Colonel, aware of her reputation, prudently waited a while before sending one of his officers to collect some honey. Miss Britain told the man to go to blazes. The honey belonged to King Idris and no one else would get so much as a spoonful. Years passed before Miss Britain left her post and retired to Syria and it was only then that Gaddafi got his hands on the honey.

The King was a charming, gentle and delightful man with a deeply-held religious faith. And he had a rather nice sense of humour. An Englishman was making a telephone call in Tobruk in the late 1950s and was inadvertently put through to His Majesty. On discovering who he was speaking to, the Englishman apologised profusely. King

Idris told him that it was a pleasure to talk to him but they had better continue while they had the chance, because it was an Arab exchange and the Englishman might never get through again when he wanted to!

****

The Sultan's brother and Deputy – known as a Naib – had been a tremendous raider into Yemen in his youth. Though short of stature, he had a tremendous presence and an unrivalled reputation for courage and loyalty. Once an Englishman with his wife and baby daughter visited the town above which the Naib lived in a small fort. Leaving their child in the care of the guest house manager, they took up an invitation to dine with the Political Officer. When they returned they were considerably alarmed to find that their daughter was missing.

They woke up the manager, who told them that the child had been crying; the Naib had heard her cries and sent out a servant to find out why the child was crying because, as the manager put it, the Naib forbade children to be unhappy. The manager had explained to the servant that it was an English baby, and its parents would be back before too long. On getting this information the Naib sent out an order for the manager to bring the child up to the fort, which he did. Accordingly the parents had to walk up the hill where they found their daughter happily playing with the Naib's young son and covered from head to foot in chocolate.

The following day the Naib astonished everyone by defecting to the anti-Federation cause.

Some years later the Naib finally settled in Saudi Arabia, and the Saudi Minister of Defence thought he would be an ideal person to lead a Front for the Liberation of the Occupied Yemeni South, an organisation that would cause trouble for the communist government that had replaced the British. Accordingly the Naib was instructed to recruit a thousand men, who would be paid three riyals a day. About three years passed before the Minister of Defence suddenly announced an intention to inspect this deadly force. The Naib was deeply worried as, naturally, he hadn't actually recruited anyone, and had done quite nicely living off a million riyals a year.

As luck would have it, he met his earlier English visitor in a hotel in Jeddah and explained his difficulty. What really concerned him was not the lack of men. There would be no difficulty in getting hold of a thousand men for the day, but they would have no uniforms. And there was the added complication that as he had no men he wouldn't know what sizes of uniform to buy. His English friend comforted the Naib by telling him that there was no need for uniforms as the Front was a guerrilla force, and was supposed to merge into the landscape. The Naib, with no little relief, accepted this argument but felt that it was imperative that the men carry some sort of identification. His friend suggested that a badge of some kind would fit the bill and told the Naib that he would telephone a pal of his in London to see what could be found quickly.

London came up with the fact that there were about two thousand Metropolitan Police hat badges available at an auction of government surplus equipment in Essex the following day. With no time to lose the Naib's friend told London to buy the lot and ship them out to Jeddah with all speed. They came out by air freight in a couple of days, but the Naib was distraught when he saw them, because the wording on the badges was in English. However there was nothing else available and all hope was put into the knowledge that the Saudi Minister of Defence was very short-sighted, and if the badges were put on the Yemenis' turbans upside down all would be well. The Naib departed southwards for the Yemen with the heavy box of badges in the back of his Toyota. It was some three or four weeks before the Naib met up with his friend again. Asked how things had gone, the beaming Naib answered that everything had gone off splendidly. The

Minister had been deeply impressed and had doubled the size of the army, and additionally had doubled their pay. In the circumstances the Englishman insisted that the Naib pay for dinner that night.

Arabs in Britain

Sheikh Shakhbut of Abu Dhabi was the only Ruler from the Trucial States to be invited to the Coronation in 1953 and as such attracts a further dubious anecdote which deserves attention. It was said that like all the other Rulers he knew about impending events in London, but he received no invitation. Shakhbut forcefully demanded to know the reason why he had not been asked to attend. The reason was actually simple enough; in those days the Trucial States were notable only for their insignificance. A century earlier when the area was mentioned to the great Foreign Secretary Lord Palmerston, he had to ask for a map as he had never heard of the Trucial Coast, its inhabitants or anything about them, Indian Empire or no Indian Empire; and nothing much had changed since that time. Consequently it was not thought important at all that any of the Rulers should be invited to the Coronation of Queen Elizabeth II. Shakhbut would not accept this idea and loudly demanded to grace the august occasion with his presence. He made so much noise about it that HMG gave in and sent him an invitation. A couple of peeresses were squashed up a bit in the Abbey seating plan, and another gilt chair inserted in the gap with Shakhbut's name on it.

The Ruler of Abu Dhabi duly arrived at Heathrow to be met and welcomed by a tall young Englishman in a pinstriped suit. Sheikh Shakhbut looked up at him and politely asked how he was related to the Queen. Embarrassed, the young man replied that he was not related to Her Majesty in any way. Shakhbut was mortified and explosively retorted that he had not expected to be met personally by the Queen herself but had expected that at least some other member of the Royal Family would fill in for her. Then his eye fell on a plane on the other side of the tarmac and he decided that, following what he thought of as an insult, he could not possibly remain in England a moment longer he asked where the other aeroplane was going. He was informed that it was due to fly to Paris.

'Right' said Shakhbut, 'I shall go to Paris'. And to Paris he went; within the hour. On arrival he booked into one of the very best hotels and, having informed the management that he was the guest of the British Government, he was shown into a beautiful suite of rooms. Here for the first time in his life he met modern plumbing and delightedly put all the plugs in the basins, and the bath, and then gleefully turned on all the taps. Remembering the reputation of Paris for night time activities and frivolity, he also decided to go out on the town, which he did at once with no little enthusiasm and enormous expectations.

Rather early the following morning Shakhbut returned to his hotel, tired and in need of a bed of his own. He was met by a furious management. The basins and bath in his suite had overflowed. Water had gushed down the stairs and a priceless plaster ceiling in the dining room had collapsed onto the heads of the diners. Shakhbut, taking all this in, demanded to be taken to another and dry hotel at once, as his was now so wet he would clearly catch his death of pneumonia if he stayed in it a moment longer. As his bags were being packed the management produced an enormous bill. Sheikh Shakhbut waved it away, saying that the British would pay. They did.

✦ ✦ ✦

There is a second account of this incident, which probably has greater veracity than the foregoing. Sheikh Shakhbut was actually in the United Kingdom at the time of the Coronation, but only to receive medical treatment from an extremely eminent physician, amongst whose other patients were the inhabitants of Buckingham Palace. While the Ruler of a small barren patch of desert in the Lower Gulf would not normally be considered eligible to get an invitation to the Coronation, it was felt in official circles that, as he was already here, it would be churlish not to invite him. Space was made, it is understood, by shrinking the necessarily generous space allotted to Queen Salote of Tonga, so that a slim Sheikh and an equally slim companion could be fitted in. Queen Salote, referred to by some as the Cannibal Queen, figured in the Coronation story a bit later too. She was accompanied in her carriage by the diminutive Sultan of Zanzibar, a cousin of the Sultan of Oman. Famously, when Noel Coward was asked by a friend who was in the carriage with Her generously-proportioned Majesty, Coward retorted, 'Lunch'.

However, when the great day came the spaces devoted to Shakhbut and his companion remained empty. Enquiries led to the discovery that Sheikh Shakhbut had received information from a reliable source that the prominent doctor who was to treat him had been bribed by the Saudis to poison him. So the Sheikh fled, indeed to France. Here he put up at one of the best Paris hotels. After the exertions of the journey Shakhbut wanted a bath, but when one of his retainers turned on the taps the water ran cold. Having been told about the problem Sheikh Shakhbut did what any self-respecting desert man would do. He ordered his people to collect firewood. This they obediently did by dint of digging up the parquet floor with their daggers, and then lighting a fire under the bath to heat up the water. Finding that by luck they had some wood over they lit another fire in the sitting room of the suite and proceeded to brew up some coffee. As they all relaxed over their brew they failed to notice that as they hadn't turned off the taps, the bath was overflowing and this had extinguished the fire under the bath. The water then soaked through the floor into the rooms beneath, and the coffee party was rudely interrupted by the arrival of excited hotel staff. The inability of the hotel management to speak Arabic meant that it was not easy for Shakhbut to give a satisfactory explanation. He therefore had to leave in some haste. However, he was able to finish his trip safely and satisfactorily in Egypt.

****

The Ruler of the small Trucial State of Ajman paid a visit to the UK and was put up in a smart Park Lane hotel in London with his family and entourage. After a few days the cramped town atmosphere bore down sorely on people who were used to the huge Arabian skies at home; and who missed their usual facilities for making coffee. Accordingly the elderly Sheikh, who sported a magnificent white beard, decided to hire some twenty taxis. Into these were packed forty-odd people complete with coffee, coffee pots and cups, and all the makings. The Sheikh instructed the drivers to go out into the country to find a suitable spot, but he omitted to tell anyone – government officials or hotel management – what he was intending. The whole cavalcade then proceeded in a stately fashion until they reached a rural part of Kent. Seeing a nice large grass verge with a convenient source of firewood nearby, the Sheikh called a halt and, after everyone had disembarked, he sent the taxis back; fondly believing that replacements would be readily available.

Everything went splendidly and soon several fires were burning well, and the pots of coffee came to the boil. At this point the local policeman cycled by, and seeing what he took to be a party of gypsies – what else could these strange people be? – he dismounted and told them to move on. The Ruler of Ajman rose to offer hospitality to what he supposed to be a guest, but as neither he nor any of his family or anyone else in the party spoke any English, an impasse was quickly reached. Accordingly the Ajman party smiled and sat down again. Flummoxed, the policeman remounted his machine and rode as fast as he could to his police station and telephoned for assistance. A number of police cars now arrived at the picnic site, and one supposes that sign language let the Ruler understand that he and his party should get into the cars. This they did and all were safely conveyed to the police station, which could scarcely contain all of them, and, of course, the coffee pots.

It was about now that the Foreign Office, having sent their man round to the hotel to see if the Ruler of Ajman needed anything, discovered that he had disappeared, and no one in the hotel had any idea where he and his party had gone.

To lose a Ruler who was in a Treaty Relationship with the British Crown was, if not careless, then extremely embarrassing. However, it soon dawned on the Kent Police that their 'gypsies' were foreigners and not gypsies at all, and enquiries were made further up the chain of command. Luckily the Foreign Office had put out a call to Scotland Yard to help them find their missing Ruler, and it wasn't too long before two and two were put together, and twenty more taxis were sent winging their way into Kent.

Once, the Political Agent of the day arranged for Sheikh Muhammad Al Sharqi of Fujairah to visit the UK. The part of this plan that most interested Sheikh Muhammad concerned the number of guns that would be fired in salute on his arrival – a matter about which the Brits had long ago drawn up a detailed and comprehensive lump of bureaucracy to cover every possible sort of Ruler and occasion.

Investigation of the Foreign Service Instructions on state visits elicited the rather sad information that the Sheikh of Fujairah was entitled to only one gun. This was a bit embarrassing as the Political Agent himself was, when visiting a Sheikhdom possessed of ceremonial artillery, entitled to eleven. Nevertheless the Political Agent asked the Sheikh how many guns he would actually like. The surprising answer was, a hundred and forty four! It turned out that the reason for this number was that this was the precise quantity of shots that the Royal Navy had let loose on Sheikh Muhammad's father's fort while purportedly suppressing piracy.

During the tumultuous years leading up to British withdrawal from Aden and the Protectorates it was felt by the Colonial government in Aden that part of their difficulties was that the British people simply didn't know anything about the place, and were blissfully unaware of what was going on. It was decided that what was needed was a public relations exercise, and accordingly a small team was put together to go to England to put matters right. The wife of the Chief Minister of Aden was sent to charm the Women's Institutes and Mothers' Unions up and down the land with exciting recipes making goat taste delicious. Youth was to be educated and thrilled by a slim young Adeni guitarist accoutred in the tightest jeans imaginable. The world of business was to be intrigued and excited by a prominent Adeni businessman.

As PR exercises go, this was certainly a good thing at its inception. However, it was not realised that the businessman was a hypochondriac of a fanatic and dedicated kind. He had two very impressive briefcases. One was filled with pills to take continuously and a bit complicatedly, and the second was full of more pills which were antidotes to those in the first case, lest he made a mistake in any of the dosages. Chambers of Commerce throughout the land were truly astonished, but the impression given to British business could not be described as very businesslike. Every meeting began with a briefcase being dramatically opened on the table. The businessmen looked expectant. The Adeni asked for a glass of water and shovelled in pills, then panicked as he had forgotten which ones he had taken. The second case was thrown open and antidotes followed the first lot. No deals were struck!

Meanwhile the Adeni pop star also caused a sensation other than the one intended. He was accommodated in a Park Lane hotel as befitted the importance of his mission to British youth. He attended sundry gigs, radio stations and so on, and everyone was polite and distantly encouraging, even though he played excruciatingly badly. But it was his accommodation that really caused a problem. He had to be moved every day. The trouble was that the freedoms of life in the English capital were a lot freer and more available than those found in Aden. Outraged hotel managements objected strongly to the way he ordered breakfast for five every morning – one for himself and four more for the ladies of the night he had brought back with him when returning from the previous evening's appointments. A British official was heard to remark that the lad's jeans were clearly so tight that it was actually impossible for him to keep It in his trousers.

All hopes were pinned on the successful return of the First Minister's wife, who had been all over the place exchanging recipes and knitting notes. It so happened that the First Minister himself was in town talking to Duncan Sandys at Lancaster House. The conference concluded, the parties arranged themselves decoratively on the steps for the obligatory photograph. As the assembled press raised their cameras there came a wild shriek from the potted palms as the First Minister's wife leapt out, and started to belabour her husband with her umbrella. No one had noticed that the couple were going through what would be described with typical British understatement as an acrimonious and bloodstained divorce. It took quite a lot of time and, doubtless, money to recover the photographs from an entranced press corps.

Duncan Sandys was a great supporter of the Rulers of the Federation of South Arabia but he did like to keep discussions going well into the night, sometimes past eleven or twelve o'clock The Federal Minister of the Interior, Sharif Hussein of Bayhan, found this a little irritating. As he remarked to Sir Kennedy Trevaskis, Governor of Aden, who asked him if the Rulers needed any help in the evening, the Sharif replied that he and the Rulers appreciated the advice and help they received during the day but they had better advisers at night! The Sharif had a great sense of humour and on one occasion, at the Reception that was usually put on for the Rulers when they came to London, everyone else was smartly dressed in suits, but the Sharif arrived late in full South Arabian regalia – turban, kilt and dagger – with a very obvious professional lady on his arm. He stalked majestically up to Duncan Sandys and hugely enjoyed the embarrassment that this accompanying vision of the night occasioned as she was introduced.

These occasions were used by the British government to provide training for young diplomats who had recently joined the Foreign Service. Just emerged from the comforts of an Oxford education, they were let loose amongst the inheritors of two thousand years of South Arabian shenanigans. Like lambs, into the wolf cage they were thrown. Their elders, knowing that appearance was everything, served only orange and tomato juice at the reception. However, also knowing that their important guests liked a bit of a strengthener, they had stashed encouraging bottles in the gents' loo. Several of the innocent lambs were heard to wonder aloud that the frequent visits of the wolves to the loo must be because, as England's climate was colder than that of their homeland, the bladders of the wolves needed more frequent emptying than might have been thought usual.

PART THREE

LANGUAGE

Poetry about Arabia

Aden
by James Nash

1
Late sun restores the hills' contorted form
That midday bleached of colour, depth and line.
Sharp tongues of light
Now curl about the tomb whose lime-washed dome,
Bright half ellipse amid small fields of green,
Has stood for a millennium or two
To celebrate an ancient saint or sage,
A priest-king of an unremembered age,
Once he controlled a thriving incense trade
From towered cities at the desert's edge,
Where caravans of myrrh
Were halted, measured and assessed for tolls,
Till anarchy regained its old estate
And hungry nomads scoured the tumbled stones
In hope of gold the ruins might reveal,
Or some fine agate carved into a seal.
But surely he enjoyed the evening breeze
While sitting, as did I, among good friends,

Lean, dark men sinewed like taut springs,
Quick moving, nervous, garrulous as birds,
With bubbling laughter welling up within
At all our own absurdities.
Did he not love the evening light that fills
With reds and blues and saffrons, those stark hills

2

September, overburdened with the heat,
Makes moving of a limb an act of will.
Now patience cracks, the storms
Of blinding temper and the sand
Obliterate both landscape and the mind;
Exposure flays, the darkest recess fills
With dust and anger till pursuing rain
Restores men's reason and the land again.
But even blessings here have darker sides,
The land gives nothing but it claims its fee;
For life renewing floods
Revive vendettas that have run decades
And spill fresh blood to mingle with the old
In feuds of ownership of barren fields.
Neither your spells, old king, nor my vain threats
Could stop the killing that this land begets.
Old images persist. The snake-like files
Of hillmen, armed, dark stained with indigo,
Those twisting lines of blue,
Converging from surrounding mountainsides
To hector, parley or perhaps to pledge

A doubtful loyalty to their amir:
Their chanted rhymes of tribal escapades
Crescendo with the shouts, the fusillades.
The fear, the waiting for the raids, do you
Remember that? Seeing the work of years,
A small prosperity,
Built hand on hand, dissolving in the flames?
Yet those old battles had their recompense,
Intensity, an exultation, just to be alive;
The reputation and the pride it gave.
Old king, it must be quiet in the grave.

3
Yet did we wish to change those wilder ways,
The pride that soared with kite and lammergeyer
In knife-edged days,
When young men sought to etch an honoured name
Upon recited epics of the tribe?
We tried to force on anarchy a form,
To press amorphous dust into a mould,
Half hoping that the pattern would not hold,
Though one apart, I also loved this land
With passion just as potent as your own,
Wept for dead friends, your heirs,
And was consoled by brothers of your tribe.
Now what remains? Some fading photographs,
Curled sepia memories of past beliefs,
Whose truths are tangled into fairy tales
And turn to myths as recollection fails.

The Tribal Poets
by James Nash

How many times I heard those poets feud,
Hurling quatrains like javelins
That gleamed with waspish insult as they flew,
Each shaft applauded by the waiting crowd
Gathered to hear their gladiators' words.
Word warriors, masters of lunge,
Of metric parry and ancient form,
They fought their ritual combats with their rhymes.

Poor poets, none were destined to survive;
Caught in the harsher battles that ensued,
They died in nameless back streets, on bare hills,
But I have kept the rhythm of their songs,
The songs we used to sing as we rode home,
Through fine embalming dust that lapped,
Enshrouded us, like strangely merry ghosts,
As we rode laughing, singing slowly home.

Ode to Al Sayyid Mohammad Idris Al Sanusi, Ancestor of King Idris
Soluk, August 1944

Professor Dr Edward Evans-Pritchard to Captain Alastair MacIntosh, Resident Adviser in Mukalla, Eastern Arabian Protectorate

You have waited long for the sun to shine again on tent and palm and herds,
where once
Your forebears of the Holy Prophet's line, the Mahdi and the Grand Sanusi,
trod
Through lives of contemplation and of prayer, the Sufi's mystic rose strewn
road to God
While Ahmad 'gainst three European Powers raised high- in challenge the
Khalifa's sword,
Less tempestuous, you, counting the hours in exile, waited till divine decree
Determined a more favourable course; then headed boldly for the open sea.
Brave hearts that followed the Sanusi star to its far setting, see it rise again:
Al-Kisih, al-Ataiwish, al Abbar, and many a Shaikh of lineage, share
Your tardy triumph and the applause won long ago, on a scaffold, over there.
We too salute you, we from northern shores. Your fight became ours, in your
friendly land
We have shed our blood, mingled it with yours, and to your country where
our sons have bled
We entrust what are to us most precious, our English freedom and our
English dead.

Misunderstandings about Arabic

So bad are the English at speaking other people's languages that it has almost become a matter of national pride to refrain from having anything to do with the idea.

It has been reported that the early British military maps of the Sudan have an interesting feature – all the mountains have the same name! The reader can imagine the scene. The British officer marching across the desert in voluminous shorts getting his triangulations right. He consults his phrasebook and asks the local carrying the striped pole what the mountain is called. 'This is *Jebel* [Mountain] *Ma'araf ismu* [I don't know its name].' Getting the same reply every time, he doubtless feels that his opinion of the locals is confirmed. The poor simple chaps, fancy having only one name for all their mountains.

It is a sad fact that very few Englishmen are or have been fluent in Arabic. Some mistakenly feel they have great fluency. Thus a Brit will roar at his servant, *'Ya walad jibli wahid whisky wa soda and be bloody sari-a about it'*. I suppose every reader will have understood the instruction even if they don't know a word of Arabic. However, the speaker, because a glass of Scotch arrives at the double, felt that his Arabic must be perfect. It never occurred to the poor soul that the servant had learnt what the Sahib wanted and thought that he himself understood English!

In practice this often led to the creation of a special sort of interpreter. This was an Arabian who learned what the fractured language of the Englishman meant, and then quietly translated it into proper Arabic, for the house boy, driver, clerk etc to understand. The British attitude to the language of the natives was deeply ingrained. As early as 1903 it is related by no less an authority than the egregious Wilfrid Blunt, that the British Adviser to the Ministry of Instruction in the Egyptian government refused to have under him any Englishman who spoke a word of Arabic. He was of the opinion that any such knowledge would give the young men romantic ideas about the natives, and lead to them explaining what they taught the natives in Arabic, instead of forcing them to speak English.

Precision in all things! Leslie McLoughlin reports that while representing the Oxford University Press in the Middle East from his house in Cairo he was horrified, over breakfast one morning, to read in *The Egyptian Gazette* that the editors of the Concise Oxford English Dictionary had, in the latest edition, defined a Palestinian as 'a person seeking to remove Israel from Palestine'. The editorial in the *Gazette* furiously demanded a boycott of all OUP books throughout the Arab World. Luckily it proved possible to remove the offending text immediately.

There is a story from the Aden Protectorates which, while possibly a bit exaggerated, is also a good warning to people who make assumptions.

When important visitors came out to Aden from the UK they were provided with an Arabic speaker in case they met an Arab who couldn't speak English. Such visitors were always very keen to encourage 'the chaps on the ground', and were always exceptionally friendly to them. On one occasion a senior High Tory MP came out and, as was the custom, was introduced to a Sultan. Because he had an interpreter handy, the great man assumed that the Sultan couldn't speak English and as he settled against the cushions in the Reception Room he said to the interpreter in loud but avuncular tones, in order to be matey, 'Well, I suppose we ought to find out what the young wog wants, eh?'

Knowing that the Sultan was just back from Oxford, the interpreter, with all speed, said to the Sultan in Arabic, 'Your Highness, Sir Tiddle-Tiddle wishes to express his deep appreciation of the honour paid to him by being received by Your Highness'. The Sultan responded, also in Arabic, 'You know perfectly well that isn't what the old fool said at all'. The interpreter, turning to the MP said, 'His Highness, not wishing to appear rude by contradicting his distinguished guest, nevertheless wants to say that, on the contrary, it is he and his people who are honoured by the visit of such an eminent person'. The MP said, 'He didn't say as much as that'. The interpreter then explained to the MP that courtesies in Arabic, when translated into English, were much more long-winded than they at first appeared. He then addressed the Sultan saying, 'Sir Tiddle-Tiddle was deeply touched by the Sultan's gracious courtesy'. In Arabic the Sultan replied, 'You are doing a splendid job, but I don't know how much longer I can keep this up with a straight face'. The MP asked what it was the Sultan had just said. Fighting to hold on to the gravity of the situation, if any was left, the interpreter said, 'His Highness, and his people, are always gratified for any opportunity to strengthen the already strong bond between them and the great British people'.

The MP expressed his thanks and the Sultan, trying hard to suppress a fit of the giggles, indicated that it was time to have lunch. Coping with eating bits of sheep and rice without the benefit of cutlery fortunately curtailed further conversation. However, over dinner at Government House subsequently, Sir Tiddle-Tiddle did tell the Governor that he thought the Sultan was a charming and merry soul because he laughed a lot!

The fact that an interpreter's life is actually not that easy is wonderfully illustrated by a tale related by Leslie McLoughlin. He tells how the little Arabic word 'yaani' can cause a difficulty or two. It means 'it means', but has many other connotations, such as 'er', 'what I mean to say is', 'I'm not saying yes and I'm not saying no' and, importantly, 'I'm not sure I agree'. On one occasion of interpreting at No. 10 Downing Street between a Saudi Prince and Mrs Thatcher, the interpreter on the Arab side was a Saudi whose use of language was wonderfully sonorous and orotund. During the exchange Mrs Thatcher elicited the simple reply 'yaani' from the Prince. The British Arabists leant forward, eager not to miss how the Saudi interpreter would render this little word. He said, 'Having regard to all the circumstances and taking into account the probable ramifications of what you have suggested we would prefer to reserve our position'. *Yaani* indeed!

Linguistic matters have naturally played an important role in relations between the Arab World and the British. One of the nicest from the point of view of the British is the way in which, during the heady days of President Nasser's career, Egyptian propaganda had rather less impact on the Sultanate of Oman and the Trucial States than might have been expected. The reason is that throughout the Middle East the word *misri* means an Egyptian. In Oman and the Trucial States it means a donkey. Despite this, Egyptian propaganda did have some effect and a little girl on the beach at Khor Fakkan warned the Political Agent to 'watch out or Abdalnasir will get you'.

When Queen Elizabeth visited Aden in 1954, naturally there would have to be a speech to welcome her. It was decided that Sultan Salih Al Qu'aiti from the Eastern Aden Protectorate, being the most senior Ruler, should deliver the welcoming speech in Arabic, while the Sultan of Lahej read the address in English. However, the rendering of Her Majesty's title of Defender of the Faith in the Arabic form gave rise to a lot of concern. The Faith referred to was of course that of the Church of England and the text of the speech had consequently been the subject of a huge amount of revision and counter-revision, with the British authorities adamant that this title of hers, along with her other titles, must be translated in full without any modification. This course would possibly give offence locally and there were two views as to what should be done. One was to leave the title out altogether. The other was that the faith of which she was the Defender should be specified. Agreement was reached to use the second option. However in the confusion the approved version only surfaced just prior to the delivery of the speech itself, so that in the event Sultan Salih failed to notice this decision and accordingly gave the speech, loud and clear, in its original text which was relayed by loudspeaker to all corners of the Colony. Yet such was the respect that the Sultan commanded as a scholar, above all of Islamic jurisprudence, that the *faux pas* passed completely unnoticed by the general public, and with Sultan Salih likewise unaware, until much later, that he had made it.

In an effort to encourage business from the Kingdom, Air France decided to paint the company name on their aircraft in Arabic. The reader should know that the classical Arabic for penis is '*air*' – and an aeroplane is roughly the right shape, isn't it? A saintly and elderly merchant was watching the comings and goings of the planes at Jeddah's old International Airport when a French plane landed, and its logo, Air Faransa, was brazenly paraded for all to see, despite the fact that Arabic has a perfectly good word for 'airline'. The old man caustically remarked, with a twinkle in his eye, that this was progress indeed.

The French, though having a long colonial association with North Africa and the Lebanon (which should perhaps have given them some familiarity with the language) also had another problem – with a record sleeve. The hit song *Ya Mustapha* appeared in a sleeve cunningly and decoratively covered in Arabic script. The only problem was that the script concerned was simply copied from an Arabic leaflet which, unfortunately, no one had thought to translate. It was one issued by Algerian terrorists and in essence exhorted its readers to shoot every Frenchman they met! Due to the immense popularity of the song the terrorist leaflet was widely distributed, not just in the Middle East, but globally.

However, the French are by no means the only ones to suffer in this way. Sweden's Saab cars did not enjoy huge sales in Arabian lands. Saab means 'difficult' in Arabic.

The English, too, have made several quite impressive errors of this sort. One concerns the book *Colloquial Arabic (Levantine)* by Leslie McLoughlin. This was produced in 2002 by Routledge with a cover showing a map demonstrating that the Levant was made up of Lebanon, Syria and Palestine. The publishers tactfully sent this map to the Syrian Embassy for agreement. The response was explosive. It transpired that the map used a border between Syria and Turkey totally unacceptable to the former. Accepting it would mean agreeing with the border laid down in 1939 to appease Turkey at the expense of Syria. However, and most deliciously, the publishers sent Leslie McLoughlin a replacement design devoid of contentious borders. Instead it was a picture of a peaceful street scene in an Arabian city. Men in Arabian headdress walked with dignity in front of a wall. On the wall was some attractive Arabic writing. It said, 'Do Not Urinate Here'.

****

King Idris of Libya disapproved of the new Algerian President, Ben Bella. The President was driving eastwards up the coast to Egypt to see President Nasser, and stopped in Tobruk on the way. After an exchange of courtesies and the consumption of tea, the President sped on his way and someone asked King Idris what he had thought of his guest. The King replied that he didn't think very much of him, and felt that the man had no right to be the President of an Arab country because (being happier with French) he couldn't speak Arabic properly.

The State of Sharjah, like Fujairah, was also once divided into three bits, and its distinguished ruling family divided into two branches. One branch ruled Sharjah itself, the other ruling Ras Al-Khaimah, the Headland of the Tent. The bits of Sharjah were called Kalba, Khor Fakkan and Dibba, which last was completely separated from the other two and situated on the far side of the mountains, on the Gulf of Oman. This led an early Ruler of Sharjah to style himself on his visiting cards, quaintly, as 'Ruler of Sharjah and its Independencies'. His successor corrected this to 'Dependencies'.

****

At this point it might be possible, without too much risk, to mention that Thani in Arabic is a derivative of the root for the numeral two. One would never mention this in Qatar, of course, but being called the Al Thani can imply a potentially insulting second place in life – an insult much used by the rest of the Arab world, of course! The Qataris as a whole are anyway referred to by the rest of the Gulf as Awlad Liftons, that is 'Children of Lipton' (there is no equivalent for the letter 'p' in Arabic), because the black rope holding their headdress in place has two long tails resembling a teabag hanging down the back. Omanis however are referred to as the Awlad Television – because the tie at the throat of their *dishdashas* looks like a little television aerial. Naturally the inhabitants of the Gulf, demonstrating the close-knit unity of their really quite small community, have other rude things to say about the people of Qatar who are reckoned to be country bumpkins. Captain R.E. Cheesman records that, during his voyage down the west coast of Qatar into Salwa Bay in 1921, the first by a Westerner, Saudi Bedouin travelling with him expressed their opinion of the Qataris by picking up a pinch of sand and blowing it off the palm of their hand. In Bahrain they have the joke that concerns a definition of waste. They say that waste is when a six-seater vehicle goes over a cliff with only five Qataris in it! Recent discoveries of more oil and gas in Qatar combined with the current financial difficulties in Dubai have doubtless combined to wipe these sneers off their neighbour's faces.

British Arabic

Charles Belgrave, when Political Adviser in Bahrain, records what happens when an Arabian uses an Arabic word that an Englishman mistakes for an English one. The Arabic for 'Adviser' is '*Mustashar*'. An Englishman, clearly in the imperial mould, arrived in Bahrain by boat and took a taxi to Mr Belgrave's house. The driver said he knew where the Mustashar's house was. The Englishman angrily responded that he didn't want to see a Mr Shaw but wanted Mr Belgrave. Once again, and indeed again and again, the driver repeated that he knew perfectly well where the Mustashar's house was. On arrival the furious passenger asked Charles Belgrave, 'Who's this ruddy fellow Mr Shaw the driver kept on about?'

Colonel Boustead had many abilities, but his linguistic skills led to confusion at times, particularly where his Arabic was concerned. He used to stay at English country houses when he was on leave and would garner information from the staff that he felt might be useful in the Hadramaut. It is said that on one occasion he got instructions on how to make a compost heap from a gardener he met sweeping up leaves in early autumn. The man told the Colonel how to gather all the leaves into a heap and periodically turn them over.

Armed with this information, he returned to the Protectorate and at once issued instructions to all the farmers to collect their fallen palm leaves into piles, and then to turn the heaps over. Incongruously to local ears the Colonel got the word for 'turn it over' a bit askew, and it came out as 'inklyboo it', when it should have been *inqallabihi*. The reader who has no Arabic will doubtless get the sense of it. After the farmers of the Wadi Hadramaut had spent a year or so tossing palm leaves frantically into the air the British government sent out an agricultural adviser. This worthy was horrified, as it appears that this is quite the wrong thing to do. The Colonel was forced to issue another instruction and this was 'Un-inklyboo it'. The first year was referred to as the Year of the Inklyboo, and was naturally followed by the Year of the Uninklyboo.

To be fair, the Colonel had learnt his Arabic in the Sudan, where the language is somewhat different, and on another occasion he caused surprised offence due to a misuse of the words for mosquitoes and honour. When used for the insect the word has a plural collective sense. When used for honour there is a proper and different plural. The Colonel told a meeting of very honour-conscious tribesmen in the Wadi Hajar that he was pleased to hear that they had got rid of their honour! They were much offended, not appreciating that the excellent Colonel thought he was talking about mosquitoes.

Mosquitoes are sucking
My blood like sweet wine,
And hey noddy-noddy
They merrily sing

How nimbly they're plucking,
These minstrels divine!
Their lute is my body,
Each vein is a string.
Al Sumaisir of Cordoba, 11th century

Misunderstandings about English

Much far to the south of El Adem in Libya, close to the border with Egypt, lies the oasis of Al Jaghbub. Here is the tomb of the late King's grandfather, the Grand Sanusi. It was also the place where a Libyan Government meteorologist fulfilled his function. Twice a day he inflated a large balloon and released it over the Sahara. This gentleman had been batman to a Second World War British officer, who was in the habit of greeting any English visitors by saying, 'I say, how frightfully nice of you to call. You will be staying to luncheon, won't you?' The batman thought that this was simply an expanded English greeting meaning 'Hello'. Consequently many an unsuspecting visitor often sat until after sundown waiting in vain for a meal that never came.

****

How could anyone accuse the nation that invented cricket of perfidy? There are times when circumstantial evidence does give some of our closest friends cause to wonder. In the 1960s the government of Kuwait was encouraged by the British Council to send some five hundred young Kuwaitis to England to learn English. Two hundred and fifty were sent to Glasgow and the other half were confidently despatched to Cardiff. All went well, everyone passed their exams and so returned joyfully home. It was at this point that suspicions began to emerge. The ones who went to Cardiff couldn't understand a word the ones who went to Glasgow uttered, and vice versa. It was mooted that this was all part of a nasty plot to divide the Emirate into two – the Welsh Kuwaitis and the Scots Kuwaitis. Incidentally, the Kuwaitis tend to pronounce their 'k's' as 'ch's' – thus Kirk becomes Church. What can be made of that?

PART FOUR

SOME KEY PERSONALITIES

Arabians

Oh, Mankind surely we have created you from a male and a female, and made you into tribes and families, that you may know each other.
Interpretation of Quran 49:13

Every Arab considers himself worthy to rule and it is rare to find one of them submitting to another, be it his father or brother or head of his clan.
Ibn Khaldun, 14th-century Arab historian

The Imam Ahmad Bin Yahya Hamid Al Din, Ruler of Yemen

The great Caliphs of the Abbasid dynasty had titles like Al Muwaffaq, God Aided; or Al Rashid, God Guided; or Al Mu'tazz, God Empowered. A blood-soaked and ruthless conqueror once asked Joha what his title should be. 'You should be God Forbid', replied Joha.

In the theatre of history Imam Ahmad will star in the role of the last of the well-bred tyrants, being a descendant of the Prophet Muhammad. It was against his medieval and excessively firm rule that the revolution of September 1962 was mounted. However, the old devil was cunning to the end and died a few days before the revolution against him actually broke out.

He had a predilection for ruling by dint of sending out his orders by telegram, and his forthright and at times somewhat profligate use of the ultimate penalty to maintain control was as famous as it was quixotic. During the visit of the then Governor of Aden, Sir William Luce, in 1959, the Aden party was to meet the Director of Protocol, Ali Raji, at the airfield. Ali failed to turn up and several reasons were given. He wasn't well, his daughter had fallen out of a window, and so on. Later in the day Ali turned up for tea at the British Legation saying that he had had a cold. However, it later transpired that actually he had been in prison during the morning and he was going back there after tea, the reason being that the previous day he and his brother had got drunk and they had tried to kill each other. Apparently he was sentenced to two weeks in the clink and at the end of that time would be released to resume his duties as Director of Protocol.

Ali Raji had a tendency to get into trouble. In 1952, during an attempted coup, the rebels had opened fire from the windows of Ali's house: Ali had been hiding under the bed while this was going on but when the coup failed his story was not believed. Accordingly the Imam sentenced him to death and when he was brought out to be beheaded he fainted, and was returned to prison until the following day when it was thought he would be fit enough to be killed. He was brought out again with another group of people. The Imam suddenly remarked 'That's old Ali Raji, why do you keep coming out to be executed? You have a job in the Foreign Office, go back and do some work'.

In many ways Imam Ahmad was the original control freak. The British Consul until 1962, Ronald Bailey, had to ask the Imam's permission if he wanted to go for a walk. This permission could take a couple of weeks to be granted and, you guessed it, arrived by telegram. But this telegram also contained conditions. The Consul could take his stroll but he had to carry an open umbrella so that anyone he met would treat him with respect.

Imam Ahmad's father Yahya, who successfully liberated his country from the Turks in 1918, and was assassinated in 1948, is recorded as asking the representative of an American oil company who offered him two million dollars for exploration rights, 'And how much will it cost to get you out?' He had a much gentler reputation than the one acquired by his son, but was still pretty firm, brooking no opposition whatsoever!

Sultan Said Bin Taimur Al Bu Saidi, Ruler of Muscat and Oman

The Sinner who goes to Muscat has a foretaste of what is coming to him in the afterlife.

Persian saying

The Sultan is reviled in his absence only.

Egyptian proverb

The heat was so intense that it burned the marrow in the bones, the sword in its scabbard melted into wax and the gems which adorned the handle of the dagger were reduced to coal. In the plains the chase became a matter of perfect ease, for the desert was strewn with roasted gazelles.

Abdalrazak, 14th-century geographer

Sultan Said was another Ruler ousted by the British in a coup in 1971, which replaced him on the throne with his son Sultan Qaboos Bin Said; of whom one of his subjects remarked that he hoped he could rely on the British as much as his father had! Said Bin Taimur, whose son is rightly regarded as the Great Liberator of Oman, is often regarded as the last of the old-fashioned tyrants, but in the writer's opinion this may be a little unfair. Said certainly handled the British rather well, and he ruled more of the territory in the bottom right-hand corner of Arabia than any of his ancestors had, and he did it all by himself. If only he had reigned a hundred years earlier. When he ascended the throne the Sultanate was broke and Said set about saving halfpennies to get things straight; this engendered a pathological dislike for spending money. No wonder he got on well with Sheikh Shakhbut of Abu Dhabi.

Although it may have taken a while, the way he overcame the grip of the Imamate in the mountainous interior was, though opportunistic, little short of brilliant in a 'softly, softly, catchy monkey' sort of way. While he also overcame major tribal powers looking to get hold of any available oil wealth for themselves, the essentially tribal government that he brought in following these successes was too outdated to continue, and Said's parsimony and increasing remoteness from his people were to lead to his downfall. His attitude to education is well explained by his remark that the British lost India because they educated the natives! He behaved in a way that no other Arab Ruler did and his co-rulers in the Gulf referred to him as 'that Indian'. Sultan Said responded tartly by calling them whippersnappers; and he was also rather irritated by the British, who entitled him Royal Highness. He himself, probably rightly, thought that the title of Sultan merited Majesty!

Said was the Government – all of it, acting as his own Minister of Defence, Minister of Education, Minister of Home Affairs and Minister of Foreign Affairs. In order to keep things clear he devoted one day a week to each Ministry which was accommodated in its own room in his Salala Palace in Dhofar, in the south of the country. This meant that if something cropped up in the field of foreign affairs it could only be dealt with on one day a week, and the correct day at that. In his later years he had moved to Dhofar, to avoid the necessity of being approachable in his capital of Muscat, where he was always being pestered by his subjects for money. It was not easy to get to Dhofar and Said was adept at dealing with unwanted visitors. He just kept them waiting. One Bedouin Sheikh was kept waiting for two years before being admitted to the presence. He did have one Minister other than himself, however, the Minister of the

Interior, Sayyid Ahmad Al Bu Saidi, who did live in Muscat and who communicated with the Ruler by radio, a machine he also used to keep in touch with favoured Governors. (This process is reminiscent of the way in which the Imam Ahmad of Yemen communicated with everyone by telegram.)

When receiving supplicants the Minister was wont to file their letters and petitions in his hat. At the end of a morning's work this gave him the appearance of a somewhat aged but benevolent hedgehog, and it also made it practically impossible to retrieve any document for a second look. He was also adept at delay, a device much in vogue with Arabian Governments. A supplicant from the mountains travelling to Muscat for perhaps three weeks by camel, and complaining of a neighbour, would be lavishly praised for his clear trust in government and, after expressions of gratitude and the issue of a letter giving judgement in the supplicant's favour, would be told that the Minister of the Interior would surely tell the Sultan himself of the man's devotion and loyalty. Off the supplicant would go and, three weeks later, would triumphantly flaunt his letter at his adversary. This fellow would feel deeply wronged and would at once decide to put the matter right by travelling to Muscat to see the Minister of the Interior. Three weeks later he too would arrive and have an audience with the Minister, who would tell him how grateful he was that the man had taken all this trouble to let the Minister know what terrible lies the original supplicant had told. The rest followed as usual and the man would return triumphantly with a letter, taking three weeks to get home. Then the first man would furiously travel back to Muscat, and so on and on, ad infinitum. Some people collected small suitcases of letters in this way.

In fact the oil company became involved in one of these exchanges when they drilled a well in the Wadi Halfayn. In order to follow the Sultan's instructions with regard to the hiring of unskilled labour, it was necessary to determine exactly where the well site was in relation to local tribal boundaries. Two tribes were in dispute about this, the Janaba and the Wahiba. Recourse was had to Sayyid Ahmad, who helpfully ruled that the boundary between the two was the *butn*, that is to say the 'stomach' of the wadi – the middle of the water channel. This looks simple enough. However, by the well site the wadi had several stomachs and divided into about six or seven channels. When approached again, Sayyid Ahmad reiterated his previous ruling. In order to break this impasse it was decided to negotiate directly with the two tribes themselves. Accordingly a meeting took place in an atmosphere of rising hysteria. It really boiled down to a game of snap as each party produced the correspondence that had been collected over years of argument.

The Wahiba were represented by a very smart young sheikh of the great Harth tribe, of whom they could be said to have been clients. This young man had all the letters from Sayyid Ahmad neatly and spotlessly filed in an attaché case. (Incidentally, although throughout the rest of Arabia the epithet Sayyid refers to a descendant of the Prophet Muhammad, in Oman it refers to a member of the Royal Family.) The Janaba sheikh had his letters in a dirty bundle in his pocket. The Harthi sheikh carefully unfolded and laid out his first letter on the sand.

'There,' he said. 'A clear decision from the Sayyid in our favour.' 'Rubbish,' said the Janaba sheikh, smoothing out one if his filthy documents on top of the Harthi's. The Harthi sheikh winced to see his pristine paper sullied like that but then produced his own second letter, and placed it on top of the Janaba sheikh's. And so it went on until quite a tall pile of letters stood on the sand looking like a pile of tired ham sandwiches. The negotiations ended when, with a flourish, the Janaba sheikh's last letter was trumped by the Harthi's last letter.

However, occasionally, horrendous events also have a humorous side, and the Minister of the Interior, who was affectionately nicknamed Father Christmas by the British because of his fatherly and saintly appearance, decided in the late fifties to travel to India for a holiday. In this period terrorism was much in evidence in the Sultanate. Sayyid Ahmad took passage on the British India Line ship *Dwarka*. On his first night at sea the Minister quixotically decided to sleep with his feet on the pillow and his head at the bottom of the bed. No sooner had he settled to sleep than there was a huge explosion as the time bomb set under his pillow exploded. The Minister's feet were slightly injured but he emerged from the smoke otherwise unhurt and lived, much loved, for many years more.

Sultan Said Bin Taimur had other matters to be peeved about as far as the British were concerned. The British had lost out on getting their hands on Saudi oil in a fit of imperial languor in the 1930s, which let in the more energetic Americans. However, in 1949 oil was discovered in Qatar and the British interest in the whole of the Gulf was smartly renewed, as was the interest of Saudi Arabia and the USA. The Saudis quickly revived their historical claims to the Buraimi Oasis, claims which had for years gone unrebutted by Sultan Said. Backed by Aramco, the Saudis sent a small force to threaten the oasis. Sultan Said, in concert with the Abu Dhabi Sheikhdom, sent wildly enthusiastic tribal forces to evict the Saudis. However, a terse and maladroit message from Whitehall halted these activities. The result was that the Omani and Abu Dhabi forces went home bitterly disappointed, and the rest of the world was given the strong impression that the Saudis must have had a good case.

The harbour at Muscat is surrounded by craggy rocks bearing the names of ships that have visited over the years. Sultan Said called it his marine autograph book. One commemorating the visit of HMS *Perseus* is enhanced by a white ensign said to have been painted by Nelson when a midshipman. In 1963 HMS *Eskimo* called and her visit coincided with that of Minister without Portfolio Lord Carrington. To mark the occasion Sultan Said sent down gifts. The ship was presented with a beautiful traditional Omani silver coffee pot. Lord Carrington got a large heavy suitcase which, on being opened, proved to contain a hundredweight (112 lbs, 50.8 kg) of halwa, the glutinous sticky sweet popular throughout the region. It is not known whether the two presents had got mixed up or whether Sultan Said was indulging his sense of humour.

◇ ◇ ◇

The Treaty between Oman and the British allowed for the Ruler, who usually bought his armaments out of mail-order catalogues, to call on British military aid if required. Such military aid would however remain under the control of the Sultan's Military Adviser. A story goes that in the 1960s the C-in-C at Headquarters Middle East Command in Aden realised to his dismay that the then Military Adviser was an ex-Indian Army man. To have his men under the command of such a person was something the C-in-C could not countenance. If asked to send men to help the Sultan they would remain under his own command, thank you very much! The Treaty would have to be altered accordingly. As a consequence a new Treaty was drawn up and carried on a small aeroplane up the coast to Salala. On its presentation the change was pointed out to Sultan Said who smiled in a benign way and said that he was glad to see that the C-in-C disliked his Military Adviser almost as much as he did, and signed on the dotted line.

This tale needs to be read in juxtaposition to an alternative story which may refer to the same general set of circumstances. The Sultan had need of finance to pay for an extra battalion of troops. The British agreed, provided the Sultan removed his Adviser, in whom they had little confidence. The Sultan solemnly fell in with this, so he got the money and the battalion. The British now expected Said to fulfil his part of the bargain, but were astonished to discover that instead of getting rid of his Adviser by sacking him, Sultan Said simply did it by promoting him.

The end of Said's rule was inevitable, but the events of the 1971 coup contained an element of farce that adds an air of almost theatrical comedy to what was a very serious matter – that is, if rumour current at the time carries any vestige of the truth. The oil company is said to have paid for the tickets needed to entertain the Sultan's Baluch bodyguard at the cinema on the night in question. Having got them out of the way, a detachment of other servants under the command of the son of the then Wali of Salala went to the palace with some British troops to arrest the Sultan. Sultan Said, smelling a rat, took out a gold-plated Luger from his desk drawer with which to defend himself. While skipping about the palace trying to avoid his adversaries, he inadvertently slipped on a staircase and shot himself in the foot. This proved to be the end and Sultan Said was captured.

At first he refused to leave the palace unless escorted by the British Colonel commanding the troops in Salala. When this officer was found, first aid was given, and the Sultan was whisked off to the airstrip. On arrival there, however, it was realised that while he had signed the English language version of his abdication, he hadn't signed the Arabic one, so everyone went back to the palace. The correct document was produced, but it was then also discovered that due to all the rushing about no one could lay their hands on a pen. After an embarrassing minute or two a biro was borrowed from a passing corporal, and the paperwork was satisfactorily completed. The party then drove off for the second time and delivered the by now formally ex-Sultan to the airstrip. He went via Bahrain into exile at the Dorchester hotel in London. Sultan Said died two years later and was buried at the Woking Mosque in England.

A little inaccuracy sometimes saves a ton of explanation.

Saki

There are of course very many remarkable Arabians, but those written about here have received little or no previous attention in print. The first was probably the best dressed Yemeni ever.

Sheikh Ali Salih Fidama arrived in Aden in about 1963 and proceeded to broadcast in the Royalist cause strongly anti-Republican material. He was always beautifully turned out with carefully colour coordinated robes. Beige, browns, gold; a bit of green and perhaps a splash of scarlet, yellows and oranges. He impressed the British enormously, as they hadn't seen such elegant tailoring before, and fell for this brilliant vision hook, line and sinker, though Sheikh Ali's actual station in life was somewhat lowly. Stories of the wonderful extent of his influence, and the importance of his friends relied on a large amount of imagination. Sheikh Ali Salih had served in the German Arab Legion in Russia during the Second World War, for which he had been awarded the Iron Cross, and before the coup that brought President Sallal to power he had been the Governor of a rather small Yemeni province. His activities made him serious enemies in the Republican regime, and they arranged for one of his sons to be kidnapped and taken from Aden up into Yemen itself. They then told Sheikh Ali that unless he ceased broadcasting his son would be tortured to death. With great courage the Sheikh went on with his broadcasts and it must be assumed that his son was killed, as he was not heard of again. Then, in early July 1967, Sheikh Ali Salih Fidama was himself murdered in an ambush trying to reach Royalist-held territory.

Hajji Ahmad was a servant in the Officers, Mess at Headquarters Middle East Command, at Tarshyne in Aden. Only senior officers had refrigerators in their rooms and Ahmad used to steal iced water from them to provide the junior officers with cold drinks when they came back to the Mess in the evening. On one occasion he nearly killed one young man because he was unaware that though a Squadron Leader used empty gin bottles to store water in his fridge, he also kept the gin there too. The consequence was that the junior officer poured out a pint glass of what he assumed to be cold water and downed it in one. He collapsed on the floor, to the horror of Ahmad, who rushed off as fast as he could to collect the only and best medicine he knew. This was his most precious possession – the very last of the water he had brought back from the holy well of Zamzam at Makkah, when he had made the pilgrimage some years earlier that had given him the title of Hajji. He opened the mouth of the unconscious officer and poured in the drops of foetid green water which had been lovingly and piously kept in a jerry can for about ten years. The officer recovered at once.

Later, when there was a general strike and all the Mess servants were forced to refrain from working by roving gangs of young trades union thugs, Hajji Ahmad remained at his post. However, in order to escape the notice of the strikers, he hid under a bed in the room of one of the officers. When the owner of the room got back from work he was surprised to see two enormous feet sticking out from under the end of his bed. Ahmad felt secure as he couldn't see out and so thought that no one would be able to see him either.

There is a footnote to the gin story. A similar thing happened to a parrot called Mr Pickwick. While in the Sudan with his master, Mr Pickwick was inadvertently given gin to drink due to a similar mix up over the bottles in the fridge. Apparently the sozzled bird sang wildly throughout the following night.

◇ ◇ ◇

If the reader can imagine a man who looked like an emaciated King Faisal of Saudi Arabia with bright orange hair, then he will have a pretty accurate idea of the appearance of the Qadi Al Ghazali. The Qadi had practised his profession in Taiz and had often fallen foul of the old Imam Ahmad, against whom the 1962 revolution had been plotted. The Qadi had been a quite progressive fellow and the Imam had felt in necessary to sentence him to death not once, but twice. However the Qadi Ghazali, on both these dire occasions, when he was being led away to have his head cut off, managed to retain sufficient control to crack a joke. The Imam laughed so much that he twice pardoned him. Earlier in his career Qadi Ghazali had been a Muslim missionary in, of all places, the meat markets of Detroit. This environment had been so noisy with the clanking of railway wagons, shouting and the bellowing of cattle, that he developed a strange habit of speech. He could only talk at the top of his voice which made sensitive interviews a little difficult. Sadly he too was assassinated in Aden.

****

Mention has already been made of a delightful old rogue, one of the Omani Duru' sheikhs, Sheikh Khulayfin Bin Ali Al Mahmudi Al Duru'i, to give him his full name, who used to steal camels from as far away from his home as Najran in Saudi Arabia. Returning from these expeditions he would stop off to cavort with the ladies of the Wahiba, a tribe with whom his own people were at feud, so these romps were not without danger too. The oil company had established its camp at Fahud and provided medical services for its employees only. One day the old raider turned up at the camp on a camel seeking help as one of his eyes was rotting in its socket. It was clear this condition would kill him before very long, and so the Personnel man enrolled the old man as a casual worker for the day so that he could be 'legally' treated.

The old man was flown down to the hospital on the coast where the company doctors were able to operate, and then send him back to Fahud to recuperate in the little six-bed medical centre at the oil camp. The old man could only drink camel's milk, and only milk from his own camels at that. However, after a week he was seen tottering somewhat unsteadily away from the Medical Centre making for the labour tents. On being nabbed and told he should get back to bed, he replied that he had realised that the work on the oil rigs was dangerous, and if there was an accident his bed would be needed by the young men. So he had decided that it would be better if he found a space in one of the labour tents. This unselfish act was brave as well as remarkable.

About three years later the Personnel man was visiting the old sheikh's son, Ma'ayuf, in the Wadi Halfayn and asked after his father. Ma'ayuf replied that he was dying, and would be dead by morning, but the Personnel man could see him if he wanted to. The old man was lying by a tussock of grass in the sand. It was bitterly cold and he was only wrapped in a thin piece of cotton material. He was very calm, dignified and quietly prepared to meet his Maker.

Non-Arabians

History is regularly speckled with the names of non-Arabians who have been driven more than a little potty by the pull of a mysterious East on one side, of political perceptions of national interest on the other. There can be no doubt of the romance and wonder that Arabia's inhabitants, and its geography, can conjure up. And this does not end with the possible eccentricities of Lady Stanhope and Lawrence of Arabia.

Abdulrahman Condé

Following rather bizarrely in their footsteps was His Serene Highness General the Prince Abdulrahman Bruce Alfonso de Bourbon-Condé, an American born in California in 1913. Some detractors have alleged that his mother was an unmarried lady of Scottish descent. Others report that he was adopted and took on his grandparents' family name of Condé. Whatever the circumstances of his birth this amazing person grew up with an all-consuming obsession about his ancestry, real or imagined. Years later he told an interviewer that he was a tenth-generation American from some branches of his family. He often alluded in general terms to his Spanish forebears who had a hint of noble Arabian blood, as well as his descent from Robert the Bruce who had so courageously fought the English, and there were others; but all were noble people who had battled against insuperable odds.

He surveyed the glories of the Spanish Empire in California, stretching from the Pacific to the Sierra Mountains, which was first of all sold out to the Mexicans in the 1820s and then to the USA in 1850. Condé fantasised that one day he would avenge these historical injustices. In this frame of mind he was eventually to write to every crowned monarch in the world, hoping also to enhance his stamp collection. He pledged undying allegiance in exchange for a gift of stamps, setting out as well how he was dedicated to restoring what he saw as the chivalry and nobility of previous centuries. He only got one reply, from Prince Badr of the Yemen, who invited him to the Yemen and in his turn asked for stamps.

This budding correspondence was interrupted by the outbreak of the Second World War when Condé joined the American Army, serving in Japan and North Africa. When the war was over Condé took advantage of the American GI Bill for retraining veterans to study Arabic in Beirut. He renewed contact with Badr, by now Crown Prince, and in 1953 travelled to Sana'a to join him. In 1958 he became a Yemeni citizen and adopted Islam, taking the name Abdulrahman.

He was appointed Communications Adviser to the Yemeni Government in charge of Postal Affairs. In this connection he opened a Philatelic Office and designed sets of commemorative stamps. Although the subject matter of these – space travel, European Renaissance paintings and Sir Winston Churchill – can scarcely be considered as having much to do with Yemeni culture or history, these stamps were much sought after by collectors all over the world. They provided the Imam's exchequer with a very useful income – even after the 1962 Revolution, when they sustained the Imam in his cave. The Imam continued to authorise new designs long after he had gone into exile. Some of latter issues had indeed been genuinely used, particularly those postmarked Camp Mansur. Others were not used properly and collectors came to dismiss them as mere labels. Most of Abdulrahman's designs were noteworthy for their intricacy. People said this was to prevent forgery, but the truth marks another strange turn in this tale. Poignantly Abdulrahman was by now almost completely blind and designed the stamps on huge A2 sheets of paper, drawing with the use of a powerful magnifying glass. The subsequent reduction in size meant that the designs became minutely intricate and complex. His blindness was something Abdulrahman was loath to admit, feeling that it was a sign of weakness.

Although the British community in Jeddah was unaware of the comings and goings of the Yemeni Royalists, it was a matter of great interest to the British Embassy. So an official from the Embassy arranged to meet Abdulrahman when he was staying at the Quraish Palace Hotel, to gain some idea as to the military strength of the Royalists in Yemen. The Englishman sent up word of his arrival and waited at the bottom of the Grand Staircase. There was a rustle from upstairs and an extraordinary trio appeared from the top floor. In the centre there was Prince Abdulrahman Condé with his hands clasped in front of him over the pommel of his ceremonial sword. On his right elbow hung his aide, Captain Ahmad Oshaysh. His left elbow was supported by a rather ragged servant boy. This amazing sight descended step by step in dignified unison, bobbing and turning at each landing before tackling the next floor. At the half-flight above the Reception area the floor to ceiling mirrors began. The Prince, dimly discerning his own reflection and assuming it was the Englishman, gave a warm welcoming smile and walked slap into the glass and dropped his sword. After a bit of a scuffle composure was restored and the Prince completed his descent as though nothing had happened.

During the drinking of tea later, and seeing how the Prince quite frequently placed his cup on a part of the table that wasn't there, the Englishman realised that His Serene Highness the Prince was virtually blind. Nevertheless, Condé was able to divulge a consistently exaggerated estimate of the forces available to the Imam. It seemed that this was part of his function as Minister of Communications. In earlier years when his eyesight had not been so impaired, he had been to Aden to do the same thing, and had shown a predilection for cream sponge cake. Those Englishmen involved with the covert British support for the Imam were strongly advised to avoid Abdulrahman Condé at all costs. He was thought to be an agent of the CIA where the United States had recognised the Republican Government in Yemen and, as Duff Hart-Davis says in his book *The War that Never Was,* his list of titles was weird enough to make any British officer uneasy. However there can be no doubt of his absolute loyalty to the Imam Badr and so this estimate of Abdulrahman is surely wide of the mark.

The final chapter of Prince Abdulrahman's colourful life continued when his loyalty to the Imam was rewarded and Muhammad al Badr gave him the last £6,000 he had so that he could go to the best eye surgeon in Spain. The operation was only partially successful and Abdulrahman Condé spent the rest of his life, without a passport, in Morocco. There he had one last flight of fancy. He met a senior British diplomat who reports that, on being teased about his lengthy list of titles, Abdulrahman told how he had only recently almost become King of a Japanese island. It would seem that he had been about to marry its Queen, a Japanese princess, but she had died before the wedding. As did Abdulrahman, in 1992.

Wilfred Thesiger

A British Embassy official got the chance to make the acquaintance of another kind of obsession during this same tour of duty. This time, instead of an American romantic living in a make-believe world of almost Arthurian chivalry, he met an Englishman who was the last exponent of the Victorian idea of the magnificent and noble savage – the great Wilfred Thesiger.

It is a matter of no little curiosity to Arabians that we exalt our fellow citizens when they do things that Arabs have been doing for years. We rightly praise Wilfred Thesiger for his tremendous journeys over the Empty Quarter and the privations he suffered amongst the Marsh Arabs of Iraq, quite forgetting that Arabs have been doing that sort of thing since time began. For instance Sheikh Khulayfin of the Omani Duru' tribe, father of Sheikh Ma'ayuf mentioned elsewhere, did it the long way across from east to west and back again, three times. He was actually stealing camels from Najran some thousands of miles away from his home!

Wilfred is thought rightly by his many admirers to be the last of the great British Arabist explorers: his detractors thought he was a bit of a fool. He arrived in Jeddah from Yemen, where he had travelled through Royalist-held territory on foot and by camel for five months meeting and communicating with the various Royalist leaders, and collecting information for MI6. However his sojourn with some of his fellow countrymen who were helping the Royalists was not without lighter moments.

One moonlit night he arrived in the midst of a little group, avoiding being shot by quietly asking at the mouth of their cave, 'Good evening, may I come in?' He impressed them by accepting orders, and entranced one of the group by announcing out of the blue that the only thing his grandfather had ever done was to lose the Battle of Isandlwana during the Anglo-Zulu War. But he irritated some of the men by what they saw as his affectations. 'Gentlemen don't travel by automobile in Arabia,' he once announced. He also ate all their food and only left when the group was advised to play pop music to get rid of him. However, on reaching Jeddah he brought important news of bombing and gassing by the Egyptian Air Force. This news was suppressed by both the American government of President Kennedy, and the British government of Harold Wilson.

On his arrival in Jeddah an official from the British Embassy gave a dinner party for him. Sadly the great explorer upset most of his fellow guests with his outspoken criticism of everything that was progressive in Arabia. He decried the building of hospitals, and disapproved of the building of schools and the introduction of motor cars and air travel. He thought that the only good Arab was one who had passed through the fire of privation in the desert. Rigorous selection by harsh living was the only right thing for them. Eventually feelings ran so high that his host was forced to eject him from the house and the 'greatest living explorer' had to walk back to his hotel in the dark. His host certainly seems to have lacked gallantry, if nothing else. Neither he nor any of his guests could ever have achieved a hundredth part of what Wilfred Thesiger had accomplished. And what a formidable list of achievements he has left, quite apart from his work for locust control and the planning for what could be done in Syria to hold the line should Montgomery have failed in North Africa. One wonders what he would have thought of the following 'Facts about living in Dhahran', rather incongruously published in *Makzan*, the Journal of the Arabian Natural History Association of Dhahran in Saudi Arabia in September 2011.

The best parking space is determined by shade instead of distance.
Hot water comes out of both taps.
You learn that a seat belt buckle makes a pretty good branding iron.
The temperature drops below 32°C and you feel a little chilly.
You discover that it only takes two fingers to steer your car.
You develop a fear of metal car door handles.
You break a sweat the moment you step outside at 6.00 a.m.
Your biggest bicycle wreck fear is, 'What if I get knocked out and end up
*   lying on the pavement and get cooked to death?'*
You realise that asphalt has a liquid state.
While walking barefoot back to your car from the beach, you do a
*   tightrope on the white lines in the parking lot.*
You wear a sweater to the office because the air conditioner is on full
*   blast.*
You learn that malls aren't shopping centers; they are actually temples
*   to worship air conditioning.*

The great man, who accused two Brits he met while strolling through the Hindu Kush of being sissies because they had a tent, would have had apoplexy.

EPILOGUE

In the Notes to his *The Kasidah of Haji Abdu El-Yezdi,* Sir Richard Burton tells how the Haji asked 'the old, old question, What is Truth?' The Haji answers himself, 'after the fashion of the wise Emperor of China, "Truth hath not an unchanging name"'. The following verse from the Kasidah itself puts the matter well.

> *As palace mirror'd in the stream,*
> *As vapour mingled with the skies,*
> *So weaves the brain of mortal man*
> *The tangled web of Truth and Lies.*

I admit that these stories are extraordinary, but I have merely quoted them from the books of learned men. If the information is at fault then I personally am not responsible.

Yaqut Bin Abdullah Al Hamawi, 15th Century

APPENDIX

Language and Things

Transliteration

Any work relating to matters Arabian inevitably attracts shrieks of opprobrium and fury about transliteration. Transliteration just means how Arabic words are best spelt in English, and presents a number of problems; and all Arabists have their own pet theories. When solved in a purely academic way the result is usually completely incomprehensible to the ordinary person, as he has to learn so many new linguistic symbols that he would probably be better off learning Arabic in the first place. The alternative is to use an English letter that sounds the same as the Arabic letter is pronounced. Thus 'G' as in Gulf. Actually the reader will be delighted to know that this 'G' sound is very often a 'Q' in Arabic. But in North Africa and the Gulf itself it often sounds like a 'G'. This is why everyone refers to Colonel Gaddafi when it would be more accurate and purist, possibly, to spell the name as Qadhafi.

It is worth mentioning here that one of the Arabic words for a cow is *baqar*, and the change to a 'G' here can cause confusion, or blushes in genteel English circles, except perhaps in the west of the United Kingdom where the word can still mean a cow. The reader will doubtless be thrilled to know that this 'Q' can also be missed out altogether. It is the first letter of the Arabic word for coffee, and in Egypt where they take most of their 'Q's as 'G's it is lost from *gahwa* (*qahwa*) altogether, which thus becomes *ahwa* or *ahwi*. I was once on a plane flying up to Q(G)atar from the lower Qulf when the Egypt Air hostess walked up the aisle with her trolley asking if anyone wanted *'ahwi'*. A staunch Gulf citizen manfully and loudly informed her that he didn't want *'ahwi'*. What he wanted was *'gahwa'*. I remarked, also quite loudly, that the man should be presented with an British passport as he was clearly an imperialist – a sally greeted with gales of laughter from the other passengers.

If you have hoisted all this in you may be able to accommodate the additional information that an Arabic 'J' can also become a 'G'. One ought not to go on about the wretched 'Q' endlessly, but it has caused lots of confusion. Yes, there are two further words whose pronunciation charmingly mixes up all the variations mentioned so far. One is the Arabic for camel, *'jamal'*. The other is the Arabic for louse, *'qaml'*. Change both the 'j' and the 'q' to 'g' and you will at once see how close the two words get to each other. A British visitor to Bahrain, who thought he spoke excellent Arabic, caused mortal offence when he told his host, in effect, that he was covered in lice rather than being the owner of lots of camels. Just to embroider this linguistic *frou-frou* it should be noted that the Arabians are accurately to be described by a neologism as being vepoless. That is to say they, classically, have no 'V', no 'E', no 'P' and no 'O'. So throughout this book the spellings may vary, firstly to follow general usage, and then the spelling used in the source of the anecdote concerned. However if the reader can read it surely that's all that matters?

It is often not realised that this mixing-up of letters and their sounds works two ways. Arabians have had a lot of the same sort of problem when using European alphabets as we have had trying to approximate to theirs. To mention but one example, consider the difficulties experienced by the Saudi Arabian national airline, Saudia. Booking tickets and the checking of passports involves the public as well as the airport staff of course, and this creates endless permutations in the spelling of names when it is done using the Roman alphabet, which leads to the most appalling confusion. Where and who taught the Saudia clerks is of paramount importance. Here we go again with the 'Q'. If someone's tribal epithet is Qurayshi he can be written down by an Egyptian, Qatari or Sudanese clerk as Gurayshi or perhaps Guraishi or Guraishy; even perhaps 'Uraishi. If he has been taught by a Europaean teacher it might also be spelt Kurayshi etc. So where to find him in the passenger list? As if that doesn't waste enough time, think about very common tribal names like al Ghamdi. Combined with a very common first name like Ali or Muhammad which one is he of the probably several hundred on the list?

Words

It is also important to mention that mispronouncing words and their imprecise usage can give unnecessary offence as well as providing cause for hilarity if not actual blasphemy. For instance the endless saying of 'Izzlam' instead of 'Isslam' is gratuitously rude. When the 's' is pronounced as a 'z' the word comes, in Arabic, to mean darkness, a water-divining twig or a cloven-footed badger, i.e. the Syrian Rock Hyrax! Much in the news of recent years is the name of a terrorist organisation, Al Qa'ida, with a long first 'a'. It is frequently pronounced Al Qa'eeda which actually means a 'female companion', or worse. Though of course as a gratuitous insult it might have a purpose! Rather like a Syrian lisping 'Ya Ukhti' at another man. Ya Ukhti means 'Oh My Sister'!

For the politically sensitive it may be worth mentioning that the epithet 'Semite' applies to all Arabians and to all Jews. Both peoples are of the same race. Consequently an anti-Semite is as much against the Arabians as he is against the Jews! There will be many who don't find that amusing at all.

When the Spanish enthusiastically shout '*Olé*' they might be a bit put out to know that it is derived from the Arabic word for The God, that is Allah. Followers of the Quorn and other prestigious English fox-hunts will doubtless likewise raise an eyebrow to know that 'Tally Ho' is derived from the Arabic words meaning 'come here'. It is thought that this derivation dates from the Crusades, when the Norman ancestors of the present Quorn membership employed Arabians as beaters as they chased foxes around the Holy Land. The Royal Navy, the Senior Service, does not escape either. They call their senior people Admirals. This most august of ranks comes from the Arabic words meaning 'Prince of the Sea'.

BIBLIOGRAPHY

Abu Athera, Said Salman and Holes, Clive. *Poetry and Politics in Contemporary Bedouin Society*. Reading, Ithaca Press, 2009.

A Collection of Quotable Quotes. Bicester, Aura Books, 2004.

Ahmed, Qanta A. *In the Land of Invisible Women*. Naperville, Illinois, Sourcebooks Inc., 2008.

Ali, Tariq. *The Duel*. London, Simon and Schuster, 2008.

Alice, H.R.H. Princess, Countess of Athlone. *For My Grandchildren: Some Reminiscences*. London, Evans Bros Ltd., 1966.

Allen, Calvin H. and Rigsbee, W. Lynn. *Oman under Qaboos: From Coup to Constitution, 1970-1996*. London, Frank Cass Publishers, 2002.

Allfree, P.S. *Warlords of Oman*. London, Robert Hale, 1967.

—— *Hawks of the Hadramaut*. London, Robert Hale, 1967.

Al Rasheed, Madawi. *A History of Saudi Arabia*. Cambridge University Press, 2002.

Arberry.A.J. *Aspects of Islamic Civilization*. London, George Allen and Unwin, 1964.

Arnold, José. *Golden Swords and Pots and Pans*. London, Victor Gollancz, 1964.

Baker, Randall. *King Husain and the Kingdom of Hejaz*. Cambridge, The Oleander Press, 1979.

Balfour-Paul, Glencairn. *Bagpipes in Babylon*. London, I.B.Tauris & Co. Ltd., 2006.

—— *The End of Empire in the Middle East*. Cambridge University Press, 1991.

Belgrave, Charles. *Personal Column*. London, Hutchinson, 1960.

Belhaven, Lord, (Hamilton, Robert). *The Uneven Road*. London, John Murray, 1955.

—— *The Kingdom of Melchior*. London, John Murray, 1949.

Bidwell, Robin. *The Two Yemens*. Harlow, Longman Group and Westview Press, 1983.

Blandford, Linda. *Oil Sheikhs*. London, W.H.Allen, 1977.

Blunt, Judith (Lady Wentworth). *The Authentic Arabian Horse*. London, George Allen and Unwin, 3rd. Ed., 1979.

Blunt, Lady Anne. *The Bedouin Tribes of the Euphrates*. London, Harper and Brothers, 1879.

——. *Journals and Correspondence 1878-1917*, ed. Archer and Fleming. Cheltenham, Alexander Heriot and Co. Ltd., 1986.

Blunt, Wilfrid Scawen. *My Diaries*. London, Martin Secker. Part One 1919 and Part Two 1920. Republished by the Best Publishing Co., Boulder, Colorado, 1960.

——. *My Diaries*. Martin Secker London 1919

Brent, Peter. *Far Arabia, Explorers of the Myth*. London, Quartet Books, 1979.

Boustead, Colonel Sir Hugh. *The Wind of Morning*. London, Chatto and Windus, 1971.

Burckhardt, John Lewis. *The Manners and Customs of Modern Egyptians*. London, John Murray, 1830.

Canton, James. *From Cairo to Baghdad*. London, I.B.Taurus & Co. Ltd., 2011.

Carter, Miranda. *The Three Emperors*. London, Fig Tree (imprint of of Penguin Books), 2009.

Clayton, Sir Gilbert. *An Arabian Diary*. Berkeley, University of California Press, 1969.

Cobbold, Lady Evelyn. *Pilgrimage to Mecca*. London, Arabian Publishing, 2008.

Crouch, Michael. *An Element of Luck: To South Arabia and Beyond*. London, The Radcliffe Press, 1993.

Daniels, John. *Kuwait Journey*. Luton, White Crescent Press Ltd., 1971

Darlow, Michael and Bray, Barbara. *Ibn Saud: The Desert Warrior and his Legacy*. London, Quartet Books, 2010.

Fiennes, Ranulph. *Where Soldiers Fear to Tread*. London, Hodder and Stoughton, 1975.

Foster, Donald. *Landscape with Arabs*. London, Clifton Books, 1969.

Graham, Helga. *Arabian Time Machine*. London, Heinemann, 1978.

Groom, Nigel. *Sheba Revealed*. The London Centre of Arab Studies, 2002.

Harding, John. *Roads to Nowhere: A South Arabian Odyssey, 1960 -1965*. London, Arabian Publishing Ltd., 2009.

Hart-Davis, Duff. *The War that Never Was*. London, Century, 2011.

Hason, Khan Saheb Syed Hamood. *Arabic Simplified*. Cairo, 1954.

Hawley, Donald. *Sudan Canterbury Tales*. Norwich, Michael Russell (Publishing) Ltd., 1999.

–– *The Emirates, Witness to a Metamorphosis*. Norwich, Michael Russell (Publishing) Ltd., 2007.

–– *Desert Wind and Tropic Storm: An Autobiography*. Norwich, Michael Russell (Publishing) Ltd., 2000.

Hemming, Henry. *Misadventures in the Middle East*. London, Nicholas Brealey Publishing, 2007.

Hollingsworth, Mark and Mitchell, Sandy. *Saudi Babylon: Torture, Corruption and Cover-up Inside the House of Saud*. London, Mainstream Publishing, 2005.

Howell, Georgina. *Daughter of the Desert: The Remarkable Life of Gertrude Bell*. London, Pan Books, 2007.

Ingrams, Harold. *The Yemen: Imams Rulers and Revolution*. London, John Murray, 1963.

–– *Arabia and the Isles*. London, John Murray, 3rd edition 1966.

Johnston, Charles. *The View From Steamer Point*. London, Collins, 1964.

Keane, John F. *Six Months in the Hejaz*. London, Ward and Downey, 1887.

Kishtainy, Khalid. *Arab Political Humour*. London, Quartet Books, 1985.

–– *By the Rivers of Babylon*. London, Quartet Books, 2008.

Klein, Shelley. *Senior Moments*. London, Michael O'Mara Books Ltd., 2006.

Korda, Michael. *Hero: The Life and Legend of Lawrence of Arabia*. London, JR Books, 2010.

Lacey, Robert. *The Kingdom: Arabia and the House of Sa'ud.* London, Hutchinson and Co (Publishers) Ltd., 1981.

Laffin, John. *The Arab Mind.* London, Cassell, 1975.

Ledger, David. *Shifting Sands: The British in South Arabia.* London, Peninsular Publishing, 1983.

Ledwidge, Frank. *Losing Small Wars.* London, Yale University Press, 2011.

Lewis, Norman. *Sand and Sea in Arabia.* London, George Routledge and Sons Ltd., 1938.

Luce, Margaret. *From Aden to the Gulf: Personal Diaries 1956-1966.* Wilby, Michael Russell Publishing, 1987.

Mackintosh-Smith, Tim. *Yemen: Travels in Dictionary Land.* London, John Murray, 1997.

McLoughlin, Leslie. *Confessions of an Arabic Interpreter: The Odyssey of an Arabist 1959-2009.* Dubai, Motivate Publishing, 2010.

More Brit Wit: The Perfect Riposte for Every Social Occasion. Chichester, Summerdale Publishers Ltd., 2005.

Morris, James (Jan). *Sultan in Oman.* London, Faber and Faber, 1957.

Nash, James. *Mainly Middle Eastern.* Private Publication. Bristol, 2008.

O'Ballance, Edgar. *The War in the Yemen.* London, Faber and Faber, 1971.

Onley, James. *The Arabian Frontier of the British Raj.* Oxford, Oxford University Press, 2007.

Phillips, Wendell. *Qataban and Sheba.* London, Victor Gollanz Ltd., 1955.

Pritzke, Herbert. *Bedouin Doctor: The Adventures of a German in the Middle East.* Trans. Richard Graves. London, Weidenfeld and Nicolson, 1957.

Rabi, Uzi. *The Emergence of States in a Tribal Society; Oman under Sa'id bin Taymur 1932-1970.* Eastbourne, Sussex Academic Press, 2006.

Sasson, Jean. *Daughters of Arabia.* London, Bantam Books, 1994.

Searle, Pauline. *Dawn Over Oman.* London, George Allen and Unwin, 1979.

Semple, Clara. *A Silver Legend: The Story of the Maria Theresa Thaler.* Manchester, Barzan Publishing Ltd., 2005.

Sherif, Gulsun and Forbis, Judith. *The Abbas Pasha Manuscript: And Horses and Horsemen of Arabia and Egypt During the Time of Abbas Pa Sha, 1800-1860.* Mena, Arkansas, Ansata Publications, 1993.

Skeet, Ian. *Muscat and Oman: The End of an Era.* London, Faber and Faber, 1974.

St Albans, Duchess of (Beauclerk, Suzanne). *Where Time Stood Still.* London, Quartet Books, 1980.

Stewart, Rory. *The Prince of the Marshes: And Other Occupational Hazards of a Year in Iraq.* New York and London, Harcourt Inc., 2006.

The Travel Chronicles of Mrs. J. Theodore Bent. Volume III: Deserts of Vast Eternity: Southern Arabia and Persia. Gerald Brisch, ed. Oxford, Archaeopress Ltd, 2010.

Townsend, John. *Oman: The Making of a Modern State.* London, Croom Helm, 1977.

Trevaskis, Sir Kennedy. *Shades of Amber: A South Arabian Episode.* London, Hutchinson, 1968.

Tweedie, Major General W. *The Arabian Horse: His Country and People.* Vista, California, Borden Publishing Company, 1961.

Walford, G.F. *Arabian Locust Hunter.* London, Robert Hale Limited, 1963.

Walker, Jonathan. *Aden Insurgency: The Savage War in South Arabia 1962-67.* Staplehurst, The History Press, 2005.

Walker, Julian. *Tyro on the Trucial Coast.* Durham, The Memoir Club, 1999.

Waterfield, Gordon. *Sultans of Aden.* London, Murray, 1968.

Waugh, Evelyn. *Remote People.* London, Penguin Classics, 2002 (First published by Gerald Duckworth and Co., 1931).

Winstone, H.V.F. *Lady Anne Blunt: A Biography.* Manchester, Barzan Publishing Limited, 2003. (To be re-published by Medina Publishing Ltd in 2013 in an edition edited by Ruth Winstone.)

Wrong, Michela. *It's Our Turn to Eat.* London, Fourth Estate (HarperCollins), 2009.

Papers, Articles and Interviews

Gillespie, Frances. Interview with Lord Denman. Doha, 2010.

Wilton, Sir John, British Political Agent, Qatar and Sharjah, 1949-1952.

Nash, James. *Quixote in a Cart.* Unpublished MS.

The Oman Flora and Fauna Survey Special Report 1975. *Journal of Oman Studies.* Dhofar.

Makzan, The Journal of the Arabian Natural History Association, Dhahran.

Index

As well as having his own anarchic approach to transliterations, T.E. Lawrence loathed indexes. He thought that books should be read as a whole. As he put it when writing the Introduction to the 1935 edition of *Seven Pillars of Wisdom:* 'Who would insult [his] *Decline and Fall* by consulting it just on a specific point?'

I could not possibly disagree with such an eminent authority.